A Guide to First Year Composition

Editor:
Tanya Long Bennett

Assistant Editors:
Donna Gessell
Diana Edelman-Young

Contributors:
Chris Bell
Tanya Long Bennett
David Brauer
Steven Brehe
Karen Dodson
Diana Edelman-Young
Donna Gessell
Shannon Gilstrap
Laura Ng
J. Stephen Pearson
J. Michael Rifenburg

Published by:
University of North Georgia Press
Dahlonega, Georgia

Printing Support by:
Booklogix Publishing Services, Inc.
Alpharetta, Georgia

Cover Design by Corey Parson and Amy Beard

ISBN: 978-1-940771-21-2

Printed in the United States of America, 2015

For more information, please visit: www.ung.edu/university-press
Or email: ungpress@ung.edu

UNIVERSITY *of*
NORTH GEORGIA®
UNIVERSITY PRESS

Table of Contents

The Drive to Communicate

Tanya Long Bennett

Most of us are aware of how essential communication is to our lives, but lest we begin to take it for granted, a case of laryngitis can be a harsh and inconvenient reminder of how important it is to our daily functions. If we counted our interactions with other people each day for a week, we might be surprised at just how pervasive this behavior really is. Communicating with others is a basic human impulse. Not only is it necessary for physical survival, but our desire to understand, connect with, and influence one another is fundamental to human behavior. It enables us to build communities, to enlist each other's help in tasks far beyond what an individual could accomplish alone, and to pursue understanding of our existence and our world.

To these ends, we communicate through verbal exchanges, gestures, images, music, and writing. Purpose and the circumstances of a given place and time determine which methods of communication are best for accomplishing that purpose. Today, academic and professional writing and oratory remain crucial skills, but new technologies and increasingly popular digital social networks demand a somewhat different set of communication skills, though there is much overlap, of course. For example, someone taking advantage of multiple venues—such as flyers, a blog, a Facebook post, and a newspaper press release—might employ a variety of English dialects, textual content, and images to achieve his or her purpose, depending on audience and context.

To illustrate how purpose and circumstance determine communication strategies, consider hypothetical student Juan Rodriguez, who serves as the Publicity Coordinator on the Student Activities Board at his college. He has been given responsibility for advertising the upcoming play, *Trifles*, which the drama group is producing. Since this event will serve as a collaborative fundraiser, the Student Activities Board would like to get a substantial turnout of not only students, but also faculty, staff, and community members. Juan understands that he will need to use a variety of strategies to draw an audience from these various populations.

He decides first to make posters for campus and community buildings. These will feature a high resolution color photo from a cast dress rehearsal along with basic information about the play's title, director, sponsors, date, time and location. In composing the poster, he uses a large stylish font and bright colors that will catch the eye of passersby. While the same poster will be placed in a variety of venues, Juan plans to establish a Facebook page for this event, as well, and through his own Facebook page, invite all his friends to "like" it. Juan's friends in this social network site are mostly students and community members. Although he is careful to include basic information about the play here, as he did on the poster, the Facebook page offers more space for visuals and text. He adds some candid photos of students engaged in stage set-building and of particular actors that his friends may know. He can also be less formal on Facebook and even posts a few funny quips in reply to comments submitted by some of the page's visitors.

Two weeks before the play begins its run, Juan takes a third measure to ensure a good turnout: He writes a press release for the college faculty/staff newsletter, which is distributed each week by email. In this release, he takes a formal tone and asks staff and professors not only to attend, but also to encourage students' attendance. He notes that since *Trifles* is a play often taught in English classes, this production will offer a great opportunity for students to experience it "live." He suggests that it would make an excellent extra credit assignment. Juan's choices in these advertising media have been determined not only by his goal of ensuring a well-attended play but also by the multiple target audiences of his advertising, his available tools and publicity budget, and the context of a college environment. His understanding of audience and context has informed each message's information, tone, and visual appearance. While these messages may differ greatly from the essay Juan will write for his English class, in both cases, for successful achievement of his goals, he must employ rhetorical understanding and skill.

Most of us make communication decisions daily, in situations ranging from personal conversations to community projects, from professional tasks to academic assignments. This book will not attempt to cover every possible situation which might demand strong rhetorical skills, but by focusing on *commonly required* skills and insights, we aim to help writers and speakers achieve their goals more effectively in a variety of venues. Rather than offering instruction in text-talk, for example (When should one choose LOL over ☺?), we will address the greater issues of communication that might help one make effective rhetorical decisions in a *range* of situations. Since this book is meant for use in a college class, it does offer specific insights regarding academic writing in addition to its more general discussion of rhetorical principles and strategies. These concepts should be applicable to any mode of communication in any context, and our focus on academic writing serves as a revealing example of how they can be effectively applied.

In our discussion so far, we have several times used the term **rhetoric**. This term, which comes to us from the Greeks, refers to *the art of persuasion*. In the following pages, we will often use the terms *rhetoric*, *persuasion* and *argument* as we explore various writing and presentation situations. The word **argument**, in this context, does not refer necessarily to heated debate, in which the parties are angry; rather the term will be used more broadly here to refer to *the case* one may make in establishing a position on a topic—that is, one's *message* to one's audience. To persuade is to influence one's audience toward a particular position or perspective. Almost always, a writer seeks to persuade a reader, even if at first glance, the writer's effort is not obvious.

Hold on! Is writing, indeed, nearly always persuasive in nature? Admittedly, this is a broad claim. Let's test the idea: What about the following essay written by student Kyle Moseley in response to a self-reflection assignment inquiring *whether the writer has met his or her writing goals for the semester*?

Fear and Loathing in Black and White Medium

I was simply not a writer. Feelings of loathing and anxiety often filled my head in previous English classes. Anxious of criticism, I would retreat from the idea of being a scrivener of my thoughts. But things change. During the current semester, all but withered into summer, I have found myself surprised at the creative outside connections—especially to my art major—that have permeated my analysis and essays, though I am quite used to the fact that my grammar and prose do not meet classroom standards.

In the "Goal Sheet" I completed at the beginning of my English Composition class, my goal for the semester summed up my feeling toward writing: "My goal is to confidently write essays, short stories, etc." This goal has been achieved. My confidence has been derived from my ability of logical analysis and application of foreign subjects and ideas (foreign, that is, in the context of the English classroom environment). For example, the Reader Response Card over John Updike's short story "Summer" inspired me to critique its weight as a piece of art. Simply, the imagery present in the short story, not to mention the subject matter, made for easy analysis; it functions as early American Romanticist Art. Making this connection from such bland repetitions of twenty-six shapes on extremely formatted canvas to a practice that I excel in, as well as have classical training in, brought new light to writing. Writing is just another form of self-expression, thus, it should be evaluated according to how well it achieves that expression, not just how well it follows a narrow set of classroom rules.

If writing can be compared to art, then my writing is folk art; sometimes I see Standard English grammar and prose as having a negative effect, just as an art critic would insist "proper" or classical brushstrokes or casting techniques can hinder some pieces. It's true that this preference for folk art can be a problem in certain contexts. Sentence structure is occasionally an issue: my brain thinks as it would speak. Papers are organized on my scatter-brained tendencies, not of classroom standard. The research paper draft was filled with comma splices and partially non-sequential ideas. Spelling is obviously still an issue.

One could say my essays are dressed formally but forgot to shower.

Honestly, grammar is just not that important to me. Computers fill students' scholarly lives and spellcheck still parents college kids. Writing is about putting ideas down in a tangible, somewhat loosely defined media. Writing isn't a task; it's a freedom. It's freedom to paint in gray and white. I will continue doing what any Art Major does: I will create with anything at hand. Thus, my goal of "Enjoy[ing] the act of writing because it can be considered as an extension of one's self" isn't a far-off dream (Moseley, Goal Paper).

Kyle's assignment was to write primarily for discovery rather than to persuade his audience (his instructor, in this case) toward a particular position. His professor wanted him to reflect on his initial goals for the course and, in retrospect, determine whether he had accomplished them and, if so, how fully. Here, the reflective writing itself is meant to serve as a learning experience. Thus Kyle's essay may serve as evidence that some communications are not intended primarily for persuasion.

What about typical writing produced in the sciences? If a researcher reports on a lab experiment in a research journal article, we expect the article to maintain *objectivity*, right? Science is expected to *avoid* bias in its pursuit of knowledge. Yet, this example does not really refute the idea that writing is "nearly always persuasive in nature." Here is why: In order to maintain his or her credibility as a scholar, the scientist-writer not only must persuade the journal editor that the project is important enough to be published in the journal, but this writer also must convince his or her fellow researchers that the article's conclusions are valid and worthwhile. The scientist may even use parts of the report to write a second, more overtly persuasive, paper: a grant proposal requesting money from a foundation for expansion of this project in a carefully justified direction.

What about Juan's poster? Is its goal persuasive? In offering information about the play in a visually pleasing format, Juan *is* trying to attract people to the play. He has not stated an "argument," *per se*, but persuasion is definitely his goal. Additional examples of daily communication designed to persuade include a text inviting a friend to help plan a birthday party, a phone call to one's mother asking her to deposit more money into one's checking account, an email from a student's father to the high school counselor requesting a change in his son's class schedule, and a job application.

As illustrated above by Kyle's essay in which he was primarily writing for discovery, there are certainly times when we communicate for purposes other than persuasion. In our daily communications, we undoubtedly engage in some that are not meant primarily as argument, such as a wave "hello" to a friend or an answer of "On the counter" to a family member's question, "Where are my keys?" Yet, as many of our examples show, much communication *does* fall into the category of persuasion, and thus this book will illuminate rhetorical principles that can aid writers and speakers in successfully making their cases to particular audiences in particular contexts.

This book's goal is to help writers improve their abilities to assess a situation, articulate their purpose, and employ effective communication strategies toward fulfillment of that purpose. We hope to convince readers that these skills are worth developing, that they will be useful whether one is writing a history paper on the gender shifts that occurred during World War I, requesting government funding for a project, marketing a new product, or trying to convince Facebook friends to consider a change in political perspective—or to attend a campus play.

A Few Notes about this Book

This text book is the work of a team of professors who all teach first-year composition; the information and insights we offer here arise from what we have learned by working with students like you to improve their writing skills. So the royal "we" used in the following chapters refers to this team. Speaking of "you," when we employ second person and use the pronoun "you," we are speaking directly to *you*, the first-year composition student. Finally, for your convenience, the terms that appear in **bold** in the text of each chapter are defined again in the Glossary of Important Terms at the end of the book.

Reading Critically/Engaging the Material

Tanya Long Bennett

Students accepted into college have likely been reading since they were five or six years old, so it may seem odd or even insulting to have an instructor suggest that their reading comprehension skills still need development. However, the kinds of texts students may encounter at this point in their education may very well offer them a challenge. This famous passage from Thomas Paine's *The Crisis*,[1] for example, takes some work for any reader to understand and interpret:

> These are the times that try men's souls. The summer soldier and the sunshine patriot will, in this crisis, shrink from the service of their country; but he that stands by it now, deserves the love and thanks of man and woman. Tyranny, like hell, is not easily conquered; yet we have this consolation with us, that the harder the conflict, the more glorious the triumph. What we obtain too cheap, we esteem too lightly: it is dearness only that gives every thing its value. Heaven knows how to put a proper price upon its goods; and it would be strange indeed if so celestial an article as FREEDOM should not be highly rated. Britain, with an army to enforce her tyranny, has declared that she has a right (not only to TAX) but "to BIND us in ALL CASES WHATSOEVER" and if being bound in that manner, is not slavery, then is there not such a thing as slavery upon earth. Even the expression is impious; for so unlimited a power can belong only to God.

If we have studied the eighteenth century historical context of this passage, we know that here Paine is attempting to rally American

1

colonists to war against Britain. But even in light of that information, what does Paine mean by "summer soldier"? What is the "dearness" he associates with the victory he hopes the colonies will achieve? How does Paine link the concepts of tax, being bound, and slavery in order to build his argument? Since this piece is an important link to the United States' formation as a country, we are motivated to understand it, and to meet this challenge, we must move beyond our approach to more ordinary reading tasks, such as skimming through a headline in *The Huffington Post* or an article in *Atlantic Monthly*. For this more difficult task, we must slow down and pay special attention to Paine's words and sentences.

In college, we are often presented with another type of challenging reading: **scholarly articles and books**. At first it may seem that we can manage our assignments without reading such complex works. We can often find basic information on a topic in internet articles and in textbooks, which are much easier to read and understand. However, by the time students begin courses in their majors, scholarly articles can no longer be avoided. They offer much needed information and perspectives on the specialized topics students are studying and are absolutely necessary for composing upper level research papers. So how can one successfully tackle this kind of material?

Consider this passage from John Mueller's scholarly article, "Changing Attitudes Towards War: The Impact of the First World War"[2]:

> [T]here may be something of an inherent and rather unpleasant mushiness in the study of the "historical movement of ideas," and analysis will tend to be inductive and after-the-fact, rather than predictive. (Or to put it another way, anyone who came up with a good method for predicting ideas whose time had come would be likely to keep it secret because the method, applied to stock markets and commodity production, would quickly make the theorist the richest person in the world.) But it does not seem wise in this area to ignore phenomena that cannot easily be measured, treated with crisp precision or probed with deductive panache.

These remarks are difficult to understand without reading the rest of the article, especially the rest of the introduction, where Mueller argues that *while it is commonly believed* that anti-war attitudes grew during the twentieth century as a result of World War I primarily because of its "sheer destructiveness,"[3] a more careful analysis of the war reveals that this destructiveness was not so unusual, as wars go. Mueller suggests that *the causes of the anti-war attitude were, instead,* that World War I 1) was preceded by anti-war agitation, 2) was also preceded by a long period of relative peace in Europe, and 3) introduced developments in warfare that threatened world annihilation. Mueller arrives at these three points by engaging in the practice he describes in the above passage: examining the "historical movement of ideas." As we can now begin to understand, in that passage, he is trying to counter the arguments of his nervous fellow historian-readers, who might not feel that this kind of research, focused on *ideas* rather than *data,* is concrete or "provable" enough. But even after reading the entire introduction, one must read this passage carefully to register Mueller's point.

Mueller's article is twenty-eight pages long, so clearly, to fully digest what he has to say in the article as a whole, a reader would need to read slowly and closely, and perhaps even *re*-read. This history article is typical of the scholarly material being produced in any field of study, whether it be history, art, biology, marketing, English, political science, or sociology. These articles are written by scholars, professionals in their fields, and their audience is fellow scholars/professionals. Thus, in academic materials, one often encounters **jargon**, or words used in a special way by people in that field. What does Mueller mean by "historical movement of ideas"? One might innocently begin investigation of the phrase by consulting a dictionary, but there will not be an entry for the phrase as a whole. Unfortunately, if a reader looks up each word individually, the definitions of "historical," "movement," and "ideas" will not lead him any closer to an understanding of the phrase—besides, he likely already knew the definitions of each of those words. The best option is to understand the phrase by its *context.*

It takes some time, and quite a bit of exposure, to begin understanding a particular field's jargon. The more often we run across a word or phrase in materials of a discipline, the deeper our understanding of the concept grows. So the first hint for improving students' reading comprehension is *not* to avoid difficult texts, but *instead* to read challenging material, particularly that of their majors and/or minors. This practice will develop the reader's vocabulary, as well as her knowledge, and as a result, her writing will gain sophistication, too.

For tackling difficult reading materials, there are several important strategies that can be employed to ensure the reader is digesting them as fully as possible:

1) Skim the piece first. Get an idea of its main focus, and try to get a sense of the piece's structure. Where does the introduction *end* and the body *begin*? Does the writer take time to provide background or a summary of pre-existing arguments before he or she begins making his or her own case? How is the evidence organized?

2) Next, read again, more closely this time. Look up words in the dictionary or in textbooks, and make an effort to understand an idea before moving on.

3) Annotate. Write on the page! Write questions raised by the text, and make a note of particularly important information and ideas. Highlighting important ideas can be helpful, but to inter-act *meaningfully* with the text, a reader must consider his *own* reaction to what the author is saying, and write it down. (Hint: If making marks in the book is not a viable option, use sticky notes for annotating.)

4) Read the whole piece. Often, a sentence or paragraph taken out of context can mislead the reader regarding the central message of the article.

5) Re-read if necessary—all or parts of the piece.

6) Summarize. Put down the article or book and walk away; go to dinner or have a cup of coffee. Then come back, and with-out looking at the article or book, write a summary of what the author seems to be saying. This method requires the reader to put the idea into *her own* words since, by now, the author's particular words and phrases will have ceased echoing in the reader's head. Afterwards, she can check her summary against the original source to make sure her version is accurate. A good summary of a text requires a full understanding of it.

Employing these steps, and making them a habit, will improve reading comprehension of challenging texts.

The following is an excerpt of a *Higher Education* article—"Lost in Transition? Student Food Consumption," by Blichfeldt and Gram[4]—an-notated by an engaged reader we will call Amir:

It is important to understand the anxieties of freshman students as their abilities and confidence in their new role are decisive for them during this key transition to higher education. Food is one important aspect of student wellbeing, but still relatively little is written about student food even though a rumbling stomach is no doubt not optimal when trying to perform well in higher education. When reading the sparse literature on student food one could get the impression that young people are floating around with no anchor points, starting from scratch and seeking to build food practices with next to no cooking skills… But is this the whole story about student food? This paper seeks to nuance the understanding of this domain through a qualitative explorative study of students' experiences with food in the transition phase from being cared for at home to taking care of their own food provision… [5]

Freshman college students are learning to be independent.

Nuance: to recognize subtle distinctions.

Qualitative: not based on numerical data but on participant survey comments and/or interviews.

In contrast to studies of student food, which tend to treat students as one (homogeneous) group, our interviewees span over a variety of levels of engagement and skills, from the very competent cooks to students mostly living on a diet of semi-prepared or cold meals. Although drawing on a relatively small (and potentially biased) sample, in the present study, very diverse presentations of student food consumption during transition emerged. Whereas some students come across as novices, virtually starting from scratch, others are well-versed in the domain of cooking. In opposition to the freshman 15 myth and stereotypical representations of student food as junk food, our interviewees seem to engage in food making, rule-setting and self-regulation with much energy even if, sometimes, dinner becomes a matter of quick fixes. Furthermore, the interviewees are, to a large extent, not starting out in a vacuum, but are entangled in their parents' food practices and the students who experience the least problems in regard to habitualisation are clearly those, who are experienced cooks from home. Nevertheless, although

Homogeneous: all the same, which we're not!

But the freshman 15 does seem to be a real thing for lots of people.

Habitualisation: when repeated actions become a pattern (and begin to take less thought).

anchored in parental practices, the students in our study are generally very aware of the opportunities and challenges student life brings them in terms of their generating their "own" food practices and habits. Apart from what is brought along from home, students talk about how they notice what partners, friends, and other students do and do not eat in order to be assured that the habits and practices they develop are "proper." The students do not automatically extend the practices and habits they were brought up with, but instead, new food practices are actively developed, often with a clear feeling of being in transit. Furthermore, the extent to which self-identity is changed depends on the competencies and skills brought along from home, the living situation and, most importantly, the students.[6]

Does <u>money</u> have anything to do with food choices?

Food is part of the adult identity students are forming.

Notice that Amir's comments respond to several of the tips given above for engaged and critical reading. He clearly had to stop at times to look up unfamiliar words, and his first and last marginal comments are brief summaries of key points being developed by the authors. Amir is likely working, as he reads, to form an idea of the article's central argument. However, he did not just passively absorb the article's meaning; he also responded *personally* to particular assertions such as the one regarding factors that shape student food choices and the one suggesting that the "freshman 15" may be a deceptive stereotype. If Amir decides to write a paper on this topic, he might choose to research *economic* factors that could offer even more "nuance" to Blichfeldt's and Gram's argument about student food choices. The reading process Amir has used here certainly takes longer than the approach we employ when reading a short newspaper article, and that is the point. Critical and engaged reading involves more work, but as a result, it is often more stimulating, as well.

When students begin college, they enter the dialogue of scholars. To become confident and knowledgeable enough to participate in this conversation, they will need to sharpen their reading comprehension skills and understanding of their fields, as well as build faith in their own abilities and ideas. It may take a while, but one day they should be able to debate confidently with fellow scholars and/or other professionals based on carefully gathered evidence. Reading critically and engaging rigorously with scholarly ideas and information are the first steps down this path.

Rhetorical Situation(s)

Tanya Long Bennett

2.1 COMMUNICATION MODELS

Traditionally, the rhetorical situation has been visually portrayed like this:

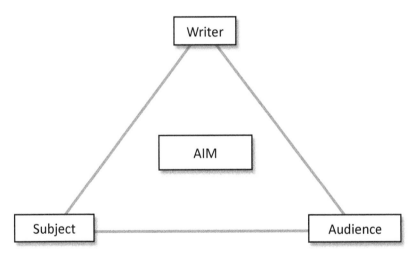

Aristotle considered *writer*, *subject*, and *audience* to be organically related to or integrated with each other in the rhetorical situation.[7]

As discussed in this book's Introduction, there *are* times when we communicate for purposes other than to persuade. Some argue that when we write about a subject in order to learn about it, the *subject*, rather than the *audience*, should be the emphasis of the writing experience. Kyle Moseley's essay, presented in the Introduction, is an example of writing for reflection or discovery. His first year composition assignment directed students to reflect on whether they had met their learning goals for the course, and to elaborate on how they had succeeded or fallen short.

Certainly, in this particular assignment the primary goal is for the writer to recognize/learn something about himself. Taking the time to consider consciously his experience in the course—and with the writing process promoted by his professor—should help Kyle progress cognitively toward his goals as a thinker and writer. Yet, as he wrote the essay, he was undoubtedly conscious of his professor, who would read and grade it not only for content, but also for how it was presented. While the assignment may prioritize the "aim" of *understanding* the subject (the student's growth as a writer), the secondary "aim" of *demonstrating* the student's writing ability (illustrating his point and persuading his professor of his writing prowess) is also a significant factor. Thus, the essay does indeed address all of the components in the diagram above.

The diagram asserts an important point about communication: While the subject is a crucial component of the communication, the writer explores the subject with a particular *purpose* (or aim) and a particular target *audience* in mind. It could be argued that in most rhetorical situations, the *purpose* is more central to the writer's decisions than the *subject* itself, though as Aristotle notes, it is difficult to separate these components from one another. As for audience, most students are accustomed to writing to a very specific reader: their teacher. In this course, we hope to broaden students' consideration of audience.

The model above gives us a simple way to think about the writing situation. Current communication venues do complicate this model, however. A Wikipedia article might be written by an expert for a general audience in order to provide basic information on the topic. But under certain conditions, a *reader* can go in and edit, delete, and/or add to the article. There is no one writer in this case, and writers and readers may switch roles. While the article's purpose may stay the same, it *is* possible that the various writers' purposes will not be completely aligned. Similarly, blogs in which readers may comment, providing hypertext to the original post, are another example of evolving models of communication.

Regardless, to write effectively, one needs to know the subject well and to consider carefully the audience and purpose of the communication.

2.2 PURPOSE AND GENRE

What do we mean by *purpose* exactly? If until this point, most student writing has been done for classes, the default purpose may have been to make an "A" on a paper and/or in a course. To that end, in addition to proving their thesis to an invisible general reader, most students have also undoubtedly worked toward a secondary purpose, which was to impress their teachers favorably. At the beginning of a course, a student may have experienced an initial "writer's anxiety" as she sought to get a "fix" on her teacher's values and preferences. This process illustrates how decisions in even this type of writing are shaped by *purpose* and *audience*.

But let's consider other, more "real world" purposes. College sophomore Katie Brown has determined that she will have to get a part-time job to help cover her college expenses. She could go to a local restaurant and complete an application for a waitressing position, but she has decided, instead, to apply for a tutoring position at the Student Success Center on her campus. Her major is math education, and she believes that experience tutoring her peers in math not only would look impressive on her resume when she graduates and enters the job market but would also give her some much-needed experience in teaching math principles effectively. The Student Success Center requires that each applicant submit a one-page résumé and a cover letter as well as letters of recommendation from two professors. Katie's *purpose*, in composing her résumé and cover letter and in carefully selecting which professors to ask for letters, is to secure the position.

In a very different situation, Katie's older brother Robert, who graduated from another state university three years ago, now works for a large environmental engineering firm. His project team has determined that, through a grant from an environmental preservation foundation, they might be able to secure funding for a new landfill project they have designed. The team believes their new design resolves several waste pollution problems associated with current landfill design. Robert's team has asked him to draft the grant proposal to the foundation. The team's *purpose* is to secure funding for the new landfill, which the company would donate to the county in which they are located.

Finally, Lee Sung has been selected by her campus's Student Activities Board to perform a stand-up comedy routine during Spring Jam week. All Lee's friends think she is hilarious, but since she will be getting paid for this performance, she wants to be sure she is received well by her fellow undergraduates in the audience. She spends two weekends writing the jokes for her act. She will perform without any notes, of course—the act should appear spontaneous. But she is using the writing process to work out ahead of time what the act should look like. Her *purpose* is to make her audience laugh—a *lot*.

In addition to the variety of purposes in these examples, each of these communication situations demands a different **genre**, meaning *type* or *category*. In writing, well-recognized genres offer guidelines or conventions that help us meet our audience's expectations and achieve our purpose. These genres include the formal letter, essay, novel, speech, research paper, news article, and many others. In the scenarios discussed above, Katie Brown writes a cover letter, the conventions of which employers know well. To meet the expectations associated with such a letter, Katie consults several examples from reliable websites. Similarly, Robert reviews sample grant proposals to be sure he is using common conventions of the genre for his team's proposal. And Lee Sung has seen many stand-up comedy routines, so she knows well the general form such acts usually follow. She uses, and sometimes purposefully breaks, the rules of common routines in order to achieve the effects she wants. Recognizing genres and understanding their common features helps us to meet our own communication goals when employing these types.

Effective Argument

As we have already established, we make the effort to communicate with others almost constantly, for specific and sometimes multiple purposes. But not all of those attempts are as successful as we would like. Further, some people seem to be much more successful than others at consistently accomplishing their communication goals. This fact haunts many of us each time we sit down to write. Are some people just born with a talent for eloquent writing? If I seem to struggle with the challenge of writing an effective persuasive argument, does this mean I am just "not good at English"?

We can look to Longinus, the Greek teacher of rhetoric, for one perspective on this issue. Longinus did not agree with the notion that only natural geniuses could write with impact. Sure, he admitted, for some people, creating work that "tears everything up like a whirlwind"[8] seems to be a breeze (pardon the pun). But Longinus argues in "On Sublimity" that powerful writing is *not magical*. The process of creating it involves recognizable, learnable features: *an important idea*, expressed in *carefully chosen words*, arranged in a particularly *effective order*. He asserts that if we study the methods that others have used to accomplish this kind of writing, and take risks, pushing ourselves beyond the mundane or the common, we may very well achieve powerful rhetoric ourselves. This chapter seeks to break down that process in order to shed light on the mystery, increasing our understanding of what makes effective argument.

3.1 PATHOS, LOGOS, AND ETHOS, *Tanya Long Bennett*

For success with an audience, we can benefit from attention to Aristotle's three categories of rhetorical appeal: *pathos, logos* and *ethos*.[9] In Chapter 2, we touched on the communication model associated with Aristotle's insights on persuasion. Considering the writer, audience, and subject as consistent components of the communication equation, Aristotle focused on these three crucial aspects of argument that influence the audience's attitudes toward the subject:

3.1.a Pathos

Pathos is the appeal to an audience's emotions. As an audience, we are subjected daily to the emotional appeal: Television commercials urging us to donate to animal rescue efforts effectively employ images of wounded and neglected dogs and cats to elicit a *sympathetic* response from the viewer. Facebook friends offer anecdotes of questionably spent tax money to generate *anger* against a particular government official, implying a desire for us to vote this politician out of office during the next election. Emotions are an integral aspect of the human experience, and since we often act more readily on our feelings than on our intellect, marketers, social activists, and even family members often rely heavily on *pathos* to persuade us toward their point of view.

3.1.b Logos

In academic and professional venues, on the other hand, we are expected to override our emotions and act more rationally and logically. Our colleagues, supervisors, and shareholders certainly demand behavior that can be justified by logic. *Logos* is the appeal to logic, which is based on either **inductive** or **deductive reasoning**.

3.1.b (1) Inductive Reasoning

By inductive reasoning, we form conclusions based on *samples*. You likely use inductive reasoning every day. Lab experiments, for example, must be repeatable in order for scientists to gather a convincing amount of data to prove a hypothesis. If a scientist hypothesizes that adding a particular substance to a rat's diet will cause the rat to develop cancer, the experiment must be carefully controlled, and must be repeated hundreds of times in order to prove that, if the rat does indeed develop cancer, it is the added dietary substance, and not some other factor, causing the cancer.

When a shopper concludes that one store sells jeans at a better price than another store, chances are that he has based this conclusion on several shopping experiences in which he has observed a consistent trend in the price differences between the two stores. Here are two other illustrations of conclusions (theses) based on inductive reasoning:

1) In Robert Frost's sonnet "Design," the color *white* is used ironically to suggest that only a devious designer would clothe the

universe's evil in so much beauty. The "dimpled spider, fat and white"; the "white heal-all" flower that "hold[s] up" the moth for the spider's feast; and the rhyming of "blight" with "white" and "right" work together to generate the poem's disturbing sense that the "order" of the natural scene is deceptively lovely.

2) There is a "devastating scale" of neglect and abuse experienced by adults with autism, a charity has warned. Many are staying at home because they are afraid of being abused or harassed, the National Autistic Society (NAS) said. People with autism can find it hard to interpret other people's motivations and as a result can be taken advantage of or manipulated, the charity said. Half of 1,300 sufferers questioned by NAS said they had been abused by someone who they thought of as a friend, 37% said they had been manipulated to do something they didn't want to do by these so-called friends and 44% said fear of abuse or harassment led them to not want to leave the house.[10]

In each of the two arguments above, the writer forwards a conclusion based on examples, or *samples*—three illustrations from the poem in the first one, and substantial percentages of 1,300 people surveyed in the second. A pattern in samples can suggest a trend, which can lead to a valid conclusion.

3.1.b (2) Deductive Reasoning

Deductive reasoning, on the other hand, is drawing a conclusion based on *a logical equation*. Sir Conan Doyle's fictional detective Sherlock Holmes is famous for employing deductive reasoning to solve mysteries. In "A Scandal in Bohemia," for example, Holmes reveals his knowledge that Watson has recently gotten very wet and that he employs "a most clumsy and careless servant girl." When Watson asks how Holmes knows these details about him, the detective explains, "It is simplicity itself . . . My eyes tell me that on the inside of your left shoe, just where the firelight strikes it, the leather is scored by six almost parallel cuts. Obviously they have been caused by someone who has very carelessly scraped round the edges of the sole in order to remove crusted mud from it. Hence, you see, my double deduction that you had been out in vile weather, and that you had a particularly malignant boot-slitting specimen of the London slavey."[11]

Such equations, when seen in their complete form, comprise a three part logical statement called a **syllogism**. This type of statement includes:

- A **warrant** (also called a *major premise*): All Southerners are friendly.
- A *minor premise*: Julie is Southern.
- And a *claim* (also called a *conclusion*: Julie must be friendly.

In the example of Holmes's deduction, above, the syllogism can be broken up as follows:

- Warrant: Parallel cuts made around the sole of a shoe area always caused by careless scraping of crusted mud.
- Minor premise: Watson's shoes exhibit such cuts.
- Claims: Not only has Watson been walking in mud, but also that mud has been scraped off by someone careless (a careless servant girl).

One can see in the above example that sometimes syllogisms are flawed, or illogical. Not *all* Southerners are friendly (no matter how narrowly this speaker defines "friendly"), and thus his assumption about Julie's disposition may be incorrect. Flawed logic is most problematic when we find the equation in its less complete form: an **enthymeme**. If we consider the warrant as an *underlying assumption*, and recognize that this premise often goes *unstated*, we see that the enthymeme is a common type of statement that often "leaps" to its conclusion unreasonably. Consider the following examples:

I.

- Enthymeme: Sarah, don't eat that leftover chicken; it came from Pete's Café.
- Warrant: Food from Pete's Café is often spoiled.
- Minor premise: That chicken came from Pete's Café.
- Claim: That chicken may be spoiled.

II.

- Enthymeme: Lori Pittsfield would be a good hire for our company; she has a degree from University of Georgia.
- Warrant: Anyone from University of Georgia would be a good employee for our company.
- Minor premise: Lori has a degree from University of Georgia.
- Claim: Lori would be a good employee for our company.

14

III.

- Enthymeme: Sam Williams should be voted out of state office because he supports Medicare.
- Warrant: Anyone who supports Medicare will damage our state.
- Minor premise: Sam supports Medicare.
- Claim: As an elected official, Sam will damage our state.

Under careful scrutiny, how do the above enthymemes fare? Are they true? If a writer asserts the above enthymemes, will readers agree with the warrant of each? Why or why not? What is the danger of reading (or hearing) only the enthymeme and not testing the underlying (unspoken) assumption?

3.1.b (3) Exercise

Test the logic of the following enthymemes:

1) The U.S. must provide effective public education in order to maintain a healthy economy.
2) Mandy Jenkins would make a bad committee chair because she is bossy.
3) Bob Richards would be an effective teacher because he exhibits a thorough knowledge of his subject area, he is highly organized, and he relates well to young people.

To test the logic of such statements, we need to question carefully the warrant, or underlying assumption. Is the assertion that *a healthy economy depends upon an educated populace* supportable with evidence? We might like for the writer to clarify the meaning of the word "healthy" here. Does it imply an economy that is at a high rate of growth *currently?* Or could it refer to a *stable* economy that yields more modest and long-reaching growth? Also, what is meant by "educated"? A high school diploma? A bachelor's degree? Once the writer establishes common ground with the audience on these points, she should provide proof, or *evidence*, linking the occurrence of *educated citizenry* to a *healthy economy*, as she has defined the terms for the purposes of this argument.

Secondly, will the audience buy the underlying assumption that "any country that desires a healthy economy should support *public* education"? If the writer presents clear evidence showing that countries with educated citizens consistently sustain a healthier economy than countries lacking in this area, the audience will likely "ride along" with her as she makes her case. However, some readers may still be skeptical. Is there any vehicle besides *public school* for educating citizens? Is there any chance that a country whose education system is predominantly run by *corporations* could affect its economy positively? If everyone were *homeschooled*, might a country produce a satisfactorily educated populace? If some readers were educated in a private school or were homeschooled, they might hesitate to go along with the warrant that a country can only produce a well-educated populace through public schools.

3.1.b (4) Logical Fallacies

Whether an assertion is based on inductive or deductive reasoning, in testing a claim, it helps to know about **logical fallacies** commonly found in weak arguments. A logical fallacy is a conclusion drawn from faulty reasoning. Here are a few of the most commonly employed fallacies:

Bandwagon argument

The band wagon claim encourages us to adopt a particular opinion because "everyone else is doing it."

> Many Americans feel that public schools are declining; therefore, an alternative educational model must be adopted.

Single cause

This kind of argument suggests that *one factor* is causing a problem when the causes may actually be multiple and complex.

> The decline of U.S. public schools has resulted in the current economic recession.

Is a publicly-educated populace the *only* factor determining whether a country's economy is "healthy"? What about natural resources, like oil? What about government policies protecting businesses and/or consumers (or failing to do so)?

Either/Or

This type of statement implies that there are only two options:

> Support public education and enjoy a healthy economy,
> or
> Don't support public education and suffer a failing economy.

Is there a third option? Are there ways to compromise between these two extremes?

Slippery slope

In this kind of argument, the writer warns that one step in the "wrong" direction will result in complete destruction.

> If the instructor allows extra credit for this assignment, students will expect extra credit opportunities on all assignments and then the course grade will have lost all its meaning.

Straw man

In this approach, the writer misrepresents the opponent's argument, which works only if the audience is ignorant of the opponent's case.

> Showing her true socialist colors, union leader Julie Burns claims that workers "should have a voice at the table" when factory owners determine salaries.

Here, the writer has taken a short passage of Burns's statement out of context, ignoring her longer, more complex argument for balancing market forces with protection of human rights.

False cause

Here, the writer offers a cause that *seems* linked to the problem but does not actually *establish* the causal relationship.

> The high school schedule changed from a block model to a seven-period day, and now I'm failing math; therefore, we should return to the original block schedule.

Ad hominem

This type of argument attacks the *character* of the opposition instead of the opposition's *logic*.

> I just don't agree with the CEO's decision to change the company's computer system; after all, this company's executives are greedy and unfriendly.

Begging the question

This approach states an argument's claim as if it were proof of its own validity (engaging in circular reasoning).

> John Doe was a great man; it says so in his autobiography.

Guarding against Fallacies

As we observe arguments—in our readings, on the internet, and in the marketplace—we should test the claims carefully to ensure that we are not deceived by illogical statements like those above. Also, we should be sure to review our *own* assertions to avoid falling into faulty logic ourselves.

3.1.c Ethos

Pathos can influence a reader's emotional response to an argument, and logic can help build a writer's credibility, or *ethos*, with the reader. If the argument is well-supported with *evidence* and is *logically presented*, the reader will be more likely to *trust* the writer. Yet ethos, the appeal to a reader's trust, is more complex than just providing sound logic and evidence. It is crucial in convincing the reader not only that the writer is *credible* but also that he *shares relevant values* with the reader. Besides good logic, what causes us to consider another person's argument? We tend to test a writer's credibility by asking ourselves the following questions:

- Is this writer knowledgeable? Is this person an expert in the area in which he/she is writing? What are his/her credentials? Has he/she done the necessary research to provide sufficient background and evidence in support of the argument?
- Is this person's argument clear and interesting?
- Does this person share key values with me? Do we agree, for example, that it is important for the U.S. economy to be strong? (Can the writer *assume* that this issue is a priority for the reader?)
- Is this person addressing me (and others) respectfully and fairly?

3.1.c (1) Exercise

A writer may safely assume that a reader will demand sound logic and proof to be convinced of an argument's or perspective's validity, but consider as well how our trust in a writer is affected when we run across a typo or a grammatical mistake. Further, a writer's use of *charged or insulting diction* can alienate a reader, especially one in the opposition's camp. Consider the writer's *ethos* in the following argument:

> A number of observable differences between people of the U.S. North and those of the South have been noted by cultural anthropologists. While Southerners tend to be open and friendly, speaking to passersby and making eye contact with them, Yankees are often gruff and cold. Reflecting this difference, people of the South tend to be community-oriented, whereas Northerners are usually more selfish and aloof in their social interactions. Finally, because the South's climate is warmer than the North's, Southerners tend to be physically active, while Northerners are lazier. These contrasting behaviors reveal a stark difference between the cultures of these two major U.S. regions.

In a class discussion, suggest ways that this writer's central point could be made without offending Northern readers. In particular, locate *charged words* that could be replaced with more objective, or neutral, diction.

3.1.c (2) Exercise

As we discussed in the section on audience in Chapter 2, writers will often need to present an argument to an audience who does not already agree with them on the issue. Yet, chances are good that a writer shares some important values with her audience that could be used to lay a foundation for the argument. To practice building ethos with such an audience, list *relevant shared values* that could use in establishing common ground between the members in each set of opposing entities:

1) Pro-Life and Pro-Choice groups
2) Gun-control advocates and gun-rights advocates
3) Local residents in favor of welcoming a Walmart into a nearby lot and those against it
4) Those in favor of expanded domestic oil drilling and those against it
5) Parents who strongly wish for their child to complete a bachelor's degree right after high school and the son or daughter who wants to work for several years before deciding whether or not to pursue a degree

Pathos, logos, and *ethos* are appeals present in most communications, though we often use them and respond to them subconsciously.

Considering on a *conscious* level how each can be generated effectively is a significant step toward thinking critically and increasing our impact as *rhetors*, or writers/speakers.

3.2 DETERMINING AND ARTICULATING AN EFFECTIVE THESIS, *Tanya Long Bennett*

The understanding of *pathos, logos,* and *ethos* is crucial to forwarding a significant and arguable thesis. The argument itself will require more than a sentence or two, but the **thesis,** the statement of the central argument, is a key to presenting a persuasive case. It should articulate the specific point around which the rest of the argument revolves and why that point is so important. It should also do so in the most effective language possible, given the target audience.

3.2.a Establishing the *Relevance* of the Thesis

In grade school, teachers may be satisfied to see students formulate a *clear* thesis that controls the rest of the essay, which of course the thesis should do. High school students may be rewarded with high grades for essays based on theses like these:

- World War I brought changes to warfare, a shift in women's social roles, and for many, a questioning of traditional religious beliefs.

- Charlotte Gilman employs elements of the Gothic style in her short story "The Yellow Wallpaper."

These theses are certainly clear and grammatically correct. Further, they may be statements used to introduce essays written for a specific purpose: to demonstrate students' understanding of a course's subject matter. Even college students may be guided to write theses like these under particular circumstances, such as for exam essays. However, if a writer's target audience includes readers *other than teachers*, he should recognize that a thesis more clearly *relevant* to a broader readership is required. Most readers demand *justification* for an argument, and one they can *relate* to, at that. A person reading a magazine in a dentist's office might consider the above-described essay on World War I (if it happened to be published in such a periodical), read the introduction, and wonder, "Why is the writer trying to cover such a broad array of World War I's effects? This article doesn't promise much depth," or about an article regarding the second topic above, "Who cares if Gilman uses the Gothic style in this story? What's the point here?"

Below are some alternate examples of theses that incorporate the *justification* for the argument into the definition of the argument, yielding much more appealing statements:

- The shift in women's social roles during World War I contributed directly to the highly-increased participation of women in today's skilled workforce.
- Charlotte Gilman's use of Gothic elements in her short story "The Yellow Wallpaper" reveals the subconscious battle many of us face in trying to fulfill our personal desires while simultaneously conforming to society's rigid expectations.

Not only are these two statements clear and grammatical, but they promise the reader insight into his/her *own experience* and a better understanding of the world *he/she lives in*. In doing so, they establish *relevance*.

3.2.b Narrowing the Thesis and Seeking Originality

In addition to establishing relevance, the second set of thesis statements in the section above accomplishes another important goal: focusing, or *narrowing*, in order to enable *depth* of development. It would take a book-length study, or perhaps even several books, to explore this statement with any thoroughness:

> World War I brought changes to warfare, a shift in women's social roles, and for many, a questioning of traditional religious beliefs.

In fact there are many books already published on each of these three subtopics. The only way to say anything original on this subject (the great effects of World War I on society) would be to narrow it substantially and find a perspective that provides *new information* and/or a *fresh angle* on World War I's effects. Readers often become impatient simply reviewing information they already know. They read to learn something new or to discover a new way of seeing the subject.

By strategically narrowing the focus, the second version of this thesis provides a fresh angle on World War I's impact on society.

> The shift in women's social roles during World War I contributed directly to the highly-increased participation of women in today's skilled workforce.

21

Readers probably already knew that women's social roles shifted as a result of the war, but they might not have considered how that historical shift can be traced to our own social practices and attitudes. Not only does this revised thesis *narrow* to women's social roles (leaving evolving warfare strategies and religious beliefs for a later study), but it *focuses* on the effects on the *contemporary* workforce and, even further, on the impact on the "skilled" portion of that workforce. And, lest a writer worry that he will run out of things to say in an essay so narrowly focused, he should relax. As the topic becomes more specific, mysteriously, he will find even *more* to say than if his task was to offer a general description of the major areas of change resulting from World War I. ☺

3.2.c Qualifying the Thesis

One common mistake writers make in articulating a thesis is *overgeneralization*. In trying to capture a whole essay's central point in one or two sentences, a writer might produce something like the following claim:

> World War I altered women's lives forever by proving to society that women could do the same work men can do.

Would most readers fully agree with this statement, or would they find themselves playing "devil's advocate"? A reader might wonder, was the change as profound as the writer suggests? Are there *no* women in the contemporary world who work primarily in the *domestic* sphere, performing duties traditionally assigned to women, like child-rearing, house-keeping, cooking, etc.? Can *all* women do *all* of the work men can do? (And *vice versa*, for that matter?) Did the shift of women toward a more public life take a *linear* historical progression or have there been times when society seemed to fluctuate back toward the pre-World War I culture? And how do we know that the current conditions, where women can flourish in the public workplace, are permanent?

To avoid introducing these kinds of doubts into a reader's mind, a writer is wise to *qualify* the argument. To qualify an assertion is to acknowledge its limits. One can narrow a thesis this way by explaining the limits of his argument and/or by adding restricting words, such as *many, often, sometimes,* and *commonly*.

> A close look at the evolution in women's roles from World War I to the present reveals that the war set into motion a *substantial* shift, *contributing to* the eventual employment of women workers in *most* traditionally male occupations.

The above thesis does *not* promise to prove that *all* women now work in traditionally male occupations; nor does it suggest that the shift was *immediate* and/or *permanent*. To avoid proposing an unsupportable argument, a writer should craft carefully the language of her thesis to qualify her claim.

3.2.d Exercise

Consider the thesis statements below. Suggest revisions that would qualify each argument to make it more supportable.

1) College is a place where young people explore their interests and form their own values before officially entering the "adult world."

2) With the emphasis on standardized testing, public schools are failing students, leaving them unable to think critically or solve problems creatively.

3) To prevent antibiotics' decreased effectiveness in treating adult infections, parents should stop giving their children these medicines.

3.3 STRUCTURING AN ARGUMENT, DAVID BRAUER

Now that we have identified the basic elements of effective argument, we need to consider strategies for organizing and developing an argument. The most critical aspect of structuring an argument is connected to your goals and purposes in a paper. Put simply, your choice of structure will depend on what you want to accomplish in the paper. Arguments have some predictable elements, but they are not formulas. As you consider your purposes, you will want to be careful to choose a structure that reflects those purposes effectively.

In discussing the basic parts of a spoken argument, Aristotle made the simple statement: "You must state your case, and you must prove it." The same is true for written arguments. An argument must be presented and then demonstrated or proven to the audience. Every effective argument will have these two parts, and in that order: 1) statement, 2) proof. With this basic template in mind, we can look at various models for structuring an argument.

3.3.a The "Three Appeals" Model

As discussed earlier, Aristotle described the three basic appeals in effective argument as pathos (emotional appeals), logos (logical appeals), and ethos (ethical credibility). If we apply these basic appeals as the main subtopics of an argument, the usually structure looks like this:

1) Pathos – in the conclusion of the paper, as this is the section in which the writer will want to convince the audience to take action. Emotional appeals usually have a stronger impact on changing the audience and on leaving a powerful impression. While we may use them in other parts of an argument, they are probably most effective at the end of the paper.

2) Logos – in the main body of the paper, as the main presentation of the argument will probably lean on logical appeals more than the other two appeals.

3) Ethos – in the introduction of the paper, as this is the section of the argument in which the writer needs to convince the audience that she is credible and ethically sound.

Keep in mind that this structure should not be overly rigid. There are many times when we will use multiple appeals in a single paragraph. But this structure gives us a solid basis for organizing a paper around these main appeals:

1) The writer demonstrates that opponent's position is understood by restating it.

2) The writer demonstrates in which contexts and under what conditions the opponent's positions may be valid.

3) The writer then offers her own position, including contexts in which it is valid.

3.3.b The Toulmin Model

The Toulmin model is the most common for persuasive essays, and its logical structure is fairly easy to understand and apply. This method is named after Stephen Toulmin, a British philosopher of the twentieth century. Toulmin believed that effective argument was built on logical appeals. But Toulmin did not believe that logic was simple and irrefutable. In this case, if someone used logic in an argument, that argument would be seen as perfect and complete, and it would be assumed that no one could challenge an argument built on logic. In contrast, Toulmin said that logic in the real world works to make an argument reasonable and convincing even if everyone does not agree with it.

Toulmin applied the idea of the enthymeme to argument structure and strategy. His model is founded on the idea that the effectiveness of a logical appeal depends on how it is perceived by the audience. Logic is critical to success, but it is not cold and impersonal. Instead, it must be shaped for an audience in order to be effective.

So how does this work? According to Toulmin, arguments have some essential components: *claims*, *evidence* (data or reasons) and *warrants*.

The claim is the summary of your argument, the point or idea that you want to prove to the audience. Claims are not facts but controversial statements that must be developed in order to convince the audience of their validity.

Evidence consists of data (often data or statistics) and reasons (examples, personal experiences, comments from authorities on the subject). Without evidence, your argument does not have the support that it needs to be convincing to the reader. The challenge for writers is to find evidence that is clear and understandable for the audience.

The warrant may be the most challenging aspect of Toulmin's model for argument. As stated earlier in this chapter, the warrant is an assumption that the writer believes to be true. More importantly, the warrant provides "glue" that connects the claim to the evidence. Without the warrant, the connection between the claim and the evidence may be weak or unconvincing.

The reason that the warrant can prove challenging is because it is not always stated directly in an argument. Instead, the writer may simply assume that the reader agrees with her about the topic at hand. The problem here is that the warrant may not be clear or convincing to the audience. In this case, the writer should work to develop and strengthen the warrant so that it does not prove a weakness in the argument.

$$\text{Claim} \quad \rightarrow \quad \text{Reasons/Evidence}$$
$$\uparrow$$
$$\text{Warrant}$$

As the graph indicates, the warrant serves as the underlying logic that connects the claim to the reasons and evidence. This connection will be made if the warrant is effective and convincing to the audience. If the warrant is not convincing to the audience, then the connection between claims and evidence may not be logical to the audience.

In an effective Toulmin argument, the warrant is an assumption that is shared by both the writer and the audience. The writer should always be conscious about the warrant or warrants that inform her argument, but she should decide whether or not to include the warrant in the *content* of her argument. The rule of thumb about warrants is as follows:

> If the warrant is strong and generally accepted by the audience, then you do not need to state it directly.

However, if the warrant is controversial, then you may need to state it directly *and* give good reasons for its validity in your argument. Although we offer examples of enthymemes in Section 3.1.b, below are two more examples for you to consider in light of Toulmin's model:

> Example 1: Marijuana should be legalized in order to allow law enforcement to concentrate on serious issues.

The warrant here is that marijuana is not as serious an issue as theft or violent crime. This warrant is relatively strong and seems to place the argument on solid footing.

> Example 2: Marijuana should be legalized because its use is already prevalent in society.

The warrant here appears to be that if a certain behavior is already prevalent, then it is useless to try to prohibit that behavior. This warrant may or may not be convincing to a wide variety of readers, so it should be developed by the writer.

A recap of the structure of the Toulmin model is as follows:

1) Make claims
2) State reasons
3) Provide evidence to support reasons
4) Discuss warrant (if necessary)

The claims will be stated in the introduction of the essay, the reasons and evidence will make up the content in the main body of the essay, and the discussion of the warrant (when needed) will follow either the introduction or the main body of the paper.

3.3.c The Rogerian Model

If we have a tendency to think about argument as a one-sided, "I'm right, you're wrong" affair, then there are alternatives to traditional argument. One of the best alternatives is the Rogerian model. This model reflects an approach to argument more committed to *understanding* and *consensus* than persuasion. This strategy was developed by a therapist named Carl Rogers and is focused more on reaching agreement and common ground than on convincing the audience that your position is valid. Writing instructors will often use the Rogerian model to help students think about argument in more subtle and creative ways.

This model has a recognizable structure that demonstrates the goal of achieving understanding and developing common ground. The structure is developed through the following specific steps:

1) The writer demonstrates that opponent's position is understood by restating it.

2) The writer demonstrates in which contexts and under what conditions the opponent's positions may be valid.

3) The writer then offers his own position, including contexts in which it is valid.

4) The writer demonstrates how opponent's position would benefit if opponent were to adopt elements of writer's position–attempts to show how sides complement each other.

The first three steps should come after an introduction that establishes the context and topic of the argument. The fourth step will likely serve as the conclusion in a Rogerian argument, and this conclusion should be somewhat longer than a traditional conclusion.

These steps are common in Rogerian argument, but writers should be careful to avoid turning these steps into a formula. Based on the topic and goals of the writer, a Rogerian approach will look different from paper to paper and from writer to writer. Nevertheless, this structure is logical and clear to readers. As a result, it is effective for writers who want to avoid traditional, one-sided approaches to discussion of a controversial topic.

3.3.d Other Common Models

There are other approaches to basic structure, and they demonstrate the close relationship between goals and structure. As with the Rogerian model, these models tend to avoid oppositional strategies in favor of specific goals determined by the assignment or by the writer. The goal of persuading the audience may prove less important in many of these models.

Here are some of the most common:

- Arguments of definition—The claim specifies that something does or does not meet the conditions or characteristics set forth in a definition; e.g., The death penalty is a deterrent to crime.
- Argument of evaluation—The claim states that something does or does not meet specific criteria.
- Causal argument—an argument that seeks to explain the effects of a cause, the cause of an effect, or a causal chain.
- Proposal—an argument in which a claim is made in favor of or opposing a particular course of action.

The claims in these respective arguments will be stated in the introduction of the paper, and the main body of the essay will develop the claim according to the writer's goals and approach to the topic. That said, the rhetorical purposes in these approaches to argument will vary. In most of these models, persuasion is secondary to analysis and explanation.

3.3.e Options for Organizing the Essay

Apart from basic structure, we may need to consider specific strategies for organizing the content within an argument. It is important to recognize that approaches to structure found in other kinds of academic writing may also help us to develop arguments. These include:

- Narrative (telling a story)
- Describing a process
- Describing an object
- Comparison and contrast

These structures are familiar to us because we use them every day to solve problems and to understand information. We can use these structures or patterns in two ways:

- To organize one section of an argument, such as a paragraph or subtopic
- To organize the argument as a whole

The advantage of these options is that they are familiar both to us and to our audience, so the argument should be logical and easy to follow for the reader. Though arguments are distinct from other kinds of writing, we should be prepared to borrow strategies from those writing situations to structure an argument.

Structure and organization are related concepts, but they are not the same. The organization of an argument will always depend on its structure, and the structure of an argument will always depend on the writer's goals. If we are able to keep these relationships in mind as we write, we will be able to use structure to our advantage in writing arguments.

3.4 THE IMPORTANCE OF AUDIENCE, *Laura Ng*

3.4.a Who is Our Audience?

As students, the default answer to this question seems to be the teacher, as we discussed earlier. On many levels, this is accurate. The instructor has the right of final evaluation of any assignment. Even then, the instructor is looking for how students, as writers, manage audience considerations in the text. This means that writers need a clear conception of who they are writing for when creating essays, proposals, or blogs. Aristotle considered audience one of the primary driving purposes of a written work.[12] Without a clear conception of who you are writing for, can you really be certain *why* you are writing? Audience is a consideration woven into all aspects of the rhetorical situation. The question, "Who is the audience?" is one that writers must answer.

The idea of audience is complex. A really daunting aspect of audience is the idea that anyone and everyone is a potential audience. There are multiple types of audiences; some conceptions of audience are very general, even in writing.[13] What will help us, as writers, is making our concept of the audience as concrete as we are able. Yes: concept. If we are going beyond creating an email, memo, or text for someone we know, then our concept of audience is theoretical. We create it in our minds.[14] On the one hand, this allows us to carefully consider who we are writing for in our work. On the other hand, thinking about a person or persons who will be reading our work can be intimidating.[15] We can deal with our nervousness by determining *how* we consider audience and *when*. There are a couple of options available to us when bearing in mind audience. First, we need to have a clear idea of *who* we are writing for in the work. Second, we have control over *when* we consider audience.

3.4.b When to Consider Audience

When thinking about audience, one needs to be as precise as one can. Who would be interested in our topic? Why? Katie Brown, discussed in Chapter 2, is writing a cover letter in order to get a job at the campus Student Success Center. She knows that education professionals will be reading her essay. She also knows that she wants this job to help build her résumé and knowledge for teaching math. In her cover letter, she must let her potential employer know how her experience makes her different from other applicants. What would the hiring committee be looking for? What parts of her job history should she highlight? How can she showcase her major in a way that shows she is a good match for the position? Her audience is going to be concerned with her knowledge base, professional skills, and ability to work with others in a tutor/student fashion. She should showcase these qualities in her cover letter as items that set her apart from other applicants. Katie's conception of her audience is theoretical, but also specific and clear.

So, when, in the writing process, should you consider the audience? The answer to this question will differ for everyone. All communication, even personal, has audience as a consideration, but when to factor in the audience depends upon the individual. Some writers may want to consider audience from the beginning. Others may find that starting off thinking about audience can be intimidating, and will want to wait until much later in the writing process to factor in outside readers.[16] What is important is that we consider our audience, their expectations, and our messages at some point, or multiple points, during the writing process. Exactly where or how often is up to us as writers.

3.4.c In the Topic-Choosing Phase

If you are comfortable, you can start at the beginning, considering your audience. This can help you with topic selection. Let's say you are writing a personal essay about a significant memory. Brainstorming, you come up with following topic choices:

- Graduating High school
- Mission trip to Guatemala
- Passing of my grandmother

These are all powerful moments that we could discuss in terms of how we felt during or were changed by the experiences. But who is the audience? Granted, the instructor is the dominant figure, but you may also share this essay with our peers in the response/critique part of the writing process. What are you comfortable sharing with the audience? Given that element, you may choose not to write about the passing of a relative. It may strike too close to home.

What about the other potential topics? Some of your instructor or some classmates may have been on mission trips, too. However, you cannot be sure. If you choose that topic, you may have to provide more background and descriptive materials just in case the audience is not familiar with mission trips. As the writer, this means you would need to spend time identifying important elements to explain so that the audience can fully understand your message and experience. As Aristotle points out, as authors, we may have to write for an audience that is not familiar or trained to follow our reasoning.[17] This trip as a topic has potential.

However, since the assignment is for a college class, it is a good bet that your audience is familiar with high school and the feeling of graduating. The topic of graduation, then, would provide a common foundation of experience to potentially work with in the essay. It is also a topic that could be easier to discuss than the others. You would not have to spend as much time providing background information or explaining elements of the experience, which would leave more time to focus on details and exploring significant moments. These elements may make high school graduation the stronger possibility for your essay topic. Walking through those steps of deciding what you are comfortable with your audience knowing, and trying to decide the knowledge level of the audience is just one way that you can use audience consideration to help craft an effective essay.

3.4.d In the Organization Phase

There are others places in the writing process where you can consider audience. When organizing essays, you may want to take a moment and consider the best approach for the audience. With the possible structures discussed in the previous section, there are aspects of organization that can determine your message's effect on the audience. If describing a significant memory or creating a process analysis, then **chronological order** would be the logical choice. It would also be the organization the audience would be expecting. You can play with that expectation as bit as the writer. Do you want to create a flashback? Or do you want to present the memory in present tense, as if experiencing it now? Maybe you want to open the essay at a climactic moment to get the audience's attention. Even when using chronological order, you have choices,.

What about other types of order? The organizational pattern used may depend, in part, on your audience. Part of this determination of organization is a combination of purpose and audience. Let's go back to Robert, from chapter two, whose environmental engineering firm is writing a grant proposal to obtain funding for a landfill. One of the aspects Robert must account for is how much background information he needs to include in the proposal. How much can he assume his audience already knows about the need for green landfills? If he needs to include background information, it should go at the beginning, so the audience will be able to understand what he is discussing in the rest of the proposal. To further his understadning of his audience, Robert should also explore any information he can obtain about the organization offering the grant to see its view of the subject.

Additionally, Robert needs to read the grant "assignment" to see what topics or criteria it stresses, just as you need to read the essay assignments to see what is being assessed and stressed in your works. Once Robert understands what his audience expects, he can create an organization that appeals to their values. He may choose to use **emphatic order** to appeal to his audience's knowledge and expectations. Emphatic order means Robert will organize his points to achieve the *emphasis* he wants to give them, arranging his points in order of *decreasing* importance, or by *building up* to the point the audience will care about the *most* by addressing points from least important to most important. Either way, Robert is using the audience's values to help structure his work.

So far, we have discussed trying to determine how familiar the audience is with various topics and how much background information to provide. This is because when we conceptualize audience, we sometimes do this in an abstract sense by creating an idealized or generic audience in our minds[18] rather than going out to survey a specific real population before writing. Often, writers have to work with a general concept of audience as you do not always personally know your audiences. This principle is true for the audience as well. They may not be familiar with you, the writer. Given that, writers are the ones who are trying to inform, persuade, or exposit, which can be a problem. The audience needs to know that you are trustworthy. Part of creating a successful work of writing is crafting a strong sense of *ethos*, or authorial credibility, in the piece.

3.4.e In the Source-Gathering Phase

You will not have the luxury of building a personal connection to each and every audience member, so one approach to building ethos is by examining the research materials used in the essay from an audience perspective. When choosing research sources, you need to select sources that the audience will be able to trust as credible. You need to look at the purpose of including each source, the source's reputation, and its strengths and weaknesses. If you decide to use it, then you need to ask yourselves if you think the audience will be familiar with the author/ agency that created the source. If Robert includes a study from the Environmental Protection Agency as a source in his grant, he can assume that this audience is familiar with the government organization. However, if he decides to include an article from *International Construction*, he may need to take a few moments in the essay and explain why the source is trustworthy. Once he has explained, then the audience will trust his information. He is setting up his ethos.

If the article does not have an author, establishing credibility can be more difficult. Sometimes you can use the publication as a way of establishing credibility for the audience. Journal or newspaper reputation can be a good place to start. Academic journals and recognized noted periodicals have established reputations that can help when explaining credibility. While the *Washington Post* is not a peer reviewed journal, it does have a nationally recognized reputation as a quality news organization. Staff writers do not always receive individual credit for their articles, so using the newspaper's reputation as the gauge will work in this case. If you encounter a journal or periodical you are uncertain about, then you can always ask a librarian.

3.4.f In the Evidence-Development Phase

Having a strong concept of your intended audience can help with choosing your examples, or *evidence*, as well. Using examples the audience can understand and relate to on some level helps create *pathos* in your writing. The emotional connection you make with the audience is important. You need to use examples that the audience realizes are typical. Using extreme examples will hurt your credibility and rapport with the audience. The audience will not trust you. Choose examples that your audience members can recognize and see as a part of their world. Let's see how Robert is doing. In his grant proposal, he wants to take a moment and catalog why traditional landfills do not meet the environmental needs of our society. He has a choice for examples. He can use an example from an EPA study discussing the millions of tons of waste in landfills[19] or a piece on exploding landfills he found on a blog. The EPA study is very credible. Robert is not certain about the blog. He will have to do more research to see who sponsors the blog and if that person is an expert. The blog piece on landfill explosions strikes an emotional chord with him, but will it also work for his audience? He needs to consider what the grant reviewers expect to see in his proposal. They would expect to see statistics from national organizations. Robert will need to consider this audience expectation when he chooses his examples.

3.4.g In the Diction-Crafting Phase

One of the last areas where you can consider audience in your work is in your **diction**, or word choice. You can review your diction and **syntax** at any point in the writing process. You can even keep this task until the end, and do this during the polishing stage. When writing to an audience, your diction establishes much more than just tone or "voice" in an essay. Diction lets the audience understand how you feel about the subject and them as well. You need to be careful that you show the readers that you are not there to insult to talk down to them. If you open that door, the audience may disconnect emotionally and intellectually with your work. All of your efforts will be for nothing. Consider again Robert. If he calls landfills, "heaping piles of putrid waste that only uneducated dupes would support in this day and age," then he has insulted his opposition and his audience. If he creates word choices that show a logical approach to the subject like, "landfills have been a staple of municipal waste recycling for decades. As new innovations come to light, it is time for us to reconsider how we manage our solid waste," then he stands a better chance of keeping the audience sympathetic to his stance while building rapport with the reader.

A Final Note on Audience

We know that we are writing for an audience. We must also keep in mind that we *are* an audience. When we are researching our topics, we will encounter many different kinds of sources and opinions about our subjects. Analyzing those sources from the audience perspective can tell us a lot about how audience was considered in the creations of the pieces. If we run across items with confusing organization, questionable sources, bad examples, or insulting word choice, then we need to consider the intended audience. Are we a part of that group? Who is the intended audience? What is the author trying to create? What can we learn from the piece? Analyzing audience consideration in a source can help us determine the credibility of the source. It is also great practice for peer review. If you read a classmate's paper and respond to it, approaching the task from the perspective of sympathetic or disagreeing audience will help you provide the author with feedback about ways to improve the work.

Audience is everywhere. How we conceptualize the audience and when we decide to consider audience as a part of our writing process is ultimately up to us, as the authors. We can start early in the process with topic generation. We can use audience to help us organize. We can even use audience as a guide for choosing examples. We can choose the places and moments we are the most comfortable with, as writers. What is important, at the end of the day, is that we do consider audience in our work, and we use our position as an audience when we respond to others' works. Audience is a powerful part of the rhetorical triangle.

3.5 STRATEGIES FOR PARAGRAPHING, Diana Edelman-Young

We have all heard it before—a paragraph should be about *one* idea and one idea *only*. Paragraphs shouldn't be too long or too short. The problem is that words like "idea" and "long" and "short" are subjective terms. What I mean by "long" is not the same as what you mean by "long." In the "real" world of writing, whether fiction or nonfiction— newspapers, magazines, Internet articles, journal articles, short stories, novels—paragraphs can be whole pages or even just one or two sentences. Paragraphs serve different purposes depending on where they are in a text and what kind of document it is. They can function as background, ex- amples, or even as transitions between sections, and, of course, there are special paragraphs such as introductions and conclusions that are treated in a separate section in this text.

The most obvious way to identify a paragraph, for most of us, is the indented first line. The white space is a signal that the author has shifted to something new, but how do we *know* when we are supposed to do that? In a perfect world, all ideas would be neatly categorized and distinct, and there would be definitive rules for when to start new paragraphs. Ideas and the language we use to express them are complex; thus, the reasons to switch to a new paragraph are legion. You can start a new paragraph because you are really shifting to a new idea or point, or sometimes, you start a new paragraph simply because the one you are writing is just get- ting too long. Usually, though, with practice (and lots of reading), you can figure out natural places to break between ideas and can develop the skills necessary to signal to your reader why this shift is taking place.

The important thing to keep in mind is that paragraphs serve a purpose in any given piece of writing, and your job as a writer is to ensure that:

- The function of the paragraph is clearly conveyed to your reader.
- The paragraph follows the conventions of the type of writing you are doing.
- Each paragraph has a clear relationship to both the one before it and the one after it.

Sounds like a lot of work, doesn't it? No worries. There are many strate- gies for writing effective paragraphs, some traditional and some new. It is important to try different strategies and to find what works for you.

3.5.a The Paragraph

Traditionally, paragraphs are to begin with a topic sentence or a transition from the previous paragraph and then a new topic sentence. A *topic sentence*, as most of us have learned, is a sentence or two that identifies the main idea of the paragraph; it serves as a signpost to your reader. It should answer the following question, *"What is this paragraph about and how will it help prove my thesis?"* The topic sentence, like the thesis of the essay as a whole, *raises expectations* in your reader. In other words, like the thesis, the topic sentence is a *promise*, which, if left unfulfilled, will be frustrating to your reader. Think of it like a conversation. Although essays are more formal in style, they have some of the same conventions as conversation. Imagine this scenario: you and a friend are in the coffee shop. He walks up to you and says, "My teacher is such a jerk!" As a listener, you would expect to hear the specific details of what makes this professor a "jerk," perhaps even some specific examples. If he said that to you and then walked away or started talking about his weekend plans, you would be frustrated. You would want to know more about that statement, which amounts to a claim that requires proof. The same can be said for topic sentences in paragraphs.

Some schools of thought suggest that the topic sentence can be implied or can even come at the end of a paragraph; however, in the "real" world of paragraphing, Francis Christensen found that topic sentences almost always come at the beginning.[20] The topic sentence is then followed by support in the form of relevant examples and quotations that the writer explains and concludes with a reiteration of the main idea. This is a useful way to think of a paragraph, particularly for beginning writers who need a place to start. Consider the following template, which you can use to help yourself stay organized, particularly if you tend to go off topic. Also, this structure can be used after you have written a draft in order to identify information that might go better elsewhere.

3.5.a (1) Traditional Structure

In this basic format, a topic sentence is followed by examples, each of which is given further explanation, and the main idea of the paragraph is reinforced at the end. The template below has two examples, but there can be more or fewer depending on the purpose of the paragraph or how much detail each example requires.

Topic Sentence:_____

    Example 1:_____
    _____

        Explanation of example 1:_____
        _____

    Example 2:_____
    _____

        Explanation of example 2:_____
        _____

Reiteration of main idea/transition to next paragraph:_____
_____

Let's try developing the following topic: Cats are often more independent than dogs.

Example paragraph development based on the above structure:

Topic Sentence: Cats are often more independent than dogs.

    Example 1: Cats are house-trained from the moment of birth.

        Explanation of example 1: For example, my cat Cloe has never had to be potty trained; she always uses the litter box.

    Example 2: Cats can be left alone for a couple of days with enough food and water.

        Explanation of example 2: I often leave my cat Chloe for one or two nights on the weekend. When I come home, she is fine.

Reiteration of main idea/transition to next paragraph: Because cats are immediately house-trained and can be on their own, they are much more independent than dogs.

There are many, many ways that this paragraph could be developed besides personal examples. Other options could be quotations from experts or even a brief description or story of a particular cat and/or dog. The types of examples you choose depend on your audience, your purpose, and the style of writing. If your audience is a group of veterinarians in an argument essay, you will probably want to use scholarly, scientific evidence and expert testimony. If you are writing a narrative or descriptive essay, you will want to tell a story of a particular cat with vivid descriptions that show the reader the main idea. Either way, the paragraph will develop logically from the information you are starting with, the audience, the purpose, and the method of delivery.

3.5.a (2) Exercises

Practice developing two different paragraphs for the following topic sentences based on the two different audiences and purposes identified for each. The topic sentences are worded in such a way to allow you to take any position. You may have to reword the topic sentence to be more appropriate for the audience and purpose. This exercise can be done in groups or individually, on your own or in class. You can also make up your own topic, audience, and purpose, or your instructor can provide them for you.

If you do these exercises in class, when you are finished, compare both paragraphs discussing what choices were made about how to develop the paragraphs based on the audience and purpose. Discuss what choices were made. Think about the following questions: Which choices were the most effective and why? Which were the least effective and why? What changes could be made to strengthen the paragraphs? If this paragraph were in a longer essay, what kind of paragraph might you expect to come before or after this one? What are some possible thesis statements for an essay that includes this kind of information?

1) Democracy is (or is not) an effective form of government.

   a) Audience: 5th grade students; purpose: to teach them different types of government

   b) Audience: peers in your undergraduate government course; purpose: to argue for the best type of government among the ones the class has been learning

2) Women are (or are not) naturally more emotional than men.

   a) Audience: psychology professor; purpose: an argument essay on the topic of nature vs. nurture

    b) Audience: your mom; purpose: in a letter explaining a friend's recent behavior

3) College is (or is not) much more difficult than high school.

    a) Audience: juniors and seniors in high school English class; purpose: to prepare them for the changes they will experience when they graduate

    b) Audience: your peers in college; purpose: an informative newspaper article

4) Sports organizations should (or should not) be more rigorous about punishing athletes for using steroids.

    a) Audience: NFL football coaches; purpose: to persuade them to action

    b) Audience: state lawmakers; purpose: to persuade them to pass a law regarding this issue

3.5.b Other Types of Paragraph Organization (By Genre/Mode)

The above structure that I have chosen to call "traditional" is a standard format that can be applied to almost any paragraph, but there are also some types of organization that can work well for specific genres or modes (types of writing). Genres or modes include, among others, the following types: compare/contrast, descriptive, narrative, process, illustration, cause/effect, problem/solution. For example, spatially organized paragraphs are often found in *descriptive essays*. The development of the paragraph is **spatial** in the sense that it describes a place (broadly defined) by physical features and placement of objects. Suppose you are describing your dorm room. A spatially organized paragraph might be appropriate here. You could start by describing the focal point of the room and move outward, or you could describe from the ceiling to the floors (or vice versa). If you have a roommate, you could describe the room by how each half looks. A **chronological** development tells what happened in order by time. This type of paragraph often occurs in a *narrative essay* in which the writer is telling a story—what happened first, second, and so on. Similar to chronological is **sequential**, which is used when writing a *process paragraph or essay*; you are telling your reader what steps to take and in what order. For example, in describing how to drive, you might write something like the following: "Driving a car can be easy if you follow a few easy steps. First, get in the car and put on your seatbelt. Second, adjust your mirrors, and so on." If you think about it, cause/effect and problem/solution paragraphs or essays are a form of chronological or sequential as the cause always comes before the effect and the problem before the solution. Other types of development include **emphatic** order, or items discussed in order of importance. For example, you can argue in order from best to worst, least to greatest, most to least common, or some other logical organization depending on the topic.

It is important to note, also, that many of these types of paragraphs can also be expanded to be types of longer essays. A spatial paragraph describing a room, for example, can be expanded into several paragraphs. Each paragraph can go into more and more detail about each area of the room, or the essay can describe the whole house with each paragraph focusing on one room. Again, the type of paragraph can sometimes be determined by the genre itself. See below for some examples and exercises based on the three common ones discussed above.

3.5.b (1) Spatial—organization by physical arrangement in space

Example: The kitchen in the Smith home is a complete mess. The stainless steel refrigerator is cluttered with papers hung up by garish magnets from the family's world travels—a giant cactus from Mexico, a burlesque dancer from Paris, an Australian kangaroo wearing sunglasses. The papers—pink, yellow, green, orange—seem to be calendars, homework, reminders, and sports schedules posted in no particular order. To the right of the refrigerator is the stove. Clearly, this family has just made spaghetti. There are three pots: one with strands of long, yellow pasta hanging over the side; one that is full of marinara sauce that, apparently, splattered all over the beige backsplash; and one half full of boiled collard greens. On the other side of the kitchen is the sink and dishwasher. It looks like they fed a lot of people that day and hadn't cleaned up since breakfast. Dishes and cups are piled high and spread all over the counter: half-eaten bowls of cereal, plates with dried marinara sauce, and dirty cups. The open dishwasher is full of dirty dishes. The floor isn't much better: strands of spaghetti, spilled water, and a few papers that must have fallen off the fridge door. Clearly, the Smiths' harried schedule makes for a messy kitchen.

3.5.b (2) Exercise

Describe your classroom, dorm room, or bedroom in a paragraph of seven to eight sentences.

3.5.b (3) Chronological—organization by time

Example: My first day of college writing class was both frightening and rewarding. My alarm rang at 7 o'clock in the morning. I got up, ate breakfast, and brushed my teeth. After showering and dressing, I drove to campus, but my hands were sweating. I didn't know what to expect. My first class was at 9 o'clock: English 1101! I walked in about ten minutes early to a sea of faces. Nobody smiled or talked; I think they were just as nervous as I. Right at 9, the professor walked in, threw her bag on the table, and started calling roll. She seemed pretty stern. She gave us a speech about how different high school and college writing were; my heart started beating faster. I didn't like the sound of this at all. About halfway through the class—after we had gone over the syllabus, rules, and expectations—the teacher gave us a paragraph to read and discuss in groups. At first, few people talked, but then we really got into it—pointing out the strengths and weaknesses of the paragraph. The professor smiled and made jokes, which helped us relax. When students pointed out what worked and didn't work in the essay, she praised us, saying that we were astute readers. Finally, at the end of the class, around 9:45, the professor revealed that this was her first college paragraph. Wow! We started class by grading the teacher's work, and it showed us how much we already knew. At 7 o'clock that morning, I was nervous and sweating, but less than three hours later, at 9:50, I was ready to take on the rest of my first day of college.

3.5.b (4) Exercise

Narrate an experience of any "first" (first dance, first kiss, graduation).

3.5.b (5) Other Exercises

1) Write a paragraph in which you discuss celebrities in order from best to worst dressed.

2) Write a paragraph categorizing reality stars (or other celebrities) in order from kindest to meanest (or some other relevant category).

3) Write a paragraph arranging your college classes in order from least to most difficult.

4) Write a process paragraph in which you identify the steps necessary for planning and executing an effective study session.

5) Write a cause/effect paragraph in which you identify the effects of lack of sleep.

3.5.c Understanding Paragraphs through Coordination and Subordination

A different way of understanding paragraphs is to dissect them in terms of how the sentences within the paragraphs relate to one another.[21] This method is best done on existing paragraphs from the "real" world. Most relationships can be described as **coordinating** or **subordinating**. A coordinating relationship is one of equality; both ideas are on an equal level. A subordinate relationship is one in which one idea comes from or is dependent on another. Think of this like a family tree. Siblings and cousins are in equal relationship to one another (coordinating); children, on the other hand, are dependent on parents (subordinating). Consider the following chart that displays the coordinating and subordinating relationships of the sentences from a paragraph and are numbered level 1, 2, 3.

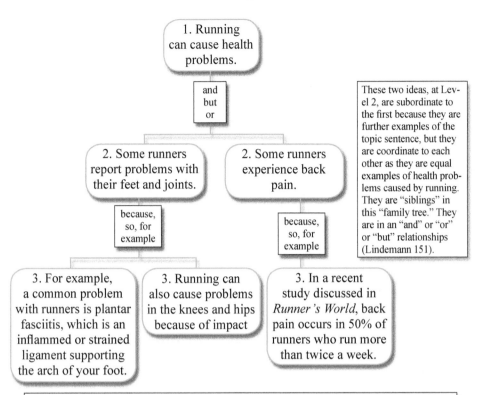

1. Running can cause health problems.

and
but
or

These two ideas, at Level 2, are subordinate to the first because they are further examples of the topic sentence, but they are coordinate to each other as they are equal examples of health problems caused by running. They are "siblings" in this "family tree." They are in an "and" or "or" or "but" relationships (Lindemann 151).

2. Some runners report problems with their feet and joints.

2. Some runners experience back pain.

because, so, for example

because, so, for example

3. For example, a common problem with runners is plantar fasciitis, which is an inflamed or strained ligament supporting the arch of your foot.

3. Running can also cause problems in the knees and hips because of impact

3. In a recent study discussed in *Runner's World*, back pain occurs in 50% of runners who run more than twice a week.

These three, at Level 3, are subordinate to the other two above because they are examples of the ideas expressed at the second level. They are the "children" of the previous level. Subordinate relationships are expressed as "because," "so," or colon relationships because they are effects or examples (Lindemann 151). They are equal or coordinate with each other because they are all at Level 3 like siblings or cousins.

Coordinating ideas are equal and can be expressed as "and" or "or" relationships. Consider the following two sentences: "Jenny went to the store. And, Jenny went to the mall." In this example, the two sentences are in a coordinating relationship because they are on an equal level. These sentences could be arranged visually as follows:

> A. Jenny went to the store.
> A. And, Jenny went to the mall.

In this case, the ideas are of equal value. They are in an "and" or coordinate relationship. Consider the following: "You can choose to get your insurance through work, or you can get insurance individually." Although this is just one sentence, it expresses two coordinating ideas, which is signaled by the word "or." Even though you choose one or the other, both options are on the same level—ways to get insured. This would be expressed in the numbering system as follows:

> A. You can choose to get your insurance through work,
> A. or you can get insurance individually.

Subordinating ideas are hierarchical as in the family generation example above. An idea is subordinate to another if it is dependent on it or further explains it. Cause/effect relationships are like this. Examples are subordinate to the idea that they are an example of. Consider the following: "My professor is mean. He always marks me late even if it's just one minute." The second sentence is subordinate to the first because it provides an example or further explanation of what was already expressed. Let's say I add a third sentence: "He also takes points off papers if I don't format the essay exactly right." This sentence is equal to the one right before it because they are both examples of the same idea regarding how mean the professor is.

If we were to create a visual for this type of relationship, we would arrange them as follows:

A. My professor is mean.
　　B. He always marks me late even if it's just one minute.
　　B. He also takes points off papers if I don't format the essay exactly right.

Notice that the topic sentence is labeled A. and that the two subordinate ideas, which are examples, are both labeled B. They are subordinate to the main idea (A), but coordinate with each other (B).

Consider the paragraph above about cats and dogs. I could arrange that one like this:

A. Cats are often more independent than dogs.
　　B. Cats are house-trained from the moment of birth.
　　　　C. For example, my cat Cloe has never had to be potty trained; she always uses the litter box.
　　B. Cats can be left alone for a couple of days with enough food and water.
　　　　C. I often leave my cat Cloe for one or two nights on the weekend.
　　　　　　D. When I come home, she is fine.
A. Because cats are immediately house-trained and can be on their own, they are much more independent than dogs.

44

In this case, the first B sentence labels a way that cats are independent (they are house trained), so it is subordinate to the topic sentence (A). The sentence about her cat Chloe and the litter box is a specific example of house-training, so it is subordinate to the first B sentence. The next sentence labeled B is another way that cats are independent. Thus, it is in a subordinate relationship to the topic sentence (A), but in a coordinating relationship to the first B sentence. The points about housetraining and about being able to leave them alone are both equal examples of independence. The same happens with the next B, which has a specific example (C) followed by more information about that example (D). Finally, the last sentence reiterates the main idea of the paragraph, so it is on the same level as the topic sentence.

3.5.d Exercises

1. Individually or in groups, try labeling the sentences in the following paragraph either using the numbering system or the family tree system shown above. Think about how the sentences relate to the ones before and after it as well as to the topic sentence. After you finish, discuss the choices you made as a class. How did you determine the relationships between sentences? Were there signal words that identified them as coordinating or subordinating?[16]

Example: The other cool thing about the college schedule is that you usually have more opportunities to explore your interests and passions. For example, you will be picking a major that will determine the types of classes you will specialize in. In high school, you have a set curriculum of classes you have to take across all subject areas. In college, think about your schedule as a pyramid. Your freshman and sophomore year, you'll take more general education classes (a mixture of everything so you walk away well-rounded) and a few classes in your major. But during your junior and senior year, you'll take fewer general education classes and more classes in your major.[22]

---

2) Gather paragraphs from your own work, a newspaper, books, or the Internet. Practice labeling the sentences in terms of coordinating and subordinating relationships. Which ideas are equal? Which are hierarchal? Discuss what the relationships between and among the sentences in the paragraph are and why. What signal words can you find that give you clues about these relationships?

3) Exchange paragraphs with a partner. See if you can label their sentences in terms of coordinating and subordinating relationships as shown in the examples above. Did you have trouble labeling any of the sentences? Why? Would signal phrases or different wording help clarify the connections between and among the sentences? Are there ideas that do not appear to fit? Is the main idea of the paragraph clear?

Dissecting paragraphs that have already been written can help you understand the relationships among sentences (and where those relationships may fall short). This, in turn, should make you more attuned to whether your paragraphs are achieving unity and coherence.

4) Before class, choose one of your own paragraphs from a draft, complete essay, or exercise. Print a copy of the paragraph on one sheet of paper. Then, go back to the file and place each sentence on a separate line of the document by hitting "enter" at the end of each sentence. Do not number or otherwise label them. Print out the document, and then cut out each sentence so that you have one strip of paper per sentence. Place the strips in a bag and bring them to class.

During class, you will exchange paragraph strips with a partner. The partner will then attempt to arrange the sentences in the correct order. You will do the same for them. Once you are both finished, compare the original paragraph to what your partner came up with. Was he able to figure out the original structure? If not, why not? Where did he struggle to figure out the proper order? Why? If he had trouble, this could indicate that you need transitions or further explanation. It might also mean that the topic sentence is not clear. Discuss ways that the paragraphs could be strengthened and rewritten.

Go home and revise the paragraph based on your discussion with your partner. Bring the paragraph back to class in the same way you did previously and choose a new partner. Do the same exercise with a new partner. Was it easier for her to identify the order of the sentences? What worked well in terms of the revision? What still needs work? Type up an analysis of this exercise. This exercise can also be done as a group with one paragraph that the instructor provides. After the students, individually or in groups, arrange the sentences into the order they think the sentences should go in, these can be projected on screen and discussed as a class using the same questions. What order did the group put the sentences in and why? Where did they have difficulty and why? Did any of the groups make different choices about the order? Why? Where can the paragraph be improved or strengthened?

Closing Remarks

The above methods can be used to structure paragraphs that have not been formed, but they can also be used to understand paragraphs that have already been written, which is a useful tool when you are revising. These strategies can help identify ways to strengthen your writing so that your reader can easily follow your description, narration, argument, or whatever other type of writing you are doing. You can also practice these methods on your own paragraphs to identify gaps, places that need transitions, or information that needs to go elsewhere in your work.

3.6 GENERATING A CONSTRUCTIVE TONE, *Tanya Long Bennett*

Tone is difficult to define, but we read the tones in our communications daily. If a roommate comes in and lists all the tasks he needs to complete before midnight, the listener can usually tell by the tone of his voice whether he is worried, depressed, or excited. How do we detect tone in *written* communications? Diction, or word choice, is usually the most revealing factor of tone in written text. If a writer chooses words like "lollygag" and "gallivant," she is likely striving for humor. Conversely, if she selects words like "composition" and "analysis," she is probably working toward a tone both serious and formal. Consider the following assignment:

Your grandmother has generously agreed to pay your college tuition as long as you uphold one condition: You maintain a 4.0 grade point average. This mandate means you must earn an A in every college course you take. She paid for this year, but she plans to discontinue her support the moment you earn any grade lower than an A. Consider your real grades this year. If you have earned anything below an A so far, you can base your letter on your actual record. If you have maintained a 4.0, pretend you made a B in one particularly difficult course. Write a persuasive letter urging your grandmother to continue paying for your tuition. Remember your <u>audience</u>: you will want to consider her values and try to find ways to show that supporting your education fulfills those values. Also, be sure to include at least two specific, concrete examples as evidence to support your assertion(s). As important tools of persuasion, consider how you might effectively employ <u>introduction</u> and <u>conclusion</u>, <u>organization</u>, <u>logic</u>, <u>evidence</u>, <u>tone</u>, and <u>grammar</u> (if she sees lots of grammar errors, she may decide that you have not been making her money count ☺).

Here is the letter Gavin wrote in response to the prompt:

Her Excellency Madam Mama B
United States of America, Planet Earth
Home

Dear Mama B,

    I done screwed up. In all seriousness, though, I need to
talk to you about my grades and our deal. I know that you
said you would fund my schooling if I maintained a 4.0
GPA, and I've been doing that. Until now at least. I made
all A's in my Military Science courses, Band, all of my
Chinese classes, my American Government course, and
my Computer Science classes. However, I've earned a B in
my English 1102 class. This is my first and only B. I wanted to take a moment to be completely honest with you, and
to ask that you would still pay for my time in college.
    I know I've broken our deal, but my English class
is both an Honors Course as well as part of the core curriculum. It's held to a different standard because it's an
Honors Course, and my writing just wasn't on par for an
A. However, English 1102 is a core course that has to be
completed by every student.
    While it does open up higher level English and Liter-
ature classes to me (so long as a grade of C or greater is
earned), it is not a course central to my Chinese degree.
I will be able to take the grammar and linguistic courses
that are required for my major, and I have made A's in
all of my classes that apply directly to my major as well.
I will still be incredibly successful so long as I continue
down this path, especially at the rate I'm going.
    On that note of success, did you know that college
graduate full-time workers earn roughly $21,528 more
per year, on average, than non-graduate full-time workers right out of school? I read a 2014 article by Karen
Farnen in the *Global Post* discussing the subject. This
degree is the difference between making $55,000 a year
compared to $30,000. That's a giant difference when

you really think about it, and I need your help to get to that point. Another point that the article makes is that college graduates, on average, make $2.422 million after forty years of work compared to the $1.371 that non-graduates make in the same amount of time. That's more than a million dollar difference, Mama B. Can you think of what I could do with an extra million dollars? I could pay for my children, your great-grandchildren, to go through college. That would be incredible. However, I do want to take a moment to say that you don't have any great-grandchildren yet, nor do I plan on giving you any for the next few years. Just wanted to make sure that we're on the same page!

I want you to know that I will work so much harder to keep your respect if you choose to continue helping me with my schooling. My GPA still maintains the Zell Miller Scholarship requirements, and I would be willing to apply for other scholarships to help ease the burden on you. I was actually just awarded a scholarship from the university for my academic excellence! It's the Richard F. Helmbold Award for Academic Excellence. The university is impressed with my grades, and I want you to be as well. It won't be easy, but I'll work harder in my courses so that I keep earning A's. I appreciate what you've done for me, Mama B. If you would give me another chance, I don't think I would be able to express my full gratitude. It would mean the world to me. Thank you for taking the time to consider all of this.

Much love,
Gavin

3.6.a Exercise: Questions for Consideration

1) What are the major points Gavin uses to support his argument that Mama B should continue funding his education? What evidence does he present to support those points?

2) Consider the organization of the letter. Why does Gavin use this arrangement? Does it seem like an effective one for achieving his purpose?

3) What kind of tone does the letter take? How does diction help to generate this tone? How does Gavin play with the conventions of a formal letter to help establish his tone? Does Gavin's choice of nonstandard grammar undermine his argument? Why or why not? Why does he use this nonstandard grammar where he does?

The next essay fulfills a more formal assignment. See if you can detect the ways in which Taylor establishes and maintains a more formal academic tone than Gavin does.

Taylor Russell
English 1101
19 November 2013

Fast Food: How McDonald's Marketing Relates to Obesity

Get up, run all day, eat, sleep. Get up, run all day, eat, sleep. Repeat, repeat, repeat. American lives are increasingly bustling, brisk, and busy. There does not seem to be enough time in the day for what has to get done, not to mention having to eat. Of course, then we do not hesitate to consume what is quickest and cheapest. But how did that come to be? Why did America choose this fast paced life style and this new fast food? The reasons for this are broad and hard to fully determine but the effects of inhaling all of the modern fast food are becoming clearer. The history of fast food is revealing about how it operates today. In particular one restaurant stands out for its contribution to both fast food's rise to prominence and the problem of obesity. Fast food is harmful to the body, potentially causing obesity, and its rise in popularity is due to a link between the McDonald's marketing strategy and children.

McDonald's is one name that has a whole lot of influence. Historically, McDonald's started out as a small restaurant owned by "Richard and Maurice McDonald, the two brothers who opened a fast food restaurant that would come to revolutionize America" ("Fast Food History in the United States"). While White Castle was the first fast food restaurant, it was not the catalyst that propelled fast food into popularity. No, rather that honor belongs to the Golden Arches ("Fast Food History in the United States"). According to Harvey Levenstein, Ray Kroc was the man behind the curtain when it came to the success of McDonald's. Kroc purchased the business from the McDonald brothers after running a McDonald's franchise for a few years. Focusing dogmatically on cleanliness, Kroc followed the patterns set by earlier restaurants (Levenstein 229). Where White Castle and McDonald's diverged, however, was on the issue of which market to target. By focusing not on the public transport system and the working class, like White Castle, McDonald's pioneered a new path by deliberately "targeting the suburbs" (Levenstein 229) and "going after the kids" (Baritz as qtd. in Levenstein 229). Levenstein credits this focus on family for the franchise's prominent rise to popularity and power. Kroc discovered that "children determined where three out of four families ate" which led him to create marketing ploys to attract more children to his stores (Levenstein 229). One of the more intuitive ploys was including special prizes in children's meals, which enabled McDonald's to overcome the competition and grow exponentially. As well, Kentucky Fried Chicken is credited with following the idea of marketing to baby boomers to increase sales (Levenstein 229). This reveals that other restaurants were taking the same steps as McDonald's to draw in costumers. These strategies would lead to fast food's rise to prominence.

One of the popular ideas today is that fast food, including McDonald's, is causing obesity in America. Seeming increasingly to permeate scientific studies is a stigma toward the unhealthiness of fast food and how it affects one's body. In the *International Journal of Behavioral Nutrition and Physical Activity*, one article released some information related to this popular opinion. By examining the proximity of one's work and home to a fast food location, a study by Jeffery, et al., sought to deduce if any relationship regarding eating habits existed between the two. Though a correlating relationship between BMI and ingesting fast food was revealed, no relationship between proximity and fast food consumption was unveiled (Jeffery et. al). More important than the primary objective, however, are the other discoveries that the study uncovered. The research of Jeffery, et al., shows that consuming fast food was positively linked "with having children, a high fat diet and Body Mass Index (BMI)." These factors reveal that fast food is related to obesity since children and a high BMI are associated with eating fast food. Having children is one of the factors that increase the chance of frequenting a fast food establishment and eating there is related to a higher BMI (Jeffery et. al). This study reveals how fast food in general affects the body and who most commonly consumes it.

Clearly, obesity is a very important issue though one could argue that fast food is relatively irrelevant in the list of causes. Jeffery, et al., acknowledge this by explaining that though linked, the "direction of causation is unclear" in relation to whether fast food causes obesity, or obesity is the cause for fast food's existence. However, when one draws the comparison between the marketing strategies of McDonald's and the research by Jeffery, et al., it becomes startlingly clear how the targeting of children by McDonald's relates to obesity. As Levenstein points out, the idea of marketing to families, more specifically children, enabled to McDonald's to gain success, and according to the study by Jeffery, et al., having children is a common reason for fast food consumption, which is linked to a higher fat diet and higher BMI. To simplify, McDonald's marketing worked and still works and is responsible at least in part for the obesity crisis.

More evidence for the danger of ingesting fast food is presented by Kristian Kilpatrick in *The Huffington Post*. In her article, she unveils some startling revelations about the nature of fast food. By comparing "the effects of a junk food meal and a Mediterranean based meal on the inner lining of the blood vessels," she shows that the blood flow is decreased dramatically within four hours of consuming the fast food meal. Clearly, fast food rapidly increases the danger to one's personal health. As well, according to Kilpatrick, studies reveal that children's caloric consumption increases when eating fast food (Kilpatrick). This article aptly seconds the revelations of the Jeffery, et al., research in regards to children being a determining factor in high fat diet and high BMI.

The evidence presented here draws a clear line between the wide-reaching effects of unhealthy fast food and McDonald's. By effectively implementing a child-centered marketing strategy, McDonald's brought fast food to prominence. Kilpatrick relates that childhood obesity is more likely with fast food consumption, supporting the theory that McDonald's plays a causal role in childhood obesity. What McDonald's knew in the 1950's and 1960's still holds true into the modern era. Children's relation to the problem of obesity is unusual because children have no real purchasing power. By operating through children's desires, however, McDonald's came to power. By influencing children's parents to eat at McDonald's and now many other fast food restaurants, this marketing strategy caused a snowball effect that is a significant factor in the current obesity problem. It is plausible that by reducing marketing targeted towards children, our society could reduce the obesity problem.

Works Cited

"Fast Food History in United States." *Fast Food Packaging*. N.p. , 1 Jan. 2011. Web. 30 Oct 2013.

Jeffery, Robert, Judy Baxter, **Maureen McGuire, and Jennifer Linde**. "Are Fast Food Restaurants an Environmental Risk Factor for Obesity?" *International Journal of Behavioral Nutrition and Physical Activity* 3.2 (2006): n. p. *JSTOR*. Web. 28 Oct. 2013.

Kirkpatrick, Kristin. "Fast Food's Immediate Damage to Your Health." *The Huffington Post*. Huffington Post. 03 Dec. 2012, Web. 30 Oct. 2013.

Levenstein, Harvey. *Paradox of Plenty: A Social History of Eating in Modern America.* New York, NY: Oxford UP, 1993. *Galileo Interconnected Libraries (GIL).* Web. 6 Nov. 2013.

Note that in addition to using diction and genre conventions to indicate a formal academic tone in his essay, Taylor also avoids using **charged language**. Charged language is highly emotional language often employed in propaganda, so if he were writing for a different kind of audience and purpose, Taylor might have described McDonald's as "greedy" and "lying." Instead, he is careful to use language less emotionally charged in order to maintain a tone of objectivity and fair-handedness. His use of a quotation in the description of the company's "going after the kids" allows him to retain his own seemingly objective stance while indicating that not everyone is so generous about the role McDonald's might have played in helping to create today's obesity problem. In any piece of writing, the author should be sure that his tone is right for his audience and purpose. An *inappropriate* tone can be off-putting to many readers, such as professors, potential employers, or customers, but an appropriate tone can enhance the effect of one's writing.

What's in Your Writing Tackle Box?

Classical rhetoric underscores the importance of considering audience, purpose, and opportunity in our writing. Writing must appeal to readers or they will not read it. Studies show that when people read magazines, they spend about three to four seconds deciding whether or not an article is worth finishing. Moving on to the next article can be accomplished even more quickly on the Internet.

So how do you attract an audience and *keep* it? You may not have considered that question yet. Throughout your school career, your teachers have been paid to read your writing. And the other people reading your texts have been mostly your close friends and family. However, in a few short years, when you are writing for your professional career or for personal reasons, no one will be paid to read your writing, and you will be writing for audiences that you may not currently know or even be able to anticipate. Therefore, you must attract and engage readers with the strategies available to you.

4.1 THE ALLURE OF TITLES, DONNA GESSELL

The first place to attract an audience is with a title. Resist the temptation to label your writing with the assignment title. "Essay #1" does nothing to make a reader salivate, nor do titles that offer little information such as "Poetry Paper" or "Dickinson's 'After great pain, a formal feeling comes'." Instead, use the opportunity to raise your readers' expectations. "Chemical Structures as Poetry" sparks curiosity.

I am a reformed title avoider. I resisted writing titles and, if forced to write a title, always waited until the last minute to stick a title on the page, one time even using the title, "Title." My notion of the value of titles was exploded by Donald Murray in his book *A Writer Teaches Writing*.[23] According to Murray, a good title works for the writer:

- It establishes the subject.
- It sets the voice.
- It points the direction.
- It limits the subject.
- It attracts the reader.[24]

In other words, it deserves to be seen as a powerful marketing device for your writing. As Murray suggests, "an effective title is not a label that simply tells us what the piece of writing is." Rather, he argues, an effective title is:

- *Honest*. The author can deliver on the promise of the title.
- *Short*.
- *Lively*. It has an individual voice.
- *Pointed*. It has an opinion or a point of view towards the subject
- *Energetic*. It has drive, or energy, often carried in a verb.[25]

Murray's text is worth consulting for strategies on how to make title writing a game. Despite his enthusiasm for title writing, only once or twice have I written more than a dozen titles for a work, never equaling his one hundred that he claims to have written for an article.

However, title writing does make an excellent brainstorming exercise for any assignment. Start short and add words, using words that are the essence of what your topic is about. Then cut to keep the title short. Use verbs to enliven your title.

Before finishing your writing, check to make certain the title still fits your essay. After all, usually the process of *writing is discovery*, and you may have shifted direction or focus.

Finally, check your title for MLA style. There are three capitalization rules:

1) Capitalize the first and last words of the title.

2) Capitalize all of the content words—nouns, verbs, adjectives, and adverbs—as well as prepositions and conjunctions over six letters long.

3) Finally, if you use a colon in the title, treat the title as if it were two titles, (for example, 'Emily Dickinson: A Crystalline Vision').

Also, be aware of a few *don'ts*:

- Don't include a period in your title.
- Don't underline your own title or put it into italics—that is, unless your work is published. For published titles, MLA italicizes titles of longer works and uses quotation marks for titles of shorter works (i.e. *War and Peace* and "A Rose for Emily").

4.1.a Exercise: Evaluating Titles

The following titles are from students' reader responses to the poem "Flower Feet" by Ruth Fainlight. Using Donald Murray's lists of traits of a good title, choose several titles that attract you as a reader and several that do not. Be ready to state your criteria for each choice.

"Flower Feet"

A Review of "Flower Feet" by Ruth Fainlight

Aching Feet

An Ancient Tradition Not Forgotten

An Extinct Custom

An Interpretation of "Flower Feet"

Fainlight's Opinion on Customs and Traditions

Harmful Traditions

Held Back

Importance of Traditions

Interpretation of a Poem

Little Feet and a Lot of Pain

Mirror Shoes

My Interpretation of the Shoe Poem

My Mother's Daughter

Painful Shoes

Painful Traditions

Poem of Pain

Points of Pain

Questions to Flower Feet

Real Women's Feet

Shoes and Traditions

Small Shoes, Bigger Feet

An Old Tradition

Beauty Is in the Feet

Changing Customs—Saving Pain

Confusion of Feet

Customs and Traditions

Damaging Traditions

The Attitude About Certain Customs

The Crunching of Feet

The Days of New

The Ethics of Tradition

The Pain of Tradition

The Pain that Traditions Sometimes Leave Behind

The Silk Shoes

The Trials of Tradition

Times of Change

Tiny Shoes

Tortured Toes

Tradition and Custom

Traditional Pressures

Traditional Silk Shoes

Traditions in Cultures

Traditions Lost

Societies' Painful Traditions	Traditions, Customs, and Culture
Just Cause It's Always Been Done That Way	The Importance of Chinese Customs and
Doesn't Make It Right	Their Negative Effects on Women

4.1.b Exercise: Writing Titles as Brainstorming

Spend fifteen minutes writing a title for your essay as a brainstorming activity. Keep writing the entire time without editing your work. Try different strategies:

1) Start with nouns stating aspects of the topic you will cover; then add verbs.

2) Make the title longer; then cut it to shorten it.

3) Pretend that you are telling your best friend what you are writing about in a short text. Then write to a parent or an older relative about it.

4) Choose one word that says it all; then try another word.

When fifteen minutes is up, go back and find out what you like best and work with it.

4.2 USING A LEAD TO HOOK YOUR READER, DONNA GESSELL

Even if a reader is attracted to a title, the decision to keep reading can change by a dull introduction. In fact, traditional introductions rarely work because they spend so much time providing background information that readers might find boring. So, instead of an introduction, learn to write **leads** that will entice your reader to want to know more about your topic.

As with titles, Donald Murray has a lot of ideas about what makes for good leads. In general, they involve getting to your subject immediately but from a less traditional approach. Murray provides an extensive list of seventeen different suggestions:

- direct statement
- anecdote
- quotation
- news
- informing detail
- dialogue

- surprise
- description
- mood
- face:
  (a person to identify with)
- scene

- third person
- tension
- problem

- first person
- process
- compelling voice

Murray also notes what does *not* work: second person, rhetorical question, background, and introductions. These strategies do not work because they do not truly address the reader or they do not get to the topic quickly enough. Murray insists that, like titles, leads need to have "honesty, simplicity, immediacy, information, and voice."[26] Using one of his seventeen suggestions will help entice a reader to want to keep on reading.

A note about process is in order here. Usually writers begin writing essays with a very focused notion of where they are going. The approaches in Section 3.3 "Structuring an Argument," suggest a variety of approaches to develop an essay. However, sometimes a writer is not ready to write a lead and may not even know exactly what the essay is about. To remedy the situation, start writing. Writers have to begin writing to come to an argument by marshaling their evidence. This dilemma is because most essays use a rhetorical strategy that follows an inductive pattern, whereas most people are trained to think deductively. The inductive pattern starts out asserting a larger idea, presents evidence to support the idea, and then interprets the idea—a powerful technique that is explained below. The deductive pattern is almost the reverse: a large body of evidence presented to be analyzed to derive an idea and then contextualized by interpretation.

INDUCTIVE	DEDUCTIVE
THEORY	INFORMATION
HYPOTHESIS	PATTERN
OBSERVATION	TENTATIVE HYPOTHESIS
CONFIRMATION	THEORY

To account for this difference, some writers begin writing and develop ideas, developing an assertion. Then, simply by using "cut and paste," the assertion can be moved to the beginning of the essay where it belongs, within a suitable lead.

In in-class essays, some writers skip several lines in order to be able to go back to insert their lead and thesis with its argument.

4.2.a Exercise: Exploring Writing Leads

Look back at the last two or three webpages or magazine articles that you read, particularly looking at the lead. Which of Murray's strategies worked?

4.2.b Exercise: Writing an Effective Lead

Write a lead for the paper you are working on that describes how you yourself connected with your topic. Use one of Murray's strategies to help your reader experience the passion that helped you to connect to the topic.

4.3 BAITING: UTILIZING THE LOGIC OF ASSERTION, EVIDENCE, AND INTERPRETATION, DONNA GESSELL

4.3.a Cut Bait: Recognize the Limitations of the Traditional Five-Paragraph Essay

Traditionally, less experienced student writers are taught to write what is called the five-paragraph essay. These essays begin with an introduction that states a thesis with a three-part argument, include a paragraph for each of the three parts, and end with a conclusion that restates the three-part argument. For writers in grade school, the five-paragraph essay can encourage the development of ideas beyond a single example. However, writers need to consider other ways of developing ideas as their thinking becomes more sophisticated.

The problem with the traditional five-paragraph essay is twofold. First of all, content should determine form and not the other way around. Seldom do topics lend themselves to a three-part analysis, that is, unless a student is discussing a topic such as the make-up of the Holy Trinity. In this case, and others similar to it, using a five-paragraph essay is fine because the form fits the content, and not the other way around. Other topics, in which the content does not easily fit into the traditional five-paragraph essay, need other strategies for development.

Further, the traditional five-paragraph essay format encourages writers to *list* ideas rather than explore *relationships* among ideas. For examples, someone might argue that "There are three things that scare me: Martians, carpet, and duct tape" and then write a paragraph about each without connecting the ideas until the conclusion that restates the thesis. Instead, imagine an essay that ties the ideas together:

> There are three things that scare me: Martians, carpet, and duct tape. They scare me because of a dream that I had as a small child. In the dream, Martians landed in my bedroom and insisted that I get out of bed and lie down on a small oriental carpet that they unrolled. Imagine my horror as they rolled me up in the carpet and then used duct tape to bind the carpet around me. Fortunately, I had managed to have my head and one hand sticking out of the carpet so that I could scratch my nose when it itched. My scratching caused me to sneeze, awakening me to find myself wound tightly up in my bed sheet. Although the experience was sheer imagination, the dream was so vivid that, to this day, I cannot shop at home do-it-yourself stores, at least not in the floor covering or adhesive tape sections.

The essay is a bit silly; however, it establishes clear connections between the three items mentioned in the thesis instead of leaving them in a disconnected list.

4.3.a (1) Exercise: Revising a Traditional Five-Paragraph Essay Thesis

Consider the following three-part thesis. How could it be rewritten to suggest the relationship among ideas?

> College should prepare students for careers, social lives, and civic responsibility.

4.3.b Evaluating Effective Techniques: Analytical Compositions

Instead of using the "gelatin-mold," limiting traditional five-paragraph essay, explore other ways of developing your ideas, using the analytical composition. Dr. Lara Whelan,[27] Berry College, provides the following comparison of the two to show the strengths of sophistication of the analytical composition. Here she calls the traditional five-paragraph essay the "Topical Theme."

The Topical Theme and the Analytical Composition: Paragraphing		
	Topical Theme	**Analytical Composition**
Thesis	• Thesis begins at a high level of generality. • Thesis includes two or three "points" or reasons loosely associated with the main claim, presented as a "list." • Thesis usually connects ideas with "and," indicating ideas are of equal importance and emphasis.	• Thesis begins at a specific relationship of ideas rather than a general idea. • Ideas within the thesis are connected by words that indicate the relationships among and between those ideas. • Ideas in the thesis are linked in a "chain" of reasoning where some ideas are subordinate to others.
Topic Sentences/ Focus Ideas	• Topic sentences repeat "points" from the thesis. • As such topic sentences usually make sweeping claims at a high level of generality.	• Each focus idea analyzes a key idea in the thesis rather than simply restating it. • The structure of the focus idea often mirrors the thesis in that it indicates a reason for or condition in which the focus idea is valid.
Paragraphs	• The connection between support ideas and the topic sentence is "topical"; i.e. the paragraph consists of a collection of ideas loosely associated with the topic established in the topic sentence.	• Each paragraph analyzes the key ideas in its focus idea and connects those ideas to the thesis (just as the focus ideas/ paragraphs analyze key ideas in the thesis).
Paragraph Development	• Body paragraphs focus heavily on the use of examples as a way of "explaining" the topic sentence.	• Paragraphs make use of a variety of analytical techniques, including comparison, analysis of cause, analysis of effect, definition, and examples as *illustrations* of a particular sequence of ideas or events.
Audience Awareness	• Essay is written for a "generic" audience and is structured as an assignment.	• Essays are directed to a particular audience for a particular purpose • Essays are structured for "real life" writing situations rather than strictly as writing "assignments."

Your instructor may even use the description for the Analytical Composition as an essay grading rubric to ensure that writing is developed with sophistication, that the essay's rhetorical strategy is developed to fit its content, and that the content fits the rhetorical strategy that you have chosen.

One way to guarantee that you construct an analytical composition is to use the model of *Assertion, Evidence, and Interpretation.* Many occupations and professions use this model, although they may use different terminology to describe each part. In simplest terms, using the model means being able to explain what the problem is (assertion), give proof that it is a problem (evidence), and then describe a solution (interpretation). In scientific writing, the abstract (assertion) is followed by the introduction, methods and materials, and results (evidence), and then put into context with the discussion (interpretation).

Well-written essays also use *assertion, evidence,* and *interpretation.* In fact, its use occurs at the essay level *and* at the paragraph level.

At the essay level, the assertion is the thesis sentence. In a shorter essay (750 words or less), it is usually included at the end of the first paragraph. That position takes advantage of the notion of "end focus," a powerful psychological fact that people usually remember the last item that they are presented when given a list. A thesis sentence sets up the argument for the entire paper; or, in other words, it indirectly asks a question that the rest of the essay will answer.

The evidence that follows develops the thesis logically. Logical strategies to present evidence may use some of these techniques, among others:

- Definition or negative-definition: Tell what it is or what it is not.

- Description: Describe what it looks like or how others see it.

- Analysis: Tell what parts make it up.

- Process: List, step by step, how it came about.

- Argument: Argue for or against it, or report how others—either experts or people on the street—receive the idea.

- Apply it: Give examples of how it plays out in reality.

- Compare and Contrast it: Explain what it is not like and what it is like.

- Narrate about it: Create a story related to the idea.

- Cause and effect: Detail how ideas are related by explaining their causal relationship.

Finally, the interpretation places your argument within a larger context. It answers the question, "So what?":

- Why is this important?
- What difference does this make?
- What's at stake?

By answering at least one of these questions, you provide your reader with the larger importance of your ideas and develop their usefulness within a larger conversation or relate them to a larger topic. If no interpretation is developed, you have squandered the opportunity that the rest of your essay created by arguing an assertion and developing ideas with evidence.

At the paragraph level, the assertion is the topic sentence, one that sets up the logical strategy that will be argued in the paragraph. The evidence represents the strategy and is developed in as many sentences as necessary. And then the final sentence—to take advantage of the concept of end focus, as described above—provides the interpretation, usually linking the idea back to the thesis sentence. This linkage provides **coherence** to the essay, the logical development that brings about a coherent picture of the whole.

Cohesion occurs with the addition of each paragraph as it develops the thesis. Each idea fits on the proceeding one, and transitional words and phrases help connect the ideas. Cohesion and coherence help the reader to understand how ideas fit together. Another way of thinking of cohesion and coherence is to think of Lego blocks: cohesion is similar to how each block fits on to the next; coherence is the end result when the whole structure looks like what was being built.

The Assertion, Evidence, and Interpretation Model occurs with quotations as well. The assertion is the **signal phrase**, one that introduces the quotation by providing information about its source, including who the speaker or author is and providing credentials. It also provides some guidance as to why the information in the quotation is important to the reader. The evidence is the quotation itself. And, the interpretation provides insights as to the importance of the quotation to the argument being developed in that paragraph.

An analogy for how *assertion, evidence,* and *interpretation* work at the quotation level is an attorney-at-law in a court case. Just as a writer would never just throw a quotation into an essay, an attorney would never just have a witness give evidence. Instead, the attorney establishes the credibility of the witness as a person and as pertinent to the case being tried. Then, the witness gives testimony appropriate to the situation. After the witness has testified, the attorney makes sure to interpret how the testimony should be understood for the jury. An attorney would never pass up the last step, simply assuming that the jury members would understand without guided analysis.

Assertion, Evidence, and Interpretation				
	Essay Level	**Paragraph Level**	**Quotation Level**	**Court Witness Analogy**
Assertion	Thesis sentence	Topic sentence	Signal phrase that introduces the quotation—including speaker and credentials	Witness is introduced and determined to be credible and pertinent to the case
Evidence	Paragraphs that develop ideas with a variety of analytical techniques	Sentences that develop ideas, usually with one or two analytical techniques	Quotation	Testimony
Interpretation	End evaluation that interprets ideas within a larger context	Final sentence that interprets the idea, usually by tying the idea back to the thesis	Contextualization to the argument being developed	Interpretation by the attorney for the jury members to guide their analysis

The interpretation at the end of an essay lies in the end focus position. Because of its position, it is what most readers—including those who are evaluating your ideas—will remember. Make sure to use the interpretation to firmly anchor the importance of your ideas within a wider framework.

4.4 CASTING COHESION AND COHERENCE, *Tanya Long Bennett*

One sign of effective writing is a quality of "tightness"—a unity of the words, sentences, and paragraphs, all in service of the essay's *purpose* (as expressed in the *thesis*). We know this kind of powerful writing when we see it, but how can we create it ourselves? Here are several tools a writer can employ to generate *cohesion*—the quality of connectedness among items near each other, or *local* unity, and *coherence*—the quality of *general* unity/connectedness around a central idea:

1) Be sure that you have not veered away from the essay's focus in any paragraph or sentence.

2) Use a well-crafted topic sentence to introduce a paragraph or section, not only indicating that section's focus, but also linking the focus to the thesis idea.

3) Use a closing sentence at the end of each paragraph/section to "tie up" that section's focus and remind the reader of how that focus has helped to develop the thesis.

4) Be sure to explain the relationships among ideas between and within paragraphs.

5) Employ "tie" words to connect the essay at a micro and macro level:

   a) Transition words: however, therefore, so, and, or, on the other hand

   b) Repeated *key words*, words that keep the reader focused on the central topic/argument

   c) Pronouns: he, she, it, they, etc., linked clearly back to their antecedent (the word each refers back to)

   d) Words linked by common meanings or connotations, for example: socket, electrical, plug, cord, power

4.4.a Exercise

To better understand the effect of *tie* words, consider the following paragraph:

> Charlotte Gilman's use of Gothic elements in her short story "The Yellow Wallpaper"[28] reveals the subconscious battle many of us face in trying to fulfill our personal desires while simultaneously conforming to society's rigid expectations. For example, the story is set at an old estate, which the narrator refers to as a "haunted house," with "hedges and walls and gates that lock." The post-partum narrator describes the room she shares with her doctor-husband as having windows that are "barred" and wallpaper that somehow disturbs her: "It is dull enough to confuse the eye in following, pronounced enough to constantly irritate and provoke study, and

when you follow the lame uncertain curves for a little distance they suddenly commit suicide—plunge off at outrageous angles, destroy themselves in unheard of contradictions." Her descriptions of the summer place's features, together generating the tone of Gothic horror, reflect not only the restrictions she feels as a result of society's standards for women, but also the psychological fragmentation caused by her struggles with those standards, ultimately breaking down her "stable" social self.

- List the paragraph's transition words.
- List any key words that are repeated throughout the paragraph.
- Underline pronouns and draw a line from each back to its antecedent.
- List groups of words with common or *linked* meanings, for example, "subconscious," "personal," "psychological."
- Discuss how these ties work as glue to unify the paragraph in support of the central point (developing *coherence*).

4.5 NETTING YOUR READER WITH A SATISFYING ENDING, DONNA GESSELL

If you have ever stayed at a hotel that has "turn down" service, you know how delightful it is to return to the room at the end of a long day to find your bed sheets turned down, ready for you to jump in. Sometimes, the staff even leaves a mint on the pillow. The result is pure satisfaction with just the right touch of closure, and a sweet experience to remember when next booking a hotel.

Writers need to leave their readers with the same degree of satisfaction. Planning the ending of an essay is just as important as planning every other part. True, you will be in your end evaluation, so the idea here is not to introduce some new idea. Nor should you repeat ideas that have already been stated; hopefully, your reader will remember them without being dunned with them a second time. Instead, use a strategy similar to those introduced in the "Lead" section of this essay. One more good idea will help secure your hold over your reader, "netting" them.

4.6 ESSAY EVALUATION CHECKLIST, *Tanya Long Bennett and Donna Gessell*

It is not uncommon for a student to complete his final draft of an essay and submit the paper, only to realize later that some components of the submission were incomplete or inadequate. The following checklist is meant to be employed *before* the essay is turned in, preferably when a student still has time for last minute revisions.

Title:

> Attracts the reader, and is honest, lively, and reasonably short; establishes voice and direction

Lead, or Introduction:

> Engaging and effective; offers insights into the topic and the writer's position

Thesis:

> Clear and interesting; asserts an argument and controls the entire essay

Organization:

> Clear and effective with cohesion (effective transitions and links among ideas) and coherence (ties to the thesis in the evaluation of each idea)

Prose:

> Clear and engaging; free of grammatical errors and awkward constructions

Evidence:

> Developed adequately to prove the writer's point

Sources:

- Effectively integrated with signal (or tag) phrases and evaluation
- Minimum (assigned) number of scholarly sources
- Quotation marks used to indicate direct quotation, and all information from sources, including paraphrased and summarized materials, cited with MLA parenthetical citation

Evaluation:

> Overall comment that answers at least one of these questions: So what? Why is this important? What difference does this make? What is at stake?

Ending, or Conclusion:

    Wraps up effectively, leaving the reader with one more specific idea that will convince the reader of the writer's point

Works Cited:

- Lists <u>only</u> sources that are mentioned in the essay
- Lists <u>all</u> sources that are mentioned in the essay
- Is alphabetized by authors' last names (and *not* numbered)
- Follows assigned format (such as MLA) in all entries

The following essays, written by both professionals and students, offer examples for analysis and discussion. Consider how these authors have used some of the rhetorical tools we have been exploring: thesis; pathos, logos, and ethos; structure; title; tone; introduction and conclusion (or lead and ending); assertion, evidence, and interpretation; and cohesion and coherence. What effects do the authors achieve through their rhetorical choices?

4.7 SAMPLES ESSAYS BY PROFESSIONAL AUTHORS

How It Feels To Be Colored Me[29]

Zora Neal Hurston

This essay was first published in 1928 in a magazine called The World Tomorrow. *Hurston (1891-1960) was born in Notasulga, Alabama, and lived much of her childhood in the all-black town of Eatonville, Florida. An anthropologist and writer, she became a well-known figure of the Harlem Renaissance, a literary, artistic, and political movement of the 1920's characterized by the blossoming of African-American culture in the U.S.*

    I am colored but I offer nothing in the way of extenuating circumstances except the fact that I am the only Negro in the United States whose grandfather on the mother's side was *not* an Indian chief.

    I remember the very day that I became colored. Up to my thirteenth year I lived in the little Negro town of Eatonville, Florida. It is exclusively a colored town. The only white people I knew passed through the town going to or coming from Orlando. The native whites rode dusty horses, the Northern tourists chugged down the sandy village road in automobiles. The town knew the Southerners and never stopped cane chewing when they passed. But the Northerners were something else again. They were peered at cautiously from behind curtains by the timid. The more venturesome would come out on the porch to watch them go past and got just as much pleasure out of the tourists as the tourists got out of the village.

The front porch might seem a daring place for the rest of the town, but it was a gallery seat for me. My favorite place was atop the gatepost. Proscenium box for a born first-nighter. Not only did I enjoy the show, but I didn't mind the actors knowing that I liked it. I usually spoke to them in passing. I'd wave at them and when they returned my salute, I would say something like this: "Howdy-do-well-I-thank-you-where-you-goin'?" Usually automobile or the horse paused at this, and after a queer exchange of compliments, I would probably "go a piece of the way" with them, as we say in farthest Florida. If one of my family happened to come to the front in time to see me, of course negotiations would be rudely broken off. But even so, it is clear that I was the first "welcome-to-our-state" Floridian, and I hope the Miami Chamber of Commerce will please take notice.

During this period, white people differed from colored to me only in that they rode through town and never lived there. They liked to hear me "speak pieces" and sing and wanted to see me dance the parse-me-la, and gave me generously of their small silver for doing these things, which seemed strange to me for I wanted to do them so much that I needed bribing to stop, only they didn't know it. The colored people gave no dimes. They deplored any joyful tendencies in me, but I was their Zora nevertheless. I belonged to them, to the nearby hotels, to the county—everybody's Zora.

But changes came in the family when I was thirteen, and I was sent to school in Jacksonville. I left Eatonville, the town of the oleanders, a Zora. When I disembarked from the river-boat at Jacksonville, she was no more. It seemed that I had suffered a sea change. I was not Zora of Orange County any more, I was now a little colored girl. I found it out in certain ways. In my heart as well as in the mirror, I became a fast brown—warranted not to rub nor run.

But I am not tragically colored. There is no great sorrow dammed up in my soul, nor lurking behind my eyes. I do not mind at all. I do not belong to the sobbing school of Negrohood who hold that nature somehow has given them a lowdown dirty deal and whose feelings are all but about it. Even in the helter-skelter skirmish that is my life, I have seen that the world is to the strong regardless of a little pigmentation more or less. No, I do not weep at the world—I am too busy sharpening my oyster knife.

Someone is always at my elbow reminding me that I am the granddaughter of slaves. It fails to register depression with me. Slavery is sixty years in the past. The operation was successful and the patient is doing well, thank you. The terrible struggle that made me an American out of a potential slave said "On the line!" The Reconstruction said "Get set!" and the generation before said "Go!" I am off to a flying start and I must not halt in the stretch to look behind and weep. Slavery is the price I paid for civilization, and the choice was not with me. It is a bully adventure and worth all that I have paid through my ancestors for it. No one on earth ever had a greater chance for glory. The world to be won and nothing to be lost. It is thrilling to think—to know that for any act of mine, I shall get twice as much praise or twice as much blame. It is quite exciting to hold the center of the national stage, with the spectators not knowing whether to laugh or to weep.

The position of my white neighbor is much more difficult. No brown specter pulls up a chair beside me when I sit down to eat. No dark ghost thrusts its leg against mine in bed. The game of keeping what one has is never so exciting as the game of getting.

I do not always feel colored. Even now I often achieve the unconscious Zora of Eatonville before the Hegira. I feel most colored when I am thrown against a sharp white background.

For instance at Barnard. "Beside the waters of the Hudson" I feel my race. Among the thousand white persons, I am a dark rock surged upon, and overswept, but through it all, I remain myself. When covered by the waters, I am; and the ebb but reveals me again.

Sometimes it is the other way around. A white person is set down in our midst, but the contrast is just as sharp for me. For instance, when I sit in the drafty basement that is The New World Cabaret with a white person, my color comes. We enter chatting about any little nothing that we have in common and are seated by the jazz waiters. In the abrupt way that jazz orchestras have, this one plunges into a number. It loses no time in circumlocutions, but gets right down to business. It constricts the thorax and splits the heart with its tempo and narcotic harmonies. This orchestra grows rambunctious, rears on its hind legs and attacks the tonal veil with primitive fury, rending it, clawing it until it breaks through to the jungle beyond. I follow those heathen—follow them exultingly. I dance wildly inside myself; I yell within, I whoop; I shake my assegai above my head, I hurl it true to the mark yeeeeooww! I am in the jungle and living in the jungle way. My face is painted red and yellow and my body is painted blue. My pulse is throbbing like a war drum. I want to slaughter something—give pain, give death to what, I do not know. But the piece ends. The men of the orchestra wipe their lips and rest their fingers. I creep back slowly to the veneer we call civilization with the last tone and find the white friend sitting motionless in his seat, smoking calmly.

"Good music they have here," he remarks, drumming the table with his fingertips.

Music. The great blobs of purple and red emotion have not touched him. He has only heard what I felt. He is far away and I see him but dimly across the ocean and the continent that have fallen between us. He is so pale with his whiteness then and I am so colored.

At certain times I have no race, I am me. When I set my hat at a certain angle and saunter down Seventh Avenue, Harlem City, feeling as snooty as the lions in front of the Forty-Second Street Library, for instance. So far as my feelings are concerned, Peggy Hopkins Joyce on the Boule Mich with her gorgeous raiment, stately carriage, knees knocking together in a most aristocratic manner, has nothing on me. The cosmic Zora emerges. I belong to no race nor time. I am the eternal feminine with its string of beads.

I have no separate feeling about being an American citizen and colored. I am merely a fragment of the Great Soul that surges within the boundaries. My country, right or wrong.

Sometimes, I feel discriminated against, but it does not make me angry. It merely astonishes me. How can any deny themselves the pleasure of my company? It's beyond me.

But in the main, I feel like a brown bag of miscellany propped against a wall. Against a wall in company with other bags, white, red and yellow. Pour out the contents, and there is discovered a jumble of small things priceless and worthless. A first-water diamond, an empty spool, bits of broken glass, lengths of string, a key to a door long since crumbled away, a rusty knife-blade, old shoes saved for a road that never was and never will be, a nail bent under the weight of things too heavy for any nail, a dried flower or two still a little fragrant. In your hand is the brown bag. On the ground before you is the jumble it held—so much like the jumble in the bags, could they be emptied, that all might be dumped in a single heap and the bags refilled without altering the content of any greatly. A bit of colored glass more or less would not matter. Perhaps that is how the Great Stuffer of Bags filled them in the first place—who knows?

Intellectual Ambition[30]
George Santayana

George Santayana (1863-1952) was born in Spain, spent many years in the U.S. after moving there as a child in 1872, and returned to Europe in 1912 to live permanently. He enjoyed a long career as a philosopher and writer, producing many philosophical works, essays, poems and novels in his lifetime. As a pragmatic naturalist, he held that "truth" was inextricable from the physical world, and he emphasized, perhaps surprisingly, the necessity of the human imagination in understanding that world and our experiences, as well as in celebrating life. "Intellectual Ambition" was included in his book The Realms of Being, *published in 1942.*

When we consider the situation of the human mind in nature, its limited plasticity and few channels of communication with the outer world, we need not wonder that we grope for light, or that we find incoherence and instability in human systems of ideas. The wonder rather is that we have done so well, that in the chaos of sensations and passions that fills the mind we have found any leisure for self-concentration and reflection, and have succeeded in gathering even a light harvest of experience from our distracted labors. Our occasional madness is less wonderful than our occasional sanity. Relapses into dreams are to be expected in a being whose brief existence is so like a dream; but who could have been sure of this sturdy and indomitable perseverance in the work of reason in spite of all the checks and discouragements?

The resources of the mind are not commensurate with its ambition. Of the five senses, three are of little use in the formation of permanent notions: a fourth, sight, is indeed vivid and luminous, but furnishes transcripts of things so highly colored and deeply modified by the medium of sense, that a long labor of analysis and correction is needed before satisfactory conceptions can be extracted from it. For this labor, however, we are endowed with the requisite instrument. We have memory and we have certain powers of synthesis, abstraction, reproduction, invention,—in a word, we have understanding. But this faculty of understanding has hardly begun its work of deciphering the hieroglyphics of sense and framing an idea of reality, when it is crossed by another faculty—the imagination. Perceptions do not remain in the mind, as would be suggested by the trite simile of the seal and wax, passive and changeless, until time wear off their sharp edges and make them fade. No, perceptions fall into the brain rather as seeds into a furrowed field or even as sparks into a keg of powder. Each image breeds a hundred more, sometimes slowly and subterraneously, sometimes (when a passionate train is started) with a sudden burst of fancy. The mind, exercised by its own fertility and flooded by its inner lights, has infinite trouble to keep a true reckoning of its outward perceptions. It turns from the frigid problems of observation to its own visions; it forgets to watch the courses of what should be its "pilot stars." Indeed, were it not for the power of convention in which, by a sort of mutual cancellation of errors, the more practical and normal conceptions are enshrined, the imagination would carry men wholly away,—the best men first and the vulgar after them. Even as it is, individuals and ages of fervid imagination usually waste themselves in dreams, and must disappear before the race, saddened and dazed, perhaps, by the memory of those visions, can return to its plodding thoughts.

Five senses, then, to gather a small part of the infinite influences that vibrate in nature, a moderate power of understanding to interpret those senses, and an irregular, passionate fancy to overlay that interpretation—such is the endowment of the human mind. And what is its ambition? Nothing less than to construct a picture of reality, to comprehend its own origin and that of the universe, to discover the laws of both and prophesy their destiny. Is not the disproportion enormous? Are not confusions and profound contradictions to be looked for in an attempt to build so much out of so little?

Some Nonsense About a Dog[31]
Harry Esty Dounce

Harry Esty Dounce (1889-1957) was born in Syracuse, New York. He worked as both a writer and editor for several well-known publications in the early 1900's, including the Syracuse Herald *and the New York* Evening Post. *This piece was published in 1921.*

"My hand will miss the insinuated nose—"
Sir William Watson

But the dog that was written of must have been a big dog. Nibbie was just a comfortable lapful, once he had duly turned around and curled up with his nose in his tail.

This is for people who know about dogs, in particular little mongrels without pedigree or market value. Other people, no doubt, will find it disgustingly maudlin. I would have found it so before Nibbie came.

The day he came was a beautiful bright, cool one in an August. A touring car brought him. They put him down on our corner, meaning to lose him, but he crawled under the car, and they had to prod him out and throw stones before they could drive on. So that when I came home I found, with his mistress-elect, a sort of potbellied bundle of tarry oakum, caked with mud, panting convulsively still from fright, and showing the whites of uncommonly liquid brown eyes and a pink tongue. There was tennis that evening and he went along—I carried him over the railroad tracks; he gave us no trouble about the balls, but lay huddled under the bench where she sat, and shivered if a man came near him.

That night he got chop bones and she got a sensible homily on the unwisdom of feeding strays, and he was left outdoors. He slept on the mat. The second morning we thought he had gone. The third, he was back, wagging approval of us and intent to stay, which seemed to leave no choice but to take him in. We had fun over names. "Jellywaggles," suggested from next door, was undeniably descriptive. "Rags" fitted, or "Toby," or

"Nig"—but they had a colored maid next door; finally we called him "Nibs," and soon his tail would answer to it.

Cleaned up—scrubbed, the insoluble matted locks clipped from his coat, his trampish collar replaced with a new one bearing a license tag—he was far from being unpresentable. A vet once opined that for a mongrel he was a good dog, that a black cocker mother had thrown her cap over Scottish mills, so to speak. This analysis accounted for him perfectly. Always, depending on the moment's mood, he was either terrier or spaniel, the snap and scrap and perk of the one alternating with the gentle snuggling indolence of the other.

As terrier he would dig furiously by the hour after a field mouse; as spaniel he would "read" the breeze with the best nose among the dog folk of our neighborhood, or follow a trail quite well. I know there was retrieving blood. A year ago May he caught and brought me, not doing the least injury, an oriole that probably had flown against a wire and was struggling disabled in the grass.

Nibbie was shabby-genteel black, sunburnt as to the mustache, grizzled as to the raggy fringe on his haunch-es. He had a white stock and shirt-frill and a white fore paw. The brown eyes full of heart were the best point. His body coat was rough Scottish worsted, the little black pate was cotton-soft like shoddy, and the big black ears were genuine spaniel silk. As a terrier he held them up smartly and carried a plumy fishhook of a tail; as a spaniel the ears drooped and the tail swung meekly as if in apology for never having been clipped. The other day when we had to say good-by to him each of us cut one silky tuft from an ear, very much as we had so often when he'd been among the burdocks in the field where the garden is.

Burrs were by no means Nibbie's only failing. In flea time it seemed hardly possible that a dog of his size could sustain his population. We finally found a true flea bane, but, deserted one day, he was populous again the next. They don't relish every human; me they did; I used to storm at him for it, and he used, between spasms of scratching, to listen admiringly and wag. We think he supposed his tormentors were winged insects, for he sought refuge in dark clothes-closets where a flying imp wouldn't logically come.

He was wilful, insisted on landing in laps when their makers wanted to read. He *would* make advances to visitors who were polite about him. He *would* get up on the living-room table, why and how, heaven knows, finding his opportunity when we were out of the house, and taking care to be upstairs on a bed—white, grimeable coverlets preferred—by the time we had the front door open; I used to slip up to the porch and catch through a window the diving flourish of his sinful tail.

One of his faults must have been a neurosis really. He led a hard life before we took him in, as witnessed the game hind leg that made him sit up side-saddle fashion, and two such scars on his back as boiling hot grease might have made. And something especially cruel had been done to him when asleep, for if you bent over him napping or in his bed he would half rouse and growl, and sometimes snap blindly. (We dreaded exuberant visiting children.) Two or three experiments I hate to remember now convinced me that it couldn't be whipped out of him, and once wide awake he was sure to be perplexedly apologetic.

He was spoiled. That was our doing. We babied him abominably—he was, for two years, the only subject we had for such malpractice. He had more foolish names than Wogg, that dog of Mrs. Stevenson's, and heard more Little Language than Stella ever did, reciprocating by kissing proffered ears in his doggy way. Once he had brightened up after his arrival, he showed himself ready to take an ell whenever we gave an inch, and he was always taking them, and never paying penalties. He had conscience enough to be sly. I remember the summer evening we stepped outside for just an instant, and came back to find a curious groove across the butter, on the dining table, and an ever-so-innocent Nibbie in a chair in the next room.

While we were at the table he was generally around it, bulldozing for tid-bits—I fear he had reason to know that this would work. One fortnight when his Missie was away he slept on his Old Man's bed (we had dropped titles of dignity with him by then) and he rang the welkin hourly, answering far-away dog friends, and occasionally came north to lollop my face with tender solicitude, just like the fool nurse in the story, waking the patient up to ask if he was sleeping well.

More recently, when a beruffled basket was waiting, he developed an alarming trick of stealing in there to try it, so I fitted that door with a hook, insuring a crack impervious to dogs. And the other night I had to take the hook, now useless, off; we couldn't stand hearing it jingle. He adopted the junior member on first sight and sniff of him, by the way; would look on beaming as proudly as if he'd hatched him.

The last of his iniquities arose from a valor that lacked its better part, an absurd mixture of Falstaff and bantam rooster. At the critical point he'd back out of a fuss with a dog of his own size. But let a police dog, an Airedale, a St. Bernard, or a big ugly cur appear and Nibbie was all around him, blackguarding him unendurably. It was lucky that the big dogs in our neighborhood were patient. And he never would learn about automobiles. Usually tried to tackle them head on, often stopped cars with merciful drivers. When the car wouldn't stop, luck would save him by a fraction of an inch. I couldn't spank that out of him either. We had really been expecting what finally happened for two years.

That's about all. Too much, I am afraid. A decent fate made it quick the other night, and clean and close at hand, in fact, on the same street corner where once a car had left the small scapegrace for us. We tell ourselves how glad we are it happened as it did, instead of an agonal ending such as many of his people come to. We tell ourselves we couldn't have had him for ever in any event; that some day, for the junior member's sake, we shall get another dog. We keep telling ourselves these things, and talking with animation on other topics. The muzzle, the leash, the drinking dish are hidden, the last muddy paw track swept up, the nose smudges washed off the favorite front window pane.

But the house is full of a little snoofing, wagging, loving ghost. I know how the boy Thoreau felt about a hereafter with dogs barred. I want to think that somewhere, some time, I will be coming home again, and that when the door opens Nibbie will be on hand to caper welcome.

4.8 SAMPLE STUDENT ESSAYS

Merle Manuel
English 1102
26 September 2011

A Cursed Life

My family has endured much pain and many hardships, but through these challenges they became better, stronger, and more capable people. For a family history project I had to do my sophomore year in high school, I interviewed my mother about any interesting things that have happened to our family. She told me that a distant and jealous relative of ours cursed our family. Apparently since my great-grandparents inherited vast acres of farmland, this relative, who thought he should have received it instead, cursed all the women in the family to live hard and unfulfilling lives. Looking back at my grandmother's life, my mother's, and finally my own, I think that the curse could be real. When I was younger, I complained that nothing interesting ever happened to us, but little did I know that even worse, an old family curse might actually decide my fate.

When I found out about the curse, I didn't quite believe in it, but I have witnessed with my own eyes that the Ruiz-Manuel family has never really had any good luck or peaceful times. Something was always going on, some scandal or family feud always surrounded us. For example, my mother had an older sister who died at an early age, and we share the same name. Speaking of my mother, she and Grandma were never quite as close as most mothers and daughters, because of the fact that Grandma worked in America while Mom grew up in the

Philippines fending for herself. Mom never made the right decisions in life, it seemed. Of course that's how I came into existence, but it seemed that she was always making her life harder because of her choices. So how can I say that the curse is not true? Of course it is true; it just took me seventeen years to figure it all out, and to think that I believed nothing interesting ever happened to my family!

Cecilia and Manuel "Manny" Manuel were two of my greatest supporters and role models; they are better known to me as Lola and Lolo (grandmother and grandfather in Tagalog). Even though they have since passed, I carry on their memories and legacies through living my life as fully as possible. I have this old black and white picture of them on their honeymoon in Baguio, Philippines. The photo was taken on November 29, 1963. They are both posing next to Our Lady Lourdes' Grotto. In the photo, both are clearly newlyweds smiling shyly at the camera. This photo reminds me of how they were innocent in the beginning. They would not have imagined all the hardships that would almost tear them apart.

The Philippines is considered as a third world country, so many of its citizens go overseas to work and send money home to support their families. My Lola, after giving birth to three children, completed nursing school and came to America to work. Lolo stayed in the Philippines to take care of the children and also got a job as a mechanic. The distance did not help their marriage, and it also didn't help Lola's relationship with my mother. Even though she was away in a different country to provide a good life for her family, Lola always wished she could have been there more for her family. Thinking about her living alone in a foreign country, where she had to learn the language on her own, amazes me because if I were in her place I would've given up after a couple of months out of shear loneliness. However, my Lola was strong and sacrificed herself in order to provide better living conditions for my mom and uncle.

In spite of her good intentions, Lola never had a close relationship with my mother because of the fact that she was away most of the time. My mother grew up pretty fast so she could take care of herself and also keep things in order at home for her father and brother. This practice of a mother's work taking her away from her children affected me, too, in that my mother and I don't have a close mother-daughter relationship either. Instead, I was always close to Lola. Mom has always been a good "friend" rather than the authoritative figure I wish she had been. Like Lola, my mother worked constantly in order to provide a better future for me. But because of her work, Lola was the one who raised me to be the person who I am today. How ironic that she would raise her estranged daughter's child.

Mom and I don't see eye to eye on everything, like for example how she remarried to a man I barely knew in 2004 and didn't even bother to tell me while I was in the Philippines with my grandparents. I have almost always forgiven her for making hard decisions that I might not like, but I don't think I'll be able to forgive her for remarrying without letting me know. Usually, though, if she made tough decisions without my support, she did so to make my future better. Like for example, she made the decision to emigrate from the Philippines to Washington D.C. with me in tow. While Lola took care of me, Mom took jobs as a maid and a babysitter, all so I could have a better life than she did. Her life has been full of many hardships, in that she worked constantly to provide for me but didn't reap the benefits of spending time with a daughter. She never really enjoyed a true mother-daughter relationship. Only now that I am about to graduate high school have we gotten somewhat closer. Even though she wasn't there for me, like Lola wasn't there for her, I still love her, and I know she did her best. I hope now that she has my little brother and has a more stable income, she can make up for what she missed with me.

Since my mother was busy with work during my childhood, my grandparents were the ones that took care of my well-being. In fact, my grandparents were more like my parents than grandparents. Lolo and Lola were my constant supporters; throughout my life they treated me as a daughter more than as a granddaughter. One reason they were so devoted to me is that out of their three children, one daughter did not live past the age of three. Her name was Merle. She had a bad heart and because of it she didn't live long. You're probably wondering why we have the same name. Well, our birthdays are separated by one day, and when Lola realized this on the day that I was born, she insisted that my mother name me after her late sister. I found a picture of Merle's gravestone in one of our photo albums.

Personally, I find it quite strange seeing my name on a gravestone before I have even lived my life yet. Maybe this twist is also part of the curse. I mean I haven't even started really living yet and I've already seen my gravestone. Something about that leaves me with a weird feeling. It's too many coincidences that Lola, Mom, Aunt Merle, and I would have lives so full of hardships. But maybe my seeing that gravestone isn't all bad: it fills me with desire to break out of the cycle.

From what I have witnessed this family curse causes the women in my family to have many regrets in life, regrets that they didn't have the life that they deserved. Instead of living, they spend all their time providing for others, working constantly to better someone else's future. They don't reap the benefits of their relationships within the family. This curse seems too strong to have it skip a generation, but it doesn't mean that I won't give up on my dreams of living my life to the fullest. Little by little, I am changing my family's legacy, away from the curse, by going to college. It was my decision, my choice to go and experience a different culture from what I've been growing up in. I have the benefit of all that my mother and my grandparents gave me, and their love will give me strength as I go forward, but I don't want to have regrets in my life like Lola and Mom. I want to become happy someday and have a close relationship with my daughter. I don't know what hardships and obstacles are in my future, but I won't stop trying to overcome them to find a new path for myself.

Samantha Fey
English 1101
19 October 2011

The Need for a Higher Minimum Wage

The federal minimum wage in America is $7.25 an hour. States can set their own legal minimum wage higher than the federal limit (U.S. Department of Labor), and many do. In some states, though, people still cannot support themselves on the state minimum wage because the cost of living in their state is so high. Even if they can cover the basics, they are not able to pay for any unexpected medical bills that might come along if they or their family members get sick or injured. For this reason, individual states should reconsider their minimum wage taking into account the average cost of living in the state.

I calculated that a person working forty hours a week every week for the federal minimum wage earns $15,080 in a year. Next, I used a cost of living calculator ("Cost of Living Wizard") to figure out the difference in disposable income for a person working for minimum wage in Columbus, Georgia, and a person working and living in New York, New York. Both Georgia and New York have a minimum wage of $7.75 (U.S. Department of Labor). However, in New York, the cost of living is 89.7% more than in Columbus. Therefore, a person would have to make $13.75 an hour in New York to maintain the same standard of living as a person working for $7.75 in Columbus.

Living on minimum wage anywhere is a struggle. Imagine a single mother of two living in Georgia and working at Wal-Mart trying to support her family. It seems almost impossible, but now imagine if the worth of her money had almost a 50% decrease. Could they survive on that in New York? They might be able to if they took welfare and shared a small apartment with another family, but maybe not. If New York increased their minimum wage to even $10.00, it would increase the family's standard of living almost to that of a family in the same situation in Georgia.

It is true that increasing minimum wage has adverse effects. For instance, employers might not be able to suddenly begin paying their employees almost three dollars more an hour, so they might have to lay off some employees. However, if consumers are making more money, they will have more money to spend, and that money could potentially come back to the employer in profits. Also, to help employers with the new costs, the government could give out temporary subsidies to businesses to prevent layoffs until the profits increased.

I have seen first-hand the difficulty of stretching minimum wage to meet financial needs. During the summer, I worked at Banana Republic as a sales associate. Originally I was paid $7.75 an hour, but I later got an eight cent raise. I did not spend any of my money; I saved it all to live off of in college. Some weeks I'd work forty hours, but it seemed like I was making almost no money after all the deductions.

I was scared about the costs of going to college. Even though my parents would be paying for my dorm, meal plan, and tuition, I wanted to make sure I'd have money for things like clothes, snacks, and cosmetics. Then I thought about the other older people I was working with who were living on only the money they were making at Banana Republic. They did not have a dorm room, a meal plan, or wealthy parents to fall back on. How were they living off their paychecks?

During the time I was working at Banana Republic, I started having a lot of problems with my shoulder. Treatment of this condition required that I go to the doctor several times, purchase medication, and get an MRI, and I may even have to get surgery eventually. I missed some work because of it, and the costs added up. What would my older colleagues do if they had a similar problem? Most of them were working part time, so they had no health insurance. If they missed a day of work, they would miss a big part of their paycheck. I do not think they would be able to afford their medical bills.

Raising the minimum wage in states where the cost of living is high would not solve everyone's financial woes, but it would help some struggling people have a better life. In general, people want to be able to support themselves and their families. If working full-time does not pay enough to cover even the basic costs of living, not only will people suffer, but many workers may become discouraged and stop working altogether. Work should help people maintain dignity and independence, and states should consider this goal when reviewing their own minimum wage rates.

Works Cited

"Cost of Living Wizard" Salary.com. International Business Machines Corporation. 2011. Web. 12 Oct. 2011.

U.S. Department of Labor, Wage and Hour Division. *Minimum Wage Laws in the States*. U.S. Department of Labor, 2011. Web. 10 Oct. 2011.

Integrating Sources into Your Writing

5.1 GATHERING YOUR SOURCES, *Chris Bell*

When writing a research paper, a task you will be required to do in a many classes, be sure to take the proper approach when gathering sources. Too often, students believe acquiring a handful of books will be a sufficient means of gathering data. In truth, books often contain too much information that can quickly become unwieldy. In addition to books, consider a variety of sources such as the following:

1) Journals
2) Magazines
3) Newspapers
4) Online resources

Furthermore, use a variety of avenues when collecting sources. In addition to books and online sources, consider academic databases, which nearly all colleges offer through electronic search engines. These databases contain hundreds of thousands of articles from a variety of source types. The information culled from databases is often considered far more useful than that found on the Internet, as sources found on web pages often cannot be verified as having been authored by an authority. Be particularly aware that many professors are highly skeptical of Internet sources.

5.2 KNOWING YOUR SOURCES, *Chris Bell*

There are two kinds of sources, **primary** and **secondary**. A primary source is one originally authored by an individual, such as a diary, speech, letter, novel, poem, play, and so on. A secondary source analyzes and comments on a primary source. An effective research paper will contain both primary and secondary sources, although this is not an absolute requirement.

5.3 EVALUATING YOUR SOURCES, CHRIS BELL

When conducting research, it is important to be able to determine the quality of a source. There are various matters to consider when determining the effectiveness of a source:

1) What are the author's credentials?
2) Has the author conducted research of his or her own and utilized it effectively?
3) Is the article contemporary (this may be more important in some disciplines than others)?
4) Is the article written effectively?

5.4 READING AND ORGANIZING EFFECTIVELY, CHRIS BELL

As you collect and evaluate your sources, take effective notes on the information which you can comment on, dispute, and amplify. Keep track of your sources by creating a bibliography. Remember to take notes carefully. When paraphrasing, be sure to make the writing distinctly different from the source in order to avoid plagiarism.

5.5 SUMMARIZING, PARAPHRASING, AND QUOTING, DIANA EDELMAN-YOUNG

As you progress through your college career, you will learn to do research in a variety of disciplines, which involves working with a variety of sources. It is important to learn how to properly quote, summarize, and paraphrase these sources as you begin to make your own arguments and respond to what others have said on a topic. Sometimes you will want to quote directly, which is when you use the source's own words verbatim (or word-for-word).

At other times, you will choose between summarizing and paraphrasing, but what is the difference, right? These two writing concepts are often confused with one another, but they are skills essential to any writers, particularly when you start using sources. In this section, we will concentrate on summarizing and paraphrasing, both of which use your own words. Then, we will discuss how to smoothly integrate direct quotations.

Students often have several questions about these areas of writing:

1) What are quoting, paraphrasing, and summarizing?
2) How do I tell the difference between paraphrasing and summarizing?
3) Only direct quotations need to be cited, right?

The following chart will help answer these questions:

Type	Definition	Citation requirements	Special markings and format required
Quotation	A transcription verbatim of the passage or parts of the passage.	Include an **in-text citation** and an entry in the Works Cited[32] page.	Use quotation marks around the words used. In the case of long quotations, use block quotations (see the MLA style section for details).
Paraphrase	A restatement of the original source in your own words. A para-phrase is about the same length as the original and touches on *all* the main ideas, sub points, and examples.	Include an in-text citation and an entry in the Works Cited page.	None
Summary	A very brief syn-opsis of the *main* idea of the pas-sage. A summary is much shorter than the original and focuses on the *main* idea of the passage as a whole.	Include an in-text citation and an entry in the Works Cited page.	None

Notice that in *all three cases*, you are required to include an in-text citation and an entry in the Works Cited page. Students often say, "But I'm changing the words to make them my own, so why do I need a citation?" The answer is that you are summarizing or paraphrasing someone else's ideas and materials. That person needs to be given credit. Also, it establishes *your* credibility to show that you have done the proper research and know what has been said already on your topic.

Examples

> **Original:** "A general rule of thumb in television advertising, then, is that daytime is the best time to reach the woman who works at home. Especially important to advertisers among this group is the young mother with children" (Craig 188).

Direct quotation: According to Steve Craig, "Gendered commercials, like gendered programs, are designed to give pleasure to the target audience, since it is the association of the product with a pleasurable experience that forms the basis for much American television advertising. Yet patriarchy conditions males and females to see their pleasure differently. Advertisers therefore portray different images to men and women in order to exploit the different deep-seated motivations and anxieties connected to gender identity" (189).[33]

Paraphrase: According to Steve Craig, because television marketing in America relies on the connection between the product and pleasure, commercials that are based on gender are supposed to target their audience through pleasure (189). The reality is that our culture believes that men and women have different ideas about what is pleasurable (Craig 189). In response, marketers use images that will take advantage of the fears that people have about their gender identities by utilizing images that capitalize on those fears (Craig 189).

Summary: Steve Craig argues that advertisers exploit our fears about gender identity by targetting men and women differently based on assumptions about what gives each of them pleasure (189).

So now you might say, "Okay, I got it, but *how* do I paraphrase? If I change every few words and substitute some synonyms, I've paraphrased, right?" Unfortunately, no. Even if you change every third word, which is a rule of thumb people often hear, that is not enough. It is possible to plagiarize someone's sentence structure. Thus, it is important to do *at least* the following:

1) Begin by changing *at least* every third word.

2) Substitute synonyms throughout.

3) Rearrange the sentence structure.

4) Condense and combine sentences (for example, you can take the main ideas of two sentences and get the gist of them in one).

5) After you do *at least* all the above, remember that you still need the in-text citation and the reference at the end. The only thing you don't need when you paraphrase is quotation marks.

Examples

Improper paraphrase: A general rule in television marketing, then, is that during the day is a good time to reach the female working at home. Particularly important is the youthful mom with children (Craig 188).

The problem with this paraphrase is that it keeps exactly the same structure as the original and changes only a few words here and there. Again, substituting synonyms every so often is not enough. A true paraphrase is a thorough restatement.

True paraphrase: Advertisers know that during the day is the most effective time to target women, especially those with young children, who work at home (Craig 188).

This paraphrase is much better because it radically restructures the sentence and changes the language without changing the meaning of the original. And, notice, even though the paraphrased information is not relayed word-for-word, the author includes an in-text citation because the *ideas* are Craig's.

Now that you have an idea on how to paraphrase, where do you place the citation? Generally, you need to *put an in-text citation at the end of each sentence, even if you paraphrase a long passage,* unless it is clear from context that you are still paraphrasing the source. Don't just put a put citation at the end of the passage. It just needs to be clear to your reader where your voice begins and ends and where the source's voice begins and ends. This also helps the reader distinguish among the sources. When you're dealing with only a few sources, this may not be as much of a problem, but as you advance your education, you will be working with more and more sources and longer and longer essays.

Examples

> **Original:** "Gendered commercials, like gendered programs, are designed to give pleasure to the target audience, since it is the association of the product with a pleasurable experience that forms the basis for much American television advertising. Yet patriarchy conditions males and females to see their pleasure differently. Advertisers therefore portray different images to men and women in order to exploit the different deep-seated motivations and anxieties connected to gender identity" (Craig 189).

Paraphrase: According to Steve Craig, because television marketing in America relies on the connection between the product and pleasure, commercials that are based on gender are supposed to target their audience through pleasure. The reality is that our culture believes that men and women have different ideas about what is pleasurable. In response, marketers use images that will take advantage of the fears that people have about their gender identities by utilizing images that capitalize on those fears (Craig 189).

Analysis of paraphrase: This paraphrase starts out well because it begins with attribution ("According to Steve Craig"). Also, it includes the parenthetical citation at the end. The paraphrase itself is strong because it restated the passage in the writer's own words. The problem here is that it is not clear from context that the *entire* selection is Craig's analysis, not theirs. Without the in-text citation at the end of every sentence or other markers that indicate the entire passage is a paraphrase, the reader might assume that some of the material is the reader's interpretation or ideas. There are two options for correction: (1) put in-text citations at the end of every sentence or (2) make it clear from context that all of the material is Craig's by continuing the attributive phrases.

Better: According to Steve Craig, because television marketing in America relies on the connection between the product and pleasure, commercials that are based on gender are supposed to target their audience through pleasure. Craig further argues that the reality is that our culture believes that men and women have different ideas about what is pleasurable. In response, marketers use images that will take advantage of the fears that people have about their gender identities by utilizing images that capitalize on those fears (Craig 189).

5.5.a The Works, Citation Requirements

A list of references at the end of your paper is not enough, partly because your reader will not know which ideas, quotations, summaries, and paraphrases in your paper come from which sources. Imagine you have 10 sources. How is your reader supposed to know which source includes the statistic you mentioned on page three? How is the reader to find that great quotation you included on page one? They can't unless you cite properly and thoroughly.

Proper citation involves several components. Various citation styles—MLA, APA, Chicago—have different formatting requirements, but essentially, they all include some form of the following:

1) Attribution

2) In-text-citation

3) End reference (for MLA, this is the Works Cited page)

Attribution—Introduce the quotation, summary, or paraphrase with words that indicate that you are now introducing someone else's words or ideas.

Example: According to Bob Smith, the advertising industry is "not only sexual but deviant on multiple levels" (12).

In-Text Citation—The specifics of these vary from discipline to discipline, but in-text citations are parenthetical citations (as in the example below), footnotes, or endnotes that go within the body of the paper to indicate where an idea or quotation comes from. In MLA, the in-text citation includes the author's last name and page number. If the author's name appears in the sentence (as in the above example under "attribution"), then only the page number is shown.

Example: Thirty percent of children are exposed to violence before age twelve (Jones 25).

End References/Works Cited—Again, the specifics of these vary from discipline to discipline, but the end references include detailed information (full name of author, title of work, publisher and location information, and date) about the source so that readers can find the information for research purposes. In MLA style, complete references are in a "Works Cited" page at the end of the document. Other disciplines might call them "References" or "Bibliography." The end citation format (what information to include where) depends on the discipline and type of source;

however, they are all more detailed than the in-text citation and generally appear at the end of the document in alphabetical order by author's last name, or by the first item in the entry if there is no author listed. Example: Smith, Bob. *Reading Advertising in the 21ˢᵗ Century*. New York: Bedford, 2012. Print.

So you hate compiling sources at the end, can't you just copy and paste the URL? Can't you just use EasyBib? Not really. The URL is not enough because those often change and are imprecise, and despite the relevance of Google, you will not find all of the relevant, credible research you need on the Internet. You can use EasyBib, but the problem there is that if you do not know what information to put in which fields (and where to find it), then the program will format the source incorrectly. EasyBib and the like are good tools, but you have to know how these things work in order to spot errors.

Here are some tips to begin:

1) Identify first which citation style your professor is using.

2) Locate the proper source guide (*MLA Handbook*, ect.). The Online Writing Lab at Purdue University (OWL) offers a free guide to several of the major style guides. This text also includes a section on MLA style. Be careful, though, as it does not include all possible sources.

3) Looking at your source, determine what type of source it is and whether it is online or just in print (or both). Is it a book, a journal article, an article on a web page, or a blog? This will help narrow your options significantly.

4) Look up in your book or online how to format that type of citation.

5) Fine-tune the citation if additional factors start to come into play. For example, suppose you have identified a hard copy book as one of your sources, but as you begin to format it, you realize that the book has two authors. You can then search for how to include both of the authors.

Now that you know how to cite quotations, summaries, and paraphrases, all you have to do is "sprinkle" in a few quotations, and you've used your sources, right? Not quite. When using quotations, it is important to consider the following:

1) Embed or weave; don't drop quotations.

2) Context, quote, comment.

Embed/Weave, Don't Drop: When citing the literature or other sources, embed rather than "drop" your quotations (this is also known as "floating" quotations). Dropping a quotation is when you simply give the quotation as a sentence by itself, "dropped," between two other sentences. Embedding is when you weave the quotation into your own sentence. When you do this, make sure the entire sentence is grammatically accurate.

Examples (MLA style for parenthetical citations):

> **Dropped**: The author hates the leaders. "They are insufferable prigs who don't care a thing about the poor" (Jones 12). He does not like them.

Notice that in this example the student simply dropped a full sentence quotation between two of his or her sentences.

> **Embedded/weaving:** The author calls the leaders "insufferable prigs who don't care a thing about the poor" (Jones 12).

Notice that in this example the entire sentence, which includes the quotation, is a complete sentence that is grammatically sound and accurately punctuated. The writer has made the quotation part of the sentence. When embedding, you need to also make sure that you

1) maintain the grammatical accuracy of the sentence as a whole,signal any changes to the quotation with square brackets (as long as it doesn't change the original meaning); and

2) do not use ellipses (. . .) at the beginning and end of the quotation, only in the middle (for MLA style), if you skip some unnecessary words.

Consider these examples using the following famous passage from Mary Shelley's novel *Frankenstein*:[34]

> **Original:** "It was on a dreary night of November that I beheld the accomplishment of my toils. With an anxiety that almost amounted to agony, I collected the instruments of life around me, that I might infuse a spark of being into the lifeless thing that lay at my feet. It was already one in the morning; the rain pattered dismally against the panes, and my candle was nearly burnt out, when, by the glimmer of the half-extinguished light, I saw the dull yellow eye of the creature open; it breathed hard, and a convulsive motion agitated its limbs" (Shelley 35).

Attempted embedding of quotation: Victor sees the creature for the first time "with an anxiety that almost amounted to agony, I collected the instruments of life around me, that I might infuse a spark of being into the lifeless thing that lay at my feet" (Shelley 35).

Notice that, although the quotation is embedded, the sentence as a whole is not grammatically accurate. It is a fused sentence or run-on. "Victor sees the creature for the first time" is a complete sentence as is the quotation. You can't "mash up" two complete sentences.

Correction to maintain grammatical accuracy: Victor sees the creature for the first time "with an anxiety that almost amounted to agony" (Shelley 35).

In the corrected version, only the part of the quotation needed to describe how Victor sees the creature is used. The sentence is now complete and is structurally accurate.

Signal changes with square brackets (only do this if necessary to maintain grammatical accuracy and if the meaning of original is unchanged): M. W. Shelley writes that it "was on a dreary night of November that [Dr. Frankenstein] beheld the accomplishment of [his] toils" (Shelley 35).

Notice that in this case, the writer changed the "I" and the "my" of the original quotation to "he" and "his" in order to make sense with the sentence as a whole. Because the subject of the sentence is "Mary Shelley," the writer did not want to write "I" or "my" because it is Victor, not Mary Shelley, who saw the creature. The square brackets indicate to the reader that the writer has adjusted the quotation to fit the overall sentence. This may also be necessary if you want to put something in a different tense (present versus past, e.g.) or if you need to change the number (singular to plural or vice versa).

Context, Quote, Comment: A good rule of thumb for incorporating quotations effectively is *to give context, to quote, and then to comment on that quotation.* Introduce the information in a context, quote the material, and then comment on how it fits in to your argument. Never assume that the quotation speaks for itself. It doesn't. Your job as the writer is to "connect the dots" for your reader. Tell us how this information fits into *your* argument. Different writers can use the same quotation for different purposes; thus, it is your job as the writer to explain how the quotation supports your claims at that particular moment.

Examples —context, quote, comment:

> The story shows how Cisneros grew up in a society governed by machismo. She complains that "only the boys mattered" to her father (Cisneros 25). Because the boys were the only ones her father cared about, she felt inferior, which affected her self-esteem, making her an easy target for domestic abuse.

5.5.b Common Errors

Sometimes students think they can embed a quotation by simply adding a comma after their sentence and then adding the quotation. This method might be okay if the sentence remains grammatically accurate and punctuated properly. Unfortunately, most often this method results in a run-on sentence.

Incorrect (comma splice/run-on): The author hates the leaders, "They are insufferable prigs who don't care a thing about the poor" (Jones 12). He does not like them.

In this case, we are dealing with two complete sentences; one is the first sentence by the writer and the second is the quotation. Each sentence can stand alone. You cannot join two complete sentences with just a comma; doing so makes the sentence a comma splice, which is a particular kind of run-on.

There are several ways to fix this problem: 1) use a colon to indicate that the quotation is an example of what you just said, 2) start a new sentence, or 3) weave the sentence into your own by cutting down the quotation.

1) **Use a colon:** The author hates the leaders: "They are insufferable prigs who don't care a thing about the poor" (Jones 12). In this statement, the author's use of the term "prigs" indicates his severe dislike. Furthermore, his attitude is affected by specific policies that the leaders have towards the poor in their country.

2) **Start a new sentence:** The author hates the leaders. He states, "They are insufferable prigs who don't care a thing about the poor" (Jones 12). The author's use of the term "prigs" indicates

his severe dislike. Furthermore, his attitude is affected by specific policies that the leaders have towards the poor in their country.

3) **Embed/weave:** The author hates the leaders because "they are insufferable prigs who don't care a thing about the poor" (Jones 12). The use of the term "prigs" indicates his disdain. Furthermore, his attitude is affected by specific policies that the leaders have towards the poor in their country.

5.6 AVOIDING PLAGIARISM, *DIANA EDELMAN-YOUNG*

Imagine the following scenario:

> You are talking to a colleague at work about a great idea that you have to save the company thousands of dollars. The next day at a meeting, your colleague pitches the idea to the boss. The boss thinks it is a great idea and offers your colleague a bunch of praise. It could even lead to a promotion. Your colleague does not mention you at all. How would you feel? Angry? Frustrated? Of course. You would feel like your colleague got credit for something he or she did not think of, and you would be right.

In the academic world, this would be called "plagiarism"—passing off someone else's words or ideas as your own. It may not seem like a big deal to "borrow" a few words here and there, but it is. Imagine if I asked my friend to go do my work out for me. Who gains the muscle? That person, not me. It works the same in academics. If you do not do the work, you do not gain the benefits.

Before you can avoid plagiarism, you have to know what information needs to be cited and what does not.

Second, the best method to avoid plagiarism is to take good notes and to be conscientious about the material. Although this may seem like a lot of information, there are several easy things you can do to avoid plagiarism.

Information that requires citation	Information that does not require citation
Statistics and studies. These were conducted by other people. They did the work, so they get the credit.	Your own research/observations (e.g., if you polled a class for a research project, that's your research. You can use it without citing yourself).[36]
Direct quotations from sources	Facts, dates, and other information that can be found in an encyclopedia (e.g., George Washington was the first President of the United States)
Paraphrases of source material	Common knowledge (e.g., Georgia is known for its peanuts and peaches.)[35]
Summaries of source material	
Ideas that did not come from your own head. If one of your sources has a particular reading/interpretation of a work of literature, for example, you can't just borrow the idea and run with it. Even if you find all your own evidence to support that idea and use all your own language, that particular idea came from someone else. Cite the idea.	

5.6.a Tips For Avoiding Plagiarism

1) Do your own writing and thinking about the topic or issue BE-FORE consulting sources. Spend some time using the various pre-writing techniques that are discussed in chapters 1 and 3, such as analyzing and/or annotating the subject (which is a text, in our examples) and formulating a perspective on it. Draft as much of the paper as you can without looking at sources.

2) As you gather sources, be sure to keep a running list, which includes all of the bibliographic information you need for each source first. Include author, title, publisher, date, location information, etc. That way, you will remember which ideas came from where (and how to find them again if you need to).

3) Whether you download a PDF or print a hard copy, highlight

important passages and make notes in the margins. If you are borrowing a book or cannot otherwise mark up the copy you have, you can take detailed notes being sure to label each source with all of the necessary information.

4) As you take notes, be sure to label the notes as source material and to list each source separately. Keep your drafts and source notes in separate files.

5) Be sure that the notes distinguish between direct quotations you might want to use and paraphrases of the material (see above). You might consider making three columns—one that summarizes the source as a whole, one that paraphrases passages that you think might be useful, and one that lists out possible direct quotations to use in your paper.

6) As you weave the sources into your paper, make sure that you have included attribution, in-text citations, and a Works Cited page for each source used.

7) A good rule of thumb when working with sources in your papers is to have *NO MORE THAN 30% of the paper from source material whether directly quoted, summarized, or paraphrased.* Most of the paper should be you and your voice. If you begin to go over this amount, the paper moves towards being a summary of sources rather than a thoughtful, original argument.

8) To ensure that most of the paper is your voice, your job as the writer is to introduce, embed, and explain the quotations in terms of *your* thesis. Use the quotations as a tool to make your point. Do not just list a bunch of quotations from sources to make your point for you. *Use the sources to support your ideas, not the other way around.*

9) And, finally, *when in doubt, cite!* You cannot get into legal trouble for citing material that did not need it, but you can for the reverse.

5.6.a (1) Exercise

Below is a paragraph from some source material with the relevant bibliographic information followed by several student attempts to incorporate the material. Identify whether the student has/has not plagiarized by choosing one of the multiple-choice options.

1) Review the original closely.
2) Compare the student version to the original.
3) Use the information discussed in this chapter to determine whether

the student cited the material properly. Is this plagiarism? After you complete the quiz (individually, in groups, or as a class), discuss the answers.

Original Source Excerpt

Zabludoff, Marc. "Fear and Longing." *Transitions.* 3rd ed. Ed. Barbara Fine Clouse. Boston: McGraw-Hill, 2006. 234-235. Print.

"We are more than our genes. We are our genes in a particular place and time, whole people interacting with others in an infinitely variable world. Only through that experience do we become who we are. A cloned Einstein reared in twenty-first-century Los Angeles will not become a tousled professor of new physics. A cloned Mozart will not reevaluate our souls or drive a cloned Salieri to distraction. A clone of a child tragically and prematurely dead will not replace wholly and without distinction the child who once was. All the clone will be for certain is the bearer of unmet expectations."

Excerpt from Student Paper #1:

In his essay "Fear and Longing," Marc Zabludoff writes that "we are more than our genes" (235). He says that we could never clone Einstein in the 21st century and expect him to perform the same intellectual feats as he did during the time when he was alive.

Works Cited

Zabludoff, Marc. "Fear and Longing." *Transitions.* 3rd ed. Ed. Barbara Fine Clouse. Boston: McGraw-Hill, 2006. 234-235. Print.

---

a) PLAGIARISM: The student uses the exact words of the source.
b) PLAGIARISM: The student does not include all of the sources.
c) NOT plagiarism: The student uses quotation marks for exact quotes, includes an in-text citation, and includes a works cited.
d) PLAGIARISM: The student uses someone else's ideas.
e) BOTH B and D

Excerpt from Student Paper #2:

> We are more than our genes because we are part of a whole people interacting with others in an infinitely variable world. We are who we are because of the time and place in which we were raised and live. Clones of Einstein and Mozart cannot be who they were in the 18th century if they are cloned in the 21st century (Zabludoff 235).
>
> ### Works Cited
> Zabludoff, Marc. "Fear and Longing." *Transitions.* 3rd ed. Ed. Barbara Fine Clouse. Boston: McGraw-Hill, 2006. 234-235. Print.

   a) PLAGIARISM: The student uses exact language without quotation marks.

   b) PLAGIARISM: The student does not include all of the sources.

   c) NOT plagiarism: It is the student's ideas.

   d) NOT plagiarism: This person has paraphrased the source and has included in-text citation and a works cited page.

   e) Both C and D.

Excerpt from Student Paper #3:

> We are more than our genes. We are our genes in a particular place and time, whole people interacting with others in an infinitely variable world. Only through that experience do we become who we are. A cloned Einstein reared in twenty-first-century Los Angeles will not become a tousled professor of new physics. A cloned Mozart will not reevaluate our souls or drive a cloned Salieri to distraction. A clone of a child tragically and prematurely dead will not replace wholly and without distinction the child who once was. All the clone will be for certain is the bearer of unmet expectations (Zabludoff 235).
>
> ### Works Cited
> Zabludoff, Marc. "Fear and Longing." *Transitions.* 3rd ed. Ed. Barbara Fine Clouse. Boston: McGraw-Hill, 2006. 234-235. Print.

   a) NOT plagiarism: The student includes the citation at the end.

   b) PLAGIARISM: The student uses exact language but does not use quotation marks.

c) NOT plagiarism: It is the student's ideas.

d) NOT plagiarism: The student uses the in-text citation.

e) ALL *except* for B.

Excerpt from Student Paper #4:

> Our genes are only part of the equation. They have a context of time and place and are subject to a large number of variables (Zabludoff 235).
>
> Works Cited
> Zabludoff, Marc. "Fear and Longing." *Transitions*. 3rd ed. Ed. Barbara Fine Clouse. Boston: McGraw-Hill, 2006. 234-235. Print.

a) PLAGIARISM: It uses the exact words of the source.

b) PLAGIARISM: The student does not include all of the sources.

c) NOT plagiarism: It is the student's ideas.

d) NOT plagiarism: This person has paraphrased the source and has included in-text citation and a works cited page.

e) Both C and D.

Excerpt from Student Paper #5: Is this plagiarism?

> Our genes are developed in a cultural context that is so variable that it affects who those genes become. Neither Einstein nor Mozart would be the geniuses they were if they were cloned in our day and age.

a) NOT plagiarism: This student paraphrased the source.

b) NOT plagiarism: This is common knowledge.

c) PLAGIARISM: This student changed the language of the original but used Zabludoff's ideas without attribution or citation.

d) NOT plagiarism: This student used her/his own words.

e) Both A and B.

Excerpt from Student Paper #6:

We are more than our genetic makeup. We are our DNA in a particular time and place, people who interact with other people in an eternally variable world.

Works Cited

Zabludoff, Marc. "Fear and Longing." *Transitions.* 3rd ed. Ed. Barbara Fine Clouse. Boston: McGraw-Hill, 2006. 234-235. Print.

---

a) NOT plagiarism: The student substituted synonyms and rearranged words.

b) PLAGIARISM: The language is too close to the original.

c) NOT plagiarism: There is a citation at the end of the paper.

d) PLAGIARISM: There is no attribution or in-text citation.

e) Both B and D.

Concluding Remarks

Basically, the idea here is to be conscientious about the material because that is professional courtesy. You would not want someone else "borrowing" your ideas and taking credit for them. As you become a part of the academic community and the professional community of your choice, you establish credibility by "doing your homework" and respecting your colleagues' thoughts and ideas.

5.7 USING *SIGNAL* OR *TAG* WORDS AND PHRASES, TANYA LONG BENNETT

As you integrate the words and ideas of other scholars into your writing, one challenge you face is making it clear whose ideas are whose and how one person's ideas relate to those of another. Tag words and phrases can be invaluable in developing clarity in this area. Consider the example below:

> Arthur Fishman and Avi Simhon <u>argue</u>, in "Division of Labor, Inequality and Growth," that the way wealth is distributed in society has a bearing on the effectiveness of the market's division of labor. They <u>assert</u> first that to

specialize, an individual must invest resources and second that when these resources are difficult to obtain (by loans, for example), struggling individuals, including entrepreneurs, may not be motivated enough to pursue further specialization. These challenges, <u>according to Fishman and Simhon</u>, may hinder society's attempts to reach more effective levels of division of labor. <u>In contrast to scholars</u> who have focused on the factors that promote effective division of labor, Fishman and Simhon <u>examine</u> the factors of "individual motivation to pursue the specialization that an improved system requires" (117-118).

Fishman, Arthur and Avi Simhon, "Division of Labor, Inequality and Growth." *Journal of Economic Growth* 7.2 (2002): 117-136. Print.

The underlined words and phrases in the passage above are *tags*, indicating for the reader whose ideas are whose. The phrase, "In contrast to scholars who . . .," provides the reader with an understanding of how Fishman and Simhon's article fits into the ongoing scholarly dialogue; it leads to an explanation of what original perspective they provide on the topic.

Tag words and phrases that you might consider in your own writing include the following list:

asserts	suggests	confirms
argues	indicates	contradicts
holds	claims	confirms
explains	interprets	disproves
examines	found ("The study found . . .")	according to
explores	reveals	In contrast to

In arguing your own point, you are not required to indicate your own ideas with phrases like "I believe," or "I think." Rather information and ideas *not* attributed to others will be *assumed to be yours*. If you employ tag words and phrases to clarify the roles of your source materials in your argument, your reader should be able to discern which ideas are yours and which come from your sources.

Documenting Sources

Chris Bell

6.1 THE PURPOSE OF CITING SOURCES

Many students, when asked, say the purpose of citing sources is so they can prove they have not plagiarized. This reason is not necessarily the best one. The most important reason for citing is to give readers of your essay the quickest route to the sources used in an essay, if they desire. When you write a research essay, you become part of a larger conversation about a topic, and readers may want to read the others who are a part of it.

6.2 COLLECTING SOURCES

The easiest way to manage sources is to be organized. Too often, students fail to collect their sources in a logical manner, leading them to have to spend unnecessary time looking up sources they have used and discarded. Therefore, as you collect sources, maintain a bibliography, simply a list of sources consulted. Many professors will assign annotated bibliographies, another excellent way of organizing and evaluating sources. For more on annotated bibliographies, see Section 7.3.

6.3 DOCUMENTING SOURCES

6.3.a What gets documented?

When writing a research essay, any information culled from sources must be cited, whether paraphrased or directly quoted.

6.3.b Know the Documentation Style your Professor Expects.

There are several documentation styles. The style you will use depends on the discipline you write for. Here is a list of the most common documentation styles:

1) American Psychological Association (APA)
2) Modern Language Association (MLA)
3) Chicago/Turabian
4) Council of Science Editors Documentation Style (CSE)

Be sure to know what documentation style you are expected to follow before you begin collecting sources for your bibliography.

6.3.c Where does one cite?

There are two areas within an essay where sources are documented.

1) **Parenthetical Citation:** Whatever sources are used must be documented within the essay itself (parenthetically). Each documentation style demands a different format. For instance, APA requires an author's name and the date of publication within the parenthetical citation, while MLA requires for only author. Chicago/Turabian and the Council of Science Editors Documentation Style are footnote based.

2) **Reference Page:** Each documentation style also calls for a reference page, a list of sources actually used (as opposed to merely consulted). As with parenthetical citation, each documentation style requires its own format. Even the names of the reference pages are different. The Council of Science Editors Documentation Style calls its reference page a "Reference List," while the appropriate heading for MLA is "Works Cited."

6.3.d A Word on Citation Generators

There are numerous, free, citation generators found online. These are useful tools that will format a reference page properly, if you enter the information correctly. Follow these steps when using a citation generator.

1) Determine the kind of source you are using
2) Locate the source type within the generator
3) Complete the areas necessary*
4) Follow the steps for downloading the reference page into a word processing program
5) Copy the reference page into your paper

*When entering criteria for a source using a citation generator, be sure to indicate where a source was procured, i.e. print, academic database, online, etc.

6.3.e Sample Citations

Below is one source documented using three different styles. Pay attention to the differences in format for each. One should note the information is generally the same, but the order in which the information is listed differs. The source is an article published in an academic journal retrieved from an academic database.

MLA Format

MLA is most concerned with crediting the author of a source.

> Sorrensen, Cynthia. "Making the Subterranean Visible: Security, Tunnels, and the United States-Mexico Border." *Geographical Review* 104.3 (2014): 328-45. *Science and Technology Collection*. Web. 30 Oct. 2014.

APA Format

APA is most concerned with dates, as contemporary publications are privileged. The citation style also prefers anonymity for authors. Another difference between APA and MLA is that the article title is not enclosed in quotation marks and only the first word, proper nouns, and the first word after a colon (the first word in a subtitle) are capitalized. APA also does not require the writer to indicate the database an article was retrieved from. Instead, APA citations should include the URL of the publisher or the homepage database URL.

> Sorrensen, C. (2014). Making the subterranean visible: Security, tunnels, and the United States-Mexico border. *Geographical Review, 104*(3), 328-345. Retrieved October 30, 2014. <http://www.wiley.com/WileyCDA/>

Chicago/Turabian Format

Chicago looks quite similar to MLA, but the arrangement and punctuation are different. Notice that the date of access is placed *before* the database in which the article is listed, and the database is not italicized. Note also the punctuation is different in various places.

Sorrensen, Cynthia. "Making the Subterranean Visible: Security, Tunnels, and the United States-Mexico Border." *Geographical Review* 104, no. 3 (2014): 328-45. Accessed October 30, 2014. SocINDEX with Full Text.

CSE

CSE is the most unique of all the styles. Like APA, CSE requires author anonymity and follows the same capitalization rules. However, the titles of publications are not italicized, and the keyword search is included, along with various differences regarding how the publication information is formatted and the where the date of retrieval appears.

Sorrensen C. Making the subterranean visible: security, tunnels, and the United States-Mexico border. Geographical Review [Internet]. 2014 Oct [cited 2014 Oct 30];104(3): 328-345. SocINDEX with Full Text. Available from: United States Border Debate.

6.3.f Final Notes, Further Resources, Etc.

There are more than fifty recognized publication types. This text does not offer a list of the different ways sources are cited, either parenthetically or on a reference page. However, innumerable sources can be found online that illustrate how to properly cite any source, such as the Purdue Online Writing Lab (OWL). If you elect to not use a citation generator for your reference page, be sure to follow the steps noted above when citing a source.

6.4 SAMPLE STUDENT RESEARCH PAPER IN MLA STYLE

Emmy Dixon
ENGL 2250
28 October 2013

At Face Value:
An Argument Against Child Beauty Pageants

"Let's not make our girls believe from a very young age that their worth is only judged by their appearance."

Chantal Jouanno

A child found strangled in her family home on Christmas would naturally make headlines; add the fact that she was part of an affluent family who participated in the mysterious sub-culture of child beauty pageants, and a perfect storm is created for the media. Images of the child in heavy make-up, dressed to look far older than her six years, accompanied every newscast for weeks, arousing a deep sense of outrage in the nation. Claiming that the act of parading her in front of the public incited a pedophile, the media initially indicted beauty pageants as the murder instrument of JonBenet Ramsey, in 1996; however, in the ensuing two decades, the original outrage over alleged child exploitation has mellowed to a bizarre voyeuristic fascination, fueling a five billion dollar-a-year industry. The high ratings of reality shows such as *Toddlers and Tiaras* reveal that childhood beauty pageants are no longer simply part of an odd sub-culture in America; rather, they have become normative and popularly accepted. There is, however, a disturbing side to this pop culture acceptance; Lindsay Lieberman warns that, "despite being one of the fastest growing industries in America, the child pageant circuit is entirely unregulated" (751). An unregulated industry profiting completely from children is ripe for controversy. While there are purported positive effects of pageants, at least as voiced by the competitors and their guardians, the negative effects clearly outweigh any possible positive outcomes. Considering the potential physical and emotional harms, as well as the vampiric exploitation and propensity for inciting pedophiles, beauty pageants are clearly an unhealthy activity for children.

In general, supporters of child beauty pageants claim that the girls gain poise, confidence, work ethic, and the ability to compete with grace. If successful, they can have significant monetary gains, sometimes in the form of scholarships. There are anecdotal instances of very shy children gaining poise and children with disfiguring disabilities gaining some measure of self-confidence about their appearance. Annette Hill, the founder of the Universal Royalty and Baby Beauty Pageants, one of

the pageants featured on *Toddlers and Tiaras*, offered
comments strongly supportive of pageants:

Pageants allow for quality family time, everyone
is involved, and everyone gets to go out for dinner
together and travel together, and it promotes positive self esteem. Children that compete are more
assertive and vocal, they aren't afraid to look you
in the eye when they talk to you, and they communicate very well . . . Besides, what is wrong with
showing off your beautiful, talented daughter to the
world? It is up to the parents to keep their children
grounded (qtd. in McKay 1).

The view that these young girls are essentially en-
joying a harmless and family-friendly hobby appears to
dominate the pageant scene; however, there is a troubling lack of scholarly research supporting the idea that
pageants are a healthy activity for a child.

On the other side of this controversy are studies
showing that this activity is profoundly, inherently, dangerous for girls, not least of which is a risk for physical
bodily harm from the various beauty regimens that they
are frequently subjected to. Procedures like eyebrow
plucking or waxing, teeth whitening, and mascara usage
can all cause pain and carry the potential for permanent
damage to the still-developing body. Spray tans are a
significant health hazard considering that their main
ingredient Dihydroxyacetone has been linked to genetic
alteration (Greenblatt and Ahuja 1). Then there is the
excess sugar and caffeine given to many of these con-
test-goers in order to give them the necessary energy to
perform at their peak (Wolfe 432-3). Pixie Stix, known
in the industry as "pageant crack," are often used, and
according to Wolfe, one pageant contestant is frequently
given a mixture of Red Bull and Mountain Dew, known
as "go-go juice," in order to get her through the demand-
ing twelve hour days. This child is six. Wolfe goes on
to warn that "a 2011 study by the American Academy
of Pediatrics reported that excessive caffeine intake can
lead to cardiovascular and neurological problems for

young children" (434). While not the obvious injury that a beating would inflict, the damage exists nonetheless.

It is not only physical bodily harm that goes hand in hand with pageantry; there are significant risks of emotional harm, as well. Ranging from mild to quite severe, various types of emotional damage can result from engaging in pageants as children, but the intense pressure from the pageant-pushing parent can be the most damaging. Commonly the parent of the contestant, most frequently the mother, is extremely domineering and ambitious. These women often exhibit a parenting style known contemporarily as overparenting or "helicopter parenting." This type of parenting has effects that can follow the child for the rest of her life, resulting in higher levels of anxiety and narcissism, as well as poor coping and problem-solving skills (Montgomery, et al., 589-91). Wolfe explains how these children are often under intense pressure from their parents to succeed, with the result being that some of these children, as young as seven, experience guilt if they do not win. That is a heavy psychological burden for a child (435). Martina Cartwright, a psychologist, explains that "the competitive pageant scene may cause young participants to believe that the love and approval of their parents hinges on their beauty and continued success in pageants" (qtd. in Wolfe 436). Considering that physical beauty is a constantly changing status, it can be especially frightening for children to feel that their parents' love is dependent upon a factor that they cannot control, impacting their self-worth in a negative, and often life-long, way.

Impacting the pageant contestant's self-worth is not the only emotional damage faced; self-esteem damage is also a very real possibility. Ironically, according to Henry Giroux, building self-esteem is a frequent rationale used for putting children in pageants. He says that a "pageant director in Murrieta, California, refuted the criticism that pageants are detrimental for young girls, arguing that 'many young girls look at pageants as a protracted game of dress up, something most young girls love.'" Ellen Mark, an editor for *Vogue*, concurred with that sentiment: "pageants made them [contestants] feel special . . . Little girls like to look pretty" (qtd. in Giroux 41). There are consequences, both social and psychological, however, when so narrowly defining appropriate self-esteem. According to Giroux, defining "self esteem in this context means embracing rather than critically challenging a gender code that rewards little girls for their looks, submissiveness, and sex appeal" (41). In other words, girls are trained from an early age that their intrinsic value is from external factors such as their facial beauty or body shape and that "others" have the ability, and perhaps most damaging, *the right*, to judge that value.

Another emotional danger from pageants, one that is often found overlapping with bodily harm, is body image issues that frequently lead to eating disorders. A psychological study conducted by Anna L. Wonderlich and colleagues showed that women who had participated in childhood beauty pageants had an increase in body dissatisfaction, interpersonal distrust, and impulse dysregulation in comparison to non-participants. The pageant participants also exhibited greater feelings of ineffectiveness (297). In addition, Cartwright believes that the constant focus on the external can lead to something called "princess syndrome" which is a drive for perfection with strong links to eating disorders later on in life (Wolfe 436). Susan Haworth-Hoeppner agrees with this assessment. "She [Susan] notes that a disproportionately high number of women who develop eating disorders participate in activities . . . in which slenderness is particularly valued" (Wolfe 436). Wolfe claims that there is an inordinate amount of emphasis placed on the concept of small size and that some child pageants even have a physical fitness category (436-7). This obsession with thinness is positively correlated with eating disorders.

The risks to a girl's personal physical and emotional health are apparent, but the risk of exploitation is far more insidious. Participation in pageants where girls are often exposed to the general public in skimpy clothing and heavy make-up has been shown to have the potential for the kind of exploitation that can set off a chain reaction of the darkest and most vile kind. Camille Paglia warns, "'[T]hese pageants mark a deep sexual disturbance in the society, a cannibalizing of youth by these vampiric adults'" (qtd. in Wolfe 439). Like vampires, the adults in this situation often derive their own pleasure through the display of these Barbie-like children. Girls as young as three are dressed in provocative clothing and shake their bodies in a sexually suggestive manner, performing "talent" dance routines to songs such as "I'm Sexy and I Know it" (Arthurs 1). One episode on *Toddlers and Tiaras* followed a three year-old girl dressed as the hooker portrayed by Julia Roberts in the movie *Pretty Woman* (Canning and Pereira 1). Wolfe says that "parents encourage this behavior because of their perception that ostentatious routines win bigger prizes" (439). In other words, the more shocking—and often more suggestive—the routines and clothing are, the more the judges are perceived to reward the young children, and through them, their parents. Lindsey Lieberman claims, "[T]he child pageant circuit focuses on ideals of perfection and beauty, with an accompanying emphasis on sexuality" (745). She goes on to say, "[E]ssentially, young pageant girls are trained to flirt and exploit their nascent sexuality in order to win" (745). The girls internalize this exploitation and apply it to their role in society, thereby doing the job of keeping them in their gendered place, already a victim.

Most disturbing of all, this exploitation can be an inducement to pedophilia, a danger that other nations are moving to mitigate. Diane Levin warns: "[T]he *Toddler's* [from the TV show] sexy outfits and dance routines 'could blur the boundaries for people who are having trouble controlling their pedophilia'" (Wolfe 440). People that may already be inclined to pedophilia could be triggered to act upon those desires by the sexualizing of children. Indeed, other scholars warn that "shows" such as these may actually push "disturbed individuals toward child pornography and pedophilic acts" (Wolfe 439). Not only are these girls sexualized, but they are exposed to the public, as well. Nancy Irwin, a psychotherapist, warns that pageant children are at an increased risk for victimization because of their high profile status (Wolfe 439). The advent of reality TV shows and social media have only heightened the visibility and intensified the danger.

The acknowledged risks have prompted France to take action. Their Senate recently passed a ban on child beauty pageants on "the grounds that they promote the 'hyper-sexualisation' of minors" ("France"). Child pageants were not highly popular in France to begin with, yet still they moved to deal with the issue (Lalisse-Jespersen). That is a weighty indictment of the exploitative and dangerous nature of pageants.

The danger from pedophiles can be deadly serious. Flash forward to 2013, and the murder of high-profile beauty queen JonBenet Ramsey has never been solved. Recently, the case was reopened when DNA evidence was concluded to have come from an unknown man. Was the killer a pedophile enamored of the little beauty queen? It is entirely possible that her time in the spotlight pretending to be a girl at least twice her age attracted the worst kind of attention. Even if she had not been murdered, studies predict that JonBenet would likely have suffered lasting harm from her pageant days, whether in the form of skin damage from the artificial tanners or emotional harm from the focus on her external beauty. Research suggests that she may have even gone on to suffer from an eating disorder later in life, or been the victim of further exploitation. France is determined to stop that from happening to its citizens. Will America continue to blindly accept the growing obsession with portraying children as miniature adults? To reiterate, *the child pageant circuit is an industry profiting completely from children with no regulation at all*. It has clear ties to physical harm, emotional trauma, sexual exploitation, and pedophilia. This is unacceptable.

Works Cited

Arthurs, Deborah. "Shock as Five-year-old Toddlers & Tiaras Girl Sings to Sexy Song on Stage in Nightclub . . . as her Mother Pushes her on." *Mail Online* 11 January 2012. Web. 28 Oct. 2013.

Baird, Julia. "Sparkle and Shine: Child Beauty Pageants in Australia." *The Monthly*. June 2011. Web. 28 Oct. 2013.

Canning, Andrea and Jennifer Pereira. "Tot Dressed as Prostitute: 'Toddlers and Tiaras' Blasted for Airing Image of 3-Y-O Pageant Contestant in Racy Costume." *ABCnews*. 12 Sept. 2011. Web. 28 Oct. 2013.

"France Moves to Ban Beauty Pageants." *BBC* 18 Sept. 2013. Web. 28 Oct. 2013

Giroux, Henry A. "Nymphet Fantasies Child Beauty Pageants and the Politics of Innocence." *Social Text* 16.4 (1998): 31-53. *Advanced Placement Source*. Web. 28 Oct. 2013.

Greenblatt, Mark and Gitika Ahuja. "Are 'Spray-On' Tans Safe? Experts Raise Questions as Industry Puts Out Warnings." *ABCnews*. 12 June 2012. Web. 28 Oct. 2013.

Lalisse-Jespersen, Priscilla. "No Honey Boo Boos in France: Parliament Moves to Ban Kiddie Pageants." *Washington Post*. 21 Sept. 2013. Web. 28 Oct. 2013.

Lieberman, Lindsay. "Protecting Pageant Princesses: A Call for Statutory Regulation of Child Beauty Pageants." *Journal Of Law & Policy* 18.2 (2010): 739-774. *Academic Search Complete*. Web. 28 Oct. 2013.

Mckay, Hollie. "Parents of Children on TLC's 'Toddlers in Tiaras' Hurting their Kids, Critics Say." *FoxNews*. 3 June 2010. Web. 28 Oct. 2013.

Montgomery, Neil, et al. "Parent and Child Traits Associated With Overparenting." *Journal of Social & Clinical Psychology* 32.6 (2013): 569-595. *Consumer Health Complete - EBSCOhost*. Web. 28 Oct. 2013.

Tamer, Christine. "Toddlers, Tiaras, and Pedophilia? The 'Borderline Child Pornography' Embraced by the American Public." *Texas Review of Entertainment &*

Sports Law 13.1 (2011): 85-101. *SPORTDiscus with Full Text.* Web. 28 Oct. 2013.

Wolfe, Lucy. "Darling Divas or Damaged Daughters? The Dark Side of Child Beauty Pageants and an Administrative Law Solution." *Tulane Law Review* 87.2 (2012): 427-455. *Academic Search Complete.* Web. 28 Oct. 2013.

Wonderlich, Anna, Diann Ackard, and Judith Henderson. "Childhood Beauty Pageant Contestants: Associations with Adult Disordered Eating and Mental Health." *Eating Disorders* 13.3 (2005): 291-301. *SPORTDiscus with Full Text.* Web. 28 Oct. 2013.

Researched Writing

You may be familiar with the traditional research paper, which requires you to investigate a topic, gather sources on that topic, and then synthesize those sources into either an in-depth report or an argument for a particular perspective on the topic. This chapter offers descriptions of common types of research assignments, such as the annotated bibliography and the prospectus, which instructors often assign to help students not only learn research skills but also plan ahead.

7.1 THE ANNOTATED BIBLIOGRAPHY, *Shannon N. Gilstrap*

7.1.a Write a What?

The first time many students encounter an annotated bibliography assignment, they feel like they face an overwhelming task. The feeling is understandable—just look at the assignment's name! It is made up of two semi-familiar words, yet here the words are coupled. The phrase "annotated bibliography" is only another way of saying "works cited entry plus a summary"—two concepts (works cited page and summary) which most students are taught in composition classes and are much more familiar with at the high school and college level. So, keep those parallels in mind as we explore what defines an annotated bibliography.

An annotated bibliography is a collection of annotations (summaries) of the individual sources you collect, often for your research paper. These sources, by reason of being presented together in one document, should all be relevant to your research question or working thesis statement. Each individual annotation is preceded by its bibliographic information (works cited entry) presented in the discipline-appropriate format. The entire collection is organized, just like a works cited page, in alphabetical order by the first word in the bibliographic information, usually—but not always—the source author's last name. The annotated bibliography is headed in appropriate format, its pages are numbered, the entire work is typed in 12 point Times New Roman font, and it is double-spaced. Very often your annotated bibliography will have a title that uniquely expresses your project's assignment, research question, or working thesis.

Keeping this definition of an annotated bibliography in mind, be aware that individual annotated bibliography assignment parameters can vary. Your instructor will give you specifics concerning how many entries you are expected to compose, as well as how long each entry should be and what it should include. An annotated bibliography may be assigned as a step towards a research paper, or it may be assigned as the research project itself. Whatever a professor's specific requirements, though, the model presented here is a good starting point. Moreover, as a skilled researcher and critical thinker, you should get into the habit of creating an annotated bibliography *whether or not one is directly assigned*. The reasons for this will become clear as we continue and, after learning the how to compose a strong annotated bibliography, getting into this habit is not very difficult.

7.1.b Writing and Compiling the Annotated Bibliography

Recall from the definition that an annotated bibliography is a *collection* of individual annotations, so here let's discuss how to compile an annotated bibliography entry. Depending on the specific requirements of your instructor's assignment, how many of these you will need to compile will vary, as stated above; however, approaching each annotation individually makes the compilation of the whole much easier.

For each entry, it may help to remember the 5 Cs:

1) Citation: Ensure that your annotated bibliography entry begins with the source's citation, presented in the format appropriate for your discipline.

2) Credentials: Present the author's *ethos*, or, if no author is given, present the source's *ethos*.

3) Complete: Ensure that, in your summary, you cover all the source's main ideas.

4) Concise: Although complete, remember that a summary is much shorter than the original source.

5) Connection: Always present, clearly, how the resource contributes to your research question or working thesis statement.

Although I have presented them as distinct, each of the above, works with the other items to contribute coherence to the entry. Let's explore how to do each of these steps, taking as a starting point a research question typical of a freshman level composition course: "Do modern horror movies like *The Cabin in the Woods, Last House on the Left,* or even *The Texas Chainsaw Massacre* have any older, literary precedents?"

Using web resources like *Galileo* databases and web-based research, I came across the following article on *Masterpiece Mystery*'s website:

Since I am writing this for my English 1101 composition class, I have been asked to use MLA formatting, so I need to format my <u>Citation</u> according to the proper format for a "Short Work Within a Website" as follows:

> Miller, Ron. "Old Dark Houses: Le Fanu's *Wyvern Mystery* Was an Early Milepost of the 'Old Dark House' Genre." "Casebook: Old Dark Houses." *Masterpiece Mystery! Case Book Index.* October 2000. Web.

Now that I have my first C finished, I need to move on to the second—<u>Credentials</u>. Taking a moment to find out more about who wrote your chosen source does wonders for your own credibility because by doing so you are letting your reader know that of all the sources available you determined that *this one* was best for your purpose. In order to do so, you must be able, in your final research paper, to establish this source's *ethos*, or authority on the topic in question. Electronic sources gathered through databases like *Galileo* make this very easy, for you can click on the author's name and immediately get a host of other articles this author has written. Check to see if they are relevant to the topic of your chosen source. If so, you can assume that the author is a recognized expert to this topic. Often at the end of an article you will be presented with a brief author biography which may contain information relevant to the author's ethos: Perhaps this author teaches at a particularly prestigious college or university, or the author holds specific degrees that make him or her an expert in the field. Include in one sentence or two (at most) a summary of these credentials, like so:

> This article was written by Ron Miller who has compiled a written history of *Masterpiece Mystery*, a long-running and well-respected show presented on the Public Broadcasting Service, titled *Mystery! A Celebration*.

Having presented the <u>Citation</u> and the author's <u>Credentials</u>, you should now *actively read* your source so that you can present a <u>Complete</u> summary of the article. By complete, I mean that you need, in your summary, to present all the author's main ideas. Do not worry here about details. Remember that a summary is presented in your own words, and follows the organization of the original (See section 5.5). Active reading can help you get started on this (See Chapter 1). As you read, look for the article's main idea, or thesis statement. Like your own writing, thesis statements are usually located early in the essay; however, you may need to also look to the source's conclusion for a full statement of the source's overarching main idea. Following the author's <u>Credentials</u>, summarize the thesis in your own words, like so:

> In this essay, Miller paints in broad strokes the characteristics associated with a particular type of perennial mystery story: the "old dark house" genre. Miller remarks over the course of the essay that the "old dark house" genre continues exerting influence on contemporary horror and mystery stories and movies, but many of the genre conventions can be traced to early practitioners of the genre, including Poe, Hawthorne, and Le Fanu.

As you continue reading the original source, take time to pause at the end of each paragraph and summarize, in one or two sentences, the paragraph's main idea on a separate sheet of paper. If you do such active reading, you will remain engaged with the text and you will internalize the text because you are processing the author's ideas through your own language and words. By the time you are finished, you will have a series of *main ideas* that you can then "thread together" into a rough summary.

However, you will need to also make this <u>Complete</u> summary <u>Concise</u>. Most annotated bibliography entries are only between 250 and 350 words. For a reference, that is about as many words as are on one page of double spaced, twelve-point Times New Roman font. If you have just read a fourteen page scholarly article, this task can be daunting! However, this point is where your research question or working thesis statement (your <u>Connection</u>) and your <u>Complete</u> rough summary work together.

As you re-read your rough summary of the article's main points, think from the perspective of your research question: What main ideas or main points *most clearly answer* your research question? What main ideas, details, or arguments provide *support* for your working thesis?

Remember, you can use more than one idea or detail from a single source to develop or prove several points in your final paper. Re-read your rough summary with that in mind, and you will find that your summary, which is itself shorter than the original, can be shortened even more. Continue working until you have met your professor's parameters for the annotation.

Finally, it is helpful to provide a few closing sentences that directly express the source's <u>Connection</u> to your research question or working thesis statement. This direct expression at the entry's conclusion helps not only close out the annotation, but calls the reader's attention to how all these individual annotations cohere as a collective assignment. Something like the following is appropriate:

> The authors that Miller brings up in his essay may provide me with excellent models to read as I try to find connections between modern horror movies and their literary precedents. Also, his definition of the genre "old dark houses" and the details he provides about what constitutes such a genre can be used as concrete points of comparison and contrast in the paper.

Now that you have fulfilled all of the <u>Five Cs</u> for several different sources, you can compile and format the entire Annotated Bibliography.

First, provide the discipline appropriate header on the first page and set up page numbers. Second, provide your reader with a unique and creative title that reflects your unique research question or your unique working thesis. Third, arrange each complete annotation entry in alphabetical order by the first word in each citation—this is usually the author's last name, but may, if no author is presented, be the essay title's first word. Fourthly, below the citation, enter in your <u>Complete</u>, <u>Concise</u>, and <u>Connected</u> annotation for this source.

All that is left for you to do now is edit your completed annotated bibliography for adherence to the assignment's parameters, documentation accuracy, grammatical responsibility, and coherence.

7.1.c Research Process and Research Tool

As mentioned earlier, your instructor may assign an annotated bibliography as both a step in the research process, or as the research project itself. Either way, internalizing the practice of creating an annotated bibliography helps you become both a better researcher (process) and helps if you are writing a final research paper (tool).

Habitually noting all the necessary bibliographic information for your <u>Citation</u> is excellent research process practice. Likewise, if you have formatted each of these <u>Citations</u> correctly, then you have, minus the annotation, essentially formatted your works cited page. The act of paying attention to an author's <u>Credentials</u> helps you choose the best sources from the best authors in the field, and briefly stating those in your annotation helps you justify using the source when you incorporate a quotation or paraphrase from it into your own argument. This builds your <u>Credentials</u>, *ethos*, with the reader. Finally, always actively reading or skimming a source with your research question or working thesis in mind and then <u>Completely</u> and <u>Concisely</u> summarizing that source in your own words helps you to internalize your own research agenda. When referencing your annotated bibliography as you develop and support your argument in your research paper, *concretely stating* that <u>Connection</u> at the annotation's end helps remind you *what details* from the source you wanted to use, *why* you wanted to use it, and *how* you envisioned it fitting into your paper. Nothing is worse for a writer than being at the opposite end of writer's block—knowing you have run across something to use in your paper, but not knowing where to find it! Finally, having thought carefully about a title for your annotated bibliography helps you formulate a title for your final research paper.

As can be seen, annotated bibliographies are not only assignments in and of themselves, but they are also an integral habit that you should develop on your own as a researcher. As both process and tool, they lend themselves to better final papers.

7.2 THE CRITIQUE, TANYA LONG BENNETT

The critique paper is a unique genre in which the author evaluates something. Sometimes called a review, this kind of essay can offer judgment on anything, from the newest model of a car to a recently released horror film. In addition to providing readers with an expert opinion on an item's *quality*, the critique is useful as a tool for scholars. Critiquing a scholarly article or book yields a helpful *analysis* of the work and enables the critique writer an opportunity to formulate a coherent *evaluation* of the work, as well.

In an article critique, the writer should include:

1) A brief summary of the article, with an emphasis on its central argument and purpose,

2) An analysis of *how* the author presented her case, including key information and ideas used to support the central argument, and

3) The critique-writer's overall evaluation of the article.

The critique essay should answer the questions, "Does the article accomplish its goal? Why or why not?" Writing such an essay helps us to examine carefully the position taken by a fellow scholar and enables us to consider how the writer's argument fits in with our own perspective on the topic. The critique can serve as a fruitful foundation as we work toward a research paper, forwarding our own argument in the context of other scholars' perspectives.

The following is an example of a critique essay written by composition student Kara Richter.

Kara Richter
Fall 2013
English 1101

Fabio Parasecoli's "Feeding Hard Bodies": A Critique

In his essay "Feeding Hard Bodies," Fabio Parasecoli offers evidence to lead his audience to believe that the magazine industry is feeding men images that subsequently result in a negative body image. He assumes a streamlined approach to the issue by showcasing two specific popular men's magazines—*Men's Health* and *Muscle and Fitness*—and some of their controversial notions about the ideal body and how to achieve it. Parasecoli's examination of the two publications poses interesting questions about what the current ideal body image for men entails, but his argument fails to effectively convince his audience that this problem is directly related to print ads, or even that the problem is severe enough to warrant the public's attention.

Parasecoli is successful in convincing his audience that men's magazines do elicit high expectations for men to strive for. He provides a plethora of excerpts from the two magazines that use language exuding "masculinity." He asserts that the writers exploit the masculine nature by presenting the idea of becoming fit as a challenge, which suggests that men who are not up to this challenge are weak and therefore feminine. One of the product ads he explores concludes with "This is hardcore. This is animal. Can you handle it?" (286). Parasecoli systematically shocks his scholarly audience with various excerpts like this that would likely seem ridiculous to them. This same ad insinuates that those who do not lift weights are crybabies; Parasecoli warns that as a result of this ad, readers who do not regularly lift weights may feel like they should start. Although a large focus of men's magazines is to encourage weight training, Parasecoli stresses their main goal, which is to raise revenue through ads. He goes on to discuss extreme "masculine" images in these publications such as skulls and excessively muscular body builders.

Parasecoli does convince the reader that these men's magazines are misguided and perhaps do not distribute the most beneficial messages to men. However, he fails to persuade his audience that men are actually affected by these messages. In his opening paragraph, Parasecoli gives his one and only piece of evidence related to the actual population of men who subject themselves to these negative images. He states that *Men's Health* "claim[s] a circulation of 1.7 million" (284). While at first glance this seems like a significant number of people, if you consider that there are approximately 7 billion people in the world today, suddenly this figure does not seem so impressive. How many men actually buy into this form of advertising if only a fraction even subscribe to these magazines? Parasecoli makes the assumptions that 1) the majority of men are reading these magazines and 2) they are being persuaded by what they see. He offers no evidence of the second. His argument would have much more validity if he offered men's testimonies on whether they personally felt influenced by said images. The entire essay's credibility is diminished because the audience is given no hard evidence of the connection between the images and men's feelings about them. Because of this, it is difficult to believe that men's body image is even a significant issue today.

Women's body image is one of the controversial topics of our current time period. It is constantly in the news and has been proven to be a dangerous problem. What we do not often, if ever, hear about is men's body image problems. Parasecoli does not offer any evidence about how many men are unhappy with the way they look. His argument would have been far more convincing had he given statistics about how many men currently have a gym membership and how many say they have been or are currently on a diet. Instead, Parasecoli offers around thirty examples from the two magazines that all basically prove the same point. His method offers shock value, but he never explores how these images negatively affect men. No possible consequences of a bad self-image, such as "mannorexia," are given. This makes it difficult for his audience to recognize a negative impact of these images created by the men's magazines.

In addition to leaving possible effects out of his essay, Parasecoli also disregards any other causes of male body issues besides the magazines. Interestingly enough, he lays the blame on the homosexual community in the beginning of his essay by stating, "After large sections of the gay community embraced the muscular body as desirable and prestigious, the same attitude became more and more visible, also in heterosexual . . . circles" (285). This statement suggests that the trend in men's obsession with body image originated somewhere besides men's fitness magazines. However, after this brief statement, he does not return to the question of the factors behind these images.

Parasecoli does not acknowledge that there may be any other possible reasons for men's desire to be fit and muscular. Could it be an effect of testosterone and other male hormones? Could it date back to ancient times when only the strongest and fittest survived? Or could it be caused by modern popular culture and the general anti-fat movement that is prevalent not only in magazines, but in every form of media? By failing to mention even one of these other possible explanations, his argument is greatly weakened.

While overall Parasecoli offers an interesting discussion on male body image projected by magazines, he does not convince the audience that it is really a problem or that the two have a direct cause and effect relationship. His argument would have been significantly more effective had he included more statistics and case studies to prove these two points. He does, however, succeed in helping his audience to understand some of the persuasive and almost manipulative techniques employed by these magazines, and makes the reader think twice about picking one up.

Work Cited

Parasecoli, Fabio. "Feeding Hard Bodies: Food and Masculinities in Men's Fitness Magazines." *Food and Culture: A Reader*. 3rd ed. Eds. Carole Counihan and Penny van Esterik. New York, NY: Routledge, 2012. 284-298. Print.

7.2.a Exercise: Questions for Consideration

1) How does Kara's essay meet the requirements of the critique essay?

2) What is Kara's central argument?

3) According to Kara, what is Parasecoli's goal? His thesis?

4) How does Kara employ signal or tag words and phrases to clarify which ideas are hers and which are Parasecoli's?

5) How is her essay structured?

6) What evidence does she use to support her claims?

7.3 THE RESEARCH PAPER PROSPECTUS,[37] Donna Gessell

Essentially your prospectus is a very detailed plan for your research paper. Whereas in your previous English classes you may have been asked to turn in a rough outline of your research paper, the prospectus requires you to put much more thought, energy, research, and effort into your paper before you actually sit down to begin writing. It requires planning by organizing your ideas and starting your research. This is a sly English professor's way of helping you to avoid procrastinating!

"Prospectus" literally means "a look forward." Of course, no one expects you to be able to foresee the future (if that is in your skillset, let's go buy lottery tickets). Instead, it is your best plan for how you will develop your topic. Because often *writing is discovery*, your plans will probably change—at least slightly—as you proceed. Instead of only offering a grade on the final project, your professor will have a timely opportunity to assess your plans and provide insights and advice for your project in its early stages.

Now, even though a prospectus is completely different from any other paper you have ever written, it is completely doable. So, take a deep breath, keep an open mind, read on, think, and write.

Again, note that this is just a plan, and your writing will probably change as you do more research, thinking, and writing. In fact, even your thesis can change as you discover more about your topic through your research, during which you will gather more evidence. Take comfort, though. Even if your plans change, you will probably be able to use a good bit of the writing you create for your prospectus in your final paper. Of course, it will have to be rearranged to fit your argument, rhetorical strategy, and content.

Your prospectus will consist of five paragraphs. Note that this structure is not that of the traditional five-paragraph essay. However, you will need five paragraphs for the content of the prospectus. Each of your paragraphs will address a slightly different topic. Below are listed the guidelines for each paragraph. Read each carefully and develop them into a planning document that can stand on its own.

Title: The title for your prospectus should be the working title for your paper (for more on effective titles, see Section 4.1).

Paragraph 1: *What is your topic and why is it worthy of discussion?* The best way to answer this question is to think of this paragraph as the beginning of your research paper. You should be able to copy and paste this first paragraph from your Prospectus to your Final Draft. Therefore, find a rhetorically interesting way to begin the paragraph—with an example, an exciting detail from research, or even a quotation. Then, begin to narrow down and focus on what exactly your topic is and why it is worthy of discussion.

Paragraph 2: *What background information is necessary in order to understand why your research begins and proceeds as it does?* Simply stated, what information does a reader need to know in order to understand your paper? For example, a reader will need to have a general understanding of your topic and its place within a larger context, as well as some of the more specific or technical terms associated with your research.

Paragraph 3: *What is your thesis statement and what does it mean?* Unless otherwise directed by your instructor, you will begin this paragraph by saying "The thesis of my paper is . . . " Now, in your final draft you will just state your thesis proper, but for the purpose of this paper, begin with the above prompt. Do exactly that—tell exactly what the thesis of your paper will be. Then, explain in a couple of sentences what various terms in your thesis mean. For example, explain what exactly is meant by "Going Green"? Although you may think this is common knowledge, pretend your reader does not have a clue and explain. Show your reader that you understand each of these terms and identifications.

Paragraph 4: *What information have you collected and what resources have you utilized?* Explain exactly what information you have found and how it is useful for your research. Be specific with titles of articles, books, or websites, and be ready to explain how they are scholarly. Do not just say that you found a website on stem cell research—what does the article tell you? What credentials make it scholarly? Does it focus on a specific aspect of this research? By explaining what information you already have, you can figure out what you are lacking and how to fill in the gaps in your research.

Paragraph 5: *How will your paper be organized?* You will begin this paragraph by stating "The thesis of this paper will be established in _____ steps. First,… Then,… Next,… And then,… Lastly, I will end by…" It will be in this paragraph where you specifically lay out the plan for the order of your paper. Remember, the more specific you are, the easier it will be to write your paper.

Communicating Outside the Box

J. Michael Rifenburg

8.1 VISUAL RHETORIC

This section is an introduction to the concept and not an exhaustive treatment of the subject of visual rhetoric. Here is what scholars of rhetoric and writing mean by the term *visual rhetoric* and what the term means for you as a college writer.

James Berlin, the late professor at Purdue and prolific historian of rhetoric, described rhetoric as concerned with *how* a text means versus *what* a text means. To be more concrete, while many scholars focus primarily on *what* a text means, a rhetoric professor is interested in *how* a text means, how a text was or is produced. To gain a stronger sense of what Berlin means by suggesting rhetoric focuses on the how, the production of text, versus the what of a text, let's consider briefly Stephen King's famous novel *It.*

While you may not have read the novel, you may be familiar with the shape-shifting villain Pennywise and the quest by a group of adults to stop the villain years after (she? he? it?) first struck. A literature professor interested in popular culture would find much to discuss in regards to what Pennywise represents; how the historical and societal context which gave birth to King's novel is reflected in this shape-shifting monster; how childhood trauma manifests itself in adulthood through narrative. These are all astute avenues for discussion and examination but a rhetorician would be interested in what makes *It* (the novel as opposed to the character) tick; what makes *It* send shivers down the reader's spine; how does *It* terrify the reader. A rhetorician would be interested in King's choice of title and how this vague pronoun increases the scare-factor. A rhetorician would be interested in the organization of the novel and how the novel moves between the childhood of the protagonists and follows them into adulthood.

Rhetoric is the how of a text. Now, let's tack on the term *visual*. I am paraphrasing Berlin here, but I think his interest in the how of rhetoric's

131

meaning makes a helpful point for entry into thinking about visual rhetoric because to understand visual rhetoric, we need to first be clear on the term rhetoric, a term that has been debated and defined since Plato in 5th century BCE Greece. Visual rhetoric is the use of *seen* images—as opposed to spoken or written words—to generate effect or amplify meaning.

Let's return to Berlin's definition of rhetoric as concerned with how a text means. The use of *text* is key; it is a broad, almost all-encompassing term. We often, and erroneously, restrict our notion of rhetoric to written documents, such as a novel, poetry, song lyrics, or oral language; political pundits love to opine on the current president's rhetoric, usually disparagingly. While Berlin is thinking about written and spoken texts, we can think of text as more than that. We can, and should, enlarge our understanding of text to include a constellation of communicative items: a t-shirt, a movie, a painting, a football play, graffiti, architecture—really, any concrete representation of meaning.

Now tacking on the term *visual* to *visual rhetoric* focuses attention, of course, to visual elements of a text's composition. So let's think of a visual piece of rhetoric.

Take Alfred Hitchcock's 1969 film *Psycho* as an example of a text that would intrigue a visual rhetorician. A visual rhetorician would be interested in how Hitchcock creates a spooky, unnerving film about a man's unhealthy obsession about his mother and taxidermy; how the murder of the leading-lady mid-way through the film throws the audience for an unexpected emotional loop; how the camera angles, lighting, dialogue, and even music—which works aurally to enhance how we process what we see—function together to create Hitchcock's desired atmosphere. Rhetoricians are interested in how the film works on a visual level.

Films form a large portion of the current research and publications in the world of visual rhetoric, but so, too, do documentary photography, advertising, and public memorials, such as the Vietnam Wall. All the visuals surrounding us are composed of a multitude of rhetorical choices on the part of the visual's designer. For example, recently I was walking across the Dahlonega, Georgia, university campus and noticed this large sign flapping in the wind.

This display is designed to persuade the viewer to a certain action. And the display is geared toward a specific audience: college students at the University of North Georgia. To appeal to UNG students and to encourage these students to a certain action, the designer of this display made several important rhetorical choices. For one, our eyes are drawn naturally to the middle, especially when what is in the middle is a different color font than the rest of the display. What jumps out visually is "Graduate on time!" This argument is easily sold, as I doubt few, if any, college students, are *not* hoping to graduate on time. As this argument is the part of the display that most would agree with, it is the most prominent aspect of the display.

The less exciting part of the display and the less exciting part of the argument surrounding the bold middle: see your advisor and take 15 hours. These are two things most college students are not as excited about. But the display has already hooked the viewer with the urge to "Graduate on time!" and now the viewer just has to do these two simple things: connect with an advisor and take a full load of course-work.

We could continue on and on with this visual; we could talk about the color choice, the font, the outline of the state of Georgia, the curiously tiny type "Best 4 years of your life!" and the choice of this display versus, say, a poster on the hallway. But this partial analysis illustrates the depth and complexity of visual rhetoric. Visual rhetoric seeks to learn more about how texts work visually and how texts persuade viewers.

8.2 MULTI-MODAL COMMUNICATION

Wanting to welcome the incoming class of 2014, the UNG Office of Student Affairs had to select the most effective method to accomplish its goal. Like any writer sitting down to compose a text, the Office of Student Affairs was faced with a wide variety of rhetorical decisions to make, decisions regarding how best to forward its message: a print advertisement in the school newspaper? A radio message? A television commercial? A Tweet, Instagram post, or Yak? If a print ad, full scale color or black and white? What should we write on this ad? What type face should we use? These rhetorical concerns, and many more, led to a final product: a banner hanging from the Hoag Student Center during the first week of fall 2014 classes. An image of this banner is shown below:

This banner is just one of many examples of multi-modal communication one encounters every day. "Multimodal communication," also called "multi-modal composition" or "multimodal rhetoric," describes how individuals put together various elements of communication into a coherent message. These elements can include color, sound, image, alphabetic text, and even smell. Visual rhetoric is, as you may have guessed, a subclass of multimodal communication.

Another example at this point may be helpful. Let's think about the movie trailer for the 2014 Best Picture winner *Twelve Years a Slave*. Prior to its release, Fox Searchlight Pictures, the production company behind the award-winning film was faced with the challenge of how best to market their film. Like the UNG Office of Student Affairs, but on a much larger scale, Fox Searchlight had to make a wide variety of rhetorical decisions that would impact how their film was to be understood and received by the public prior to its release. Fox Searchlight commissioned a trailer of just over two-minutes long which can be seen on YouTube: http://www.youtube.com/watch?v=z02Ie8wKKRg.

Throughout the brief video, various elements of communication are woven together into a coherent and powerful trailer. With a few soft notes playing, the trailer opens with a still shot of a plantation. The audience sees the setting for the film, some characters exchange dialogue, and then we get a voice-over spoken by the main character, Solomon Northrop, and alphabetic text written across the screen: "New York 1841." Quick cuts and quick changes in music lead to additional alphabetic text: "From the Acclaimed Director Steven McQueen" and then "Based on the Extraordinary True Story." The trailer ends with an ominous red hue washing out the film credits. The company responsible for the trailer made a variety of choices regarding how best to communicate the message of *12 Years a Slave* to the audience. These choices include sound, color, image, alphabetic text, and many others. Like the banner hanging from our student union welcoming the incoming class of 2014, the trailer for *12 Years a Slave* is an example of multimodal communication.

With these two different examples in mind, let's think a bit about the term "multi-modal communication" and what this term means for you as a college-level writer. Let's start with "communication." There are a lot of smart conversations currently going on between scholars about the differences between the terms "communication," "composition," and "rhetoric," but for our purposes it is helpful to think about these terms as focused on effectively transmitting a message. In this chapter, I am using the term "communication" as I find it is more commonly used among students and was covered thoroughly in the introduction to this book where Dr. Bennett thought about the communication triangle (see Chapter 2). As you already know, we are immersed in communication. We are constantly swimming in the communication triangle, attempting to tailor our subject (or message) to our intended audience. The first part of the term, "multimodal," comes into play when we start thinking about the message, which, of course, hinges on the audience.

8.2.a Mode

A well-respected and well-published scholar at the University of London, Gunther Kress, defines a mode as a "socially shaped and culturally given semiotic resource for making meaning."[38] The "making meaning" aspect of this quotation ties back into the communication triangle and the whole purpose of communication—to convey meaning to someone. Yet, how this meaning is made and then conveyed depends a great deal on context and culture, as Kress points out. Communicating—either visually or orally—in Appalachian Georgia looks a lot different than, say, communicating in an industrial city in Russia. Putting "multimodal" together, then, invites us to focus on the many cultural and social modes at our disposal when crafting our message.

So what does this mean for college-level writers? The traditional college writing assignment consists of a student typing up an essay. The font is generally a common and readable font, such as Times New Roman or Arial. The size of the font is often 12 point; the color, black. The paper is printed onto an 8 ½ x 11 sheet of white paper and handed in to the instructor—if not electronically turned it. Traditionally, the teacher directs the modes available for a college-level writer to use during the construction of an essay. Imagine what would happen if you changed your font to Algerian and turned your whole paper purple. Imagine what would happen if you inserted multiple images in your paper and printed it off on legal size paper. Some teachers would be quite irked, but that is what some college writing teachers are gravitating toward.

Well, maybe not exactly what I described, but there is a growing body of writing teachers who believe that composing and communicating in the twenty-first century demand that students select the most appropriate modes for making their argument in the wake of a proliferation of digital writing platforms and the increased access to additional communicative modes. Instead of requiring the traditional essay, typed up and delivered through the traditional channels, many college-level writing teachers are moving toward granting students the agency to select the most appropriate genre and mode for making meaning, for making their argument.

At the University of Maryland, Baltimore County, Professor Jody Shipka[39] describes an assignment her student completed. The student wrote an essay about conformity; instead of typing up and turning in the assignment in the traditional way, the student transcribed the essay by hand onto an Abercrombie & Fitch shirt. In my own English 1101 class, I had a two students film themselves leading a workshop on revision in a Lumpkin county high school English class. Another student of mine, much like Shipka's student, wrote her literacy narrative—on a poster board that she cut out to resemble a running shoe—about her love of running and writing. She even added yarn for laces. In these examples, the students were faced with a task, really, a rhetorical situation, and then selected the most effective manner in which they could make their argument.

What would you do if given the opportunity to communicate an argument in whatever mode(s) you found most effective?

Finally, I have found I used the word "traditional" throughout the last couple of paragraphs. However, it would be erroneous for me to argue that multimodal communication is a recent form of communication. A lot of scholars have argued human communication has always been multimodal. Think about hieroglyphics or the cave paintings from roughly 30,000 years ago found in France. Humans have long coordinated multiple modes of communication into a cohesive argument.

It may be more accurate to say that college writing teachers are slowly catching up with how people really communicate and are trying to value it in the classroom.

Writing About Literature

Tanya Long Bennett

9.1 WHY?

Often, English instructors teach analysis, research, and argument skills in the context of *literature*. Why? Most first year composition students will not become English majors, so they may wonder why so many of their writing assignments focus on a novel, short story, play, or poem. There are several factors that make literature a fruitful context for development of effective writing.

1) The texts themselves exemplify strategies that can be employed for powerful writing, such as metaphor, tone, and carefully chosen diction.

2) Analysis of a literary text is good practice for analysis of other subjects, such as a physical piece of courtroom evidence, student test scores, and market data.

3) Gathering and analyzing evidence for literary interpretation parallels the process as it would be used to present and interpret evidence in other situations, such as a trial, a letter of recommendation, or a scientific article.

9.2 HOW TO

To *analyze* is to break something down in order to understand it better. We hope to learn about the parts so that we may understand the whole with greater insight. In writing about literature, the first step is to read and analyze the text.

Below is a copy of Emily Dickinson's "Wild Nights—Wild Nights!"[40] along with student Sherry Parson's annotations:

She's not with her lover.	Wild nights - Wild nights! Were I with thee Wild nights should be Our luxury!	A luxury is a rare thing.
	Futile - the winds - To a Heart in port - Done with the Compass - Done with the Chart!	She doesn't need the compass or chart because she's in <u>port</u>—that's not the wild sea!
Eden—a place of innocence	Rowing in Eden - Ah - the Sea! Might I but moor - tonight - In thee!	Moor—tie off, secure

Upon first reading, Sherry believed the poem was a typical love poem, in the highly emotional tone common to poems about this subject. But on closer inspection, she reconsidered. She wondered if perhaps the speaker is torn between her desire for stability and her desire to "let go."

When Sherry reviewed her notes on the poem, she noticed a pattern: Several images of the poem suggest *security*, while others allude to *uncontrolled* or *chaotic* elements. She made a list of each so she could compare them and consider their meaning.

Stability	Uncontrolled
port	wild
Compass and chart	luxury
Eden	wind
moor	sea

She mulled over these contrasting groups, and then she wrote a working thesis to guide her as she moved forward:

> In "Wild Nights," Dickinson employs diction that suggests order and the forces that threaten it to reveal her speaker's inner fears of being lost in desire.

Because she wanted to emphasize the speaker's ultimate need for order, Sherry decided to begin with the imagery of "wildness," which seems to counter her argument, and finish with her evidence of the speaker's need for stability.

Here are her notes, before she has integrated any secondary sources into her work. We could consider these notes a rough draft:

> Dickinson's diction suggests that the speaker longs to be with her lover and to let go of the restrictions that usually govern her. "Were I with thee / Wild nights should be / Our luxury." These lines suggest that such wild nights are rare, "a luxury," implying that social codes usually rule her. The wind and the sea are uncontrollable elements, like her desire, suggesting that her longing may take her over.
>
> When she does mention the compass and the chart, tools for orienting oneself in the ocean, she says she would like to be "done" with them. Here she seems to express her wish to throw off the instruments that help us make sense of our world and experience this union in a more immediate way.
>
> However, other diction pulls back. Eden is not a wilderness, but a garden, kept perfect and innocent. The speaker paints an image of her and her lover "Rowing in Eden." She expresses her wish to "moor — / In thee!" While "thee" refers to her lover, her wish to "moor" counters her description of "wild nights."
>
> The juxtaposition of "wild" words with those like "Eden" and "moor" reveals the speaker's inability to give in to the "luxury" of her desire.
>
> The complexity and seemingly opposing forces of order and wildness reveal this poem's theme of the inner conflict most people experience when dealing with their desires.

Notice in this draft, Sherry not only provides examples of "wild" and "ordered" diction, but she *analyzes* those examples, examining *how* they work, and then provides a link back to her thesis (her overarching *interpretation* of the poem) to show how they support her argument. A helpful formula to keep in mind in argumentative writing is, as discussed in Chapter 4,

1) Make an *assertion*.

2) Provide *evidence* (including analysis of that evidence).

3) Offer your *interpretation* of that evidence.

Sherry *asserts* that key words in the poem reveal the speaker's retreat into order. She then gives *examples* of the words that prove her point, explaining how they function in the poem (*evidence*). And finally, she ties the diction discussion back to her thesis with this sentence: "The juxtaposition of 'wild' words with those like 'Eden' and 'moor' reveals the speaker's inability to give in to the 'luxury' of her desire" (Sherry's *interpretation* of the evidence). Failure to include any of these components—assertion, evidence, and interpretation—would result in a weakened argument.

Some assignments allow, or even require, the writer to incorporate *secondary* sources into the essay. Keep in mind that articles and books by other scholars do not serve to *prove* your argument; rather they provide a *context* for your argument. You utilize them to provide *background on the subject* or to help *clarify your stance*. Your evidence comes from your *primary* source, the poem itself.

Here is Sherry's final paper, including references to three secondary, scholarly sources.

Sherry Parson
English 1101
Fall 2014

Sea or Port? Desire versus Order in Dickinson's "Wild
Nights—Wild Nights!"

The desire to bond with someone romantically
is a common one. This theme is so common in movies, songs, and poetry that it might seem like humans'
main activity in life is fulfilling that desire. However,
in truth, we have to balance chasing after this pleasure
with all the other necessities of living. Working, eating,
and following social rules to keep society stable are all
activities that have to be done, in addition to pursuing
the relationships that make life interesting. Sometimes it
is hard to strike a balance. In her poem "Wild Nights—
Wild Nights!" Emily Dickinson explores the inner

struggle humans often experience between desire and order, revealing that, in the end, the need for security can override our wishes to fulfill our desires.

Dickinson herself was not a social rebel. Often referred to as a recluse, she spent much of her life in her own house in her own room. Yet, she did capture the difficulties of being human in her poetry. Gregory Orr points out that rather than being a physical adventurer, Dickinson was a "Mental Traveller" (25). He asserts that "Wild Nights" is an example of her exploring her "inner sea, the sea of subjectivity, of the rise and fall, the ebb and flow and wild, wave-torn storms of the emotional life" (27). There are stories about people whom Dickinson may have loved romantically, such as newspaper editor Samuel Bowles, Judge Otis Lorde, or even her sister-in-law Susan Gilbert Dickinson (Comment 61). These possibilities have led some readers to see "Wild Nights—Wild Nights!" as a completely sexual poem. For example, in "Emily Dickinson and the Self: Humor as Identity," Nancy Walker calls this work a "sexually explicit poem" (63) in which Dickinson does not acknowledge any guilt for her sexuality. Walker views poetry as a place where Dickinson felt liberated (58). This poem does seem more sexual than most of Dickinson's other poetry, but this poem is more complicated than just an expression of sexual desire. It shows both sides of the coin, the wish for what would most fulfill us and the need for a stable and secure life.

Dickinson's diction suggests that the speaker longs to be with her lover and to let go of the restrictions that usually control her. The lines "Were I with thee / Wild nights should be / Our luxury" (2-4) suggest that such nights are rare, "a luxury," implying that most of the time, social codes rule the speaker's decisions and behavior. The "winds" (line 5) and the "Sea" (line 10) are uncontrollable forces, like her desire, suggesting that her longing may break free of those codes and take her over. When she does mention the "compass" and the "chart," tools for finding one's way in a wild place like the ocean, she says she would like to be "done" with them (lines 7 and 8). Here she seems to express her wish to dismiss the instruments that help us make sense of our world and, instead, experience this union in a more immediate and less restricted way. These references to "Wild nights," "luxury," the "winds" and the "Sea" generate a feeling of "letting loose" in the poem.

However, other diction in the poem counters the speaker's yearning for wildness. She longs for a place where she would not need the compass and the chart, but this place is a "port" (line 6), a place of safety and comfort, away from the violent waves of the sea, or of her desire. Maybe in this port, the speaker could get rid of the instruments that help sailors orient themselves, or the rules of society, but if her love for this person does not fit society's standards, it is not likely she will find her way there in the first place. The fact that she is not there on the night she is speaking is evidence of that.

In addition, the speaker paints an image of her and her lover "Rowing in Eden" (line 9) and although it might seem she is saying that being with her lover would be like paradise, she does not use the word "paradise." Instead, she chooses the word "Eden," which is associated with human creation before sin, before all the rules governing society even had to exist. Eden is not a wilderness, but a garden, perfect and innocent. In this world, the speaker would not have needed security because there were no threats as long as Adam and Eve did not eat of the Tree of Knowledge. Along with this image of a peaceful garden, when the speaker expresses her wish to "moor—tonight / In thee!" (lines 11-12), the word "moor" contradicts the picture of "letting go" that she has been painting. While "thee" does refer to her lover, her wish to "moor" in this person suggests that the speaker's desires make her nervous and insecure. In the end, the placement of "wild" words with words like "port," "Eden," and "moor" reveals the speaker's inability to give in to the "luxury" of her unruly desire.

In "Wild Nights," Emily Dickinson reminds us how complicated life can be. While we often feel that everything we do should be leading us to romantic/sexual fulfillment, we also want, and even need, society's approval. By using images of wildness along with those of safe places in this poem, Dickinson reflects the inner turmoil of making choices between the two. Whether Dickinson ever experienced romantic or sexual love herself or not, she seems to have understood the challenges of being human.

Works Cited

Comment, Kristin M. "Wasn't She a Lesbian? Teaching Homoerotic Themes in Dickinson and Whitman" *English Journal* 98.4 (2009): 61-66. Print.

Dickinson, Emily. "Wild Nights—Wild Nights!" Poetry Foundation. *Poetry Foundation.* Web. 20 Sept. 2014.

Orr, Gregory. "Two Chapters from *Poetry for Survival.*" *American Poetry Review* 31.3 (2002): 25-27. Print.

Walker, Nancy. "Emily Dickinson and the Self: Humor as Identity." *Tulsa Studies in Women's Literature* 2.1 (1983): 57-68. Print.

9.2.a Exercise: Questions for Consideration

1) What introductory sentence best serves as Sherry's thesis? Find 2-4 other sentences in the essay that reiterate this argument.

2) How does she use her secondary sources in paragraph two to help set up her discussion? How does she make clear whose ideas are whose?

3) On what type of evidence does Sherry focus in the third paragraph? What is the shift in focus from paragraph three to paragraph four? From four to five?

4) According to Sherry how is the insight produced by her literary analysis relevant to Sherry's reader? (Here, she answers the "So what?" that your previous teachers may have posed regarding your papers.)

One last note on writing about literature: Students are often tempted to write about a novel, poem, play, or short story by tracing its parts chronologically. This choice can lead to a simple summary that never quite reaches the level of argument (interpretation). Notice that in her third paragraph, Sherry groups together all the "wild" words in the poem. She does discuss them chronologically in this paragraph then, but in paragraph four, she shifts to a discussion of all the "orderly" words, even returning to the second stanza for the first occurrence of such a word. She uses chronological order on a local level, but she has arranged the bigger sections of her paper by *common subtopic* (background, and then "wild" words followed by "orderly" words). Rather than feeling overly bound by the literary work's order, a writer should use the organization that enables her to make her argument most effectively.

Writing in the Social and Physical Sciences

J. Stephen Pearson

Whenever I talk about student writing to my colleagues in the sciences, they voice this complaint: "Our students don't think they have to write well in science classes!" They describe students who don't bother to organize their essays constructively or students who complain when they lose points for grammar errors. Many students seem to think that their writing should be graded solely on how well they know the scientific material and not also on their grammar and organization.

But writing well is important in every field—not just in English. Natural and social scientists present their findings by publishing articles in competitive journals. They expect their writing to be read by colleagues around the globe. Moreover, scientists must write proposals to get funding and other types of research support before they can even begin their projects. It is not unreasonable to say that having good writing skills is crucial to their careers.

Maybe you are not interested in a science career. But you might want to do well in your science classes in order to keep your grades competitive for internships, fellowships, study abroad opportunities, etc. So here is a tip:

> The writing skills you learned in English 1101 and 1102—how to organize your thoughts, how to express your ideas clearly, how to find the appropriate tone, how to write towards your audience, how to make persuasive arguments, how to use sources responsibly—are the same skills you need to write well in the sciences.

In fact, many of the types of essays you write for English classes can be found in science classes as well. You may be asked to *explain* in your own words what happens during a certain chemical reaction. Or you may be asked to *compare* differing theories on human development. Perhaps you are asked to *evaluate* the merits of a new proposal to increase so-lar-energy production in your neighborhood. Or maybe you were the one who wrote the solar-energy *proposal* in the first place. Or perhaps your assignment is to write a *summary* of current research on the long-term effects of bilingual education programs. All of these skills—explanation, analysis, comparison, synthesis, evaluation, and proposal—require the same skills you learned in your English composition courses: organiza-tion, clarity, proper tone, evidence, focus, thoughtfulness.

Since a fair amount of the writing in your science classes may use the same skills, techniques, and strategies you learned in your English composition courses, all you need to do is transfer them into your science topic. No matter what classes you take—sociology, biology, history, education, business, criminal justice—you should make the effort to write your best. Not only will your grades go up, but you'll be practicing a skill that will pay off for you after you graduate, whether you enter the job market or continue on to graduate school.

However, there is one common type of science writing assignment that is significantly different from the types of essays you learned in English: the "lab report," the standard report format for all your exper-iments in the natural and in the social sciences. Although these reports demand the same skills of clarity and evidence as any other assignment, they also feature a very particular organization structure that has to be carefully learned and practiced.

The rest of this chapter, therefore, will discuss the particularities of the experimental report, giving an overview of the basic structure that is found in both the natural and the social sciences. The overview will be general, as there are many stylistic issues that vary depending on your discipline. You will need to learn these variations as you go through your major; no single book chapter can cover every discipline. But I can intro-duce you to the function of each section and give you guidelines that will work in most situations. And even though you may be writing only for your professor, I am going to treat this chapter as if you are serious about a science career and want to write in a professional style right away. During your coursework, you may find a research project that you could publish on. We have plenty of opportunities for undergraduate research at UNG, and if you are serious about a career and/or about graduate work in the sciences, you should take those opportunities now. If you want to become a scientist, it is never too early to act like a future professional.

I will say this several times, but the best way for you to learn the proper report structure for your field is to look at professional scholarship in that field. Model your reports on what the experts are doing. However, if you think that you will be pursuing a research path in either the physical or social sciences, I highly recommend Angelika H. Hofmann's book *Scientific Writing and Communication.*[41] It is a very useful book that will take you through your undergraduate work and into graduate studies. I have used it in my classes, and my science majors have said it is a very helpful resource for their coursework. You will see it mentioned several times throughout this chapter. Also, note that scientific writing usually employs the documentation style of CSE (Council of Science Educators) rather than MLA, used in previous chapters of this book.

10.1 THE EXPERIMENTAL OR "LAB REPORT"

One of the biggest differences between experimental reports and other essays is that reports have a pre-set structure that is common (with only minor variations) across a wide number of disciplines. Where the humanities allow scholars a good deal of flexibility in organizing their research papers, the "lab report" structure is fairly standardized, and scientists expect new papers to follow the familiar structure. At minimum, reports will have the following sections:

- Abstract
- Introduction
- Methods
- Results
- Discussion
- References

These sections do not flow smoothly into each other, but instead are usually announced by subheadings to make the structure even easier for readers to follow.

Moreover, the content of these sections needs to be kept separate: Although it might *seem* to make sense that a Results section would include some speculation on the explanation for the data, that material must be kept in the Discussion. Hofmann points out that in the sciences, readers can handle clunky sentences but are very bothered when information is in the wrong section—or when it is simply missing.[42] The structure of the experimental report has developed into a very logical and very useful format, and scientists have learned to use that format both as writers and as readers. Therefore, you need to pay close attention to what belongs in each section so that when you are writing your own reports, there is *no content bleeding across sections.*

One major reason for this concern with keeping everything in its correct section is that *professional scientists do not always read the entire paper through the first time.* (I am not talking about your professors, who will read your entire paper in order grade it accurately.) Very often, scientists read the Abstract and Introduction, and then jump to the Discussion to see your final answers before they decide to read the Methods and Results. Or perhaps they are doing similar projects and are most interested in how you designed your experiment, or in what results you got. You may have already learned that when reading published scientific articles, it is often helpful to read the Abstract, Introduction, and Discussion sections first in order to understand the researchers' project before delving into the more technical sections in the middle. Given that readers expect to find the information they need in its customary location, it is very important for you to organize your reports correctly. If you bleed your discussion into your Results or introduce new methods information into your Discussion, that material may miss its intended audience, and your work may not get appropriate attention.

As a student writer, *your best strategy is to look at the experiment reports that you read for your classes or that you come across in your research.* Although the "lab report" structure is used in a variety of physical and social sciences, there are variations specific to each discipline, and you need to learn what is standard in your field. The social sciences, for instance, often use interviews in their research, so their reports include long quotes. But the physical sciences use very few quotes, even when citing previous studies. You will want to pay plenty of attention to how the types of research that are common in your field affect the way that research is written. And the easiest way to learn this is by analyzing published scholarship.

10.1.a Title

As a college student, I had two approaches to paper titles: they were either generic ("Final Research Essay") or were based on pop culture references but with no explicit mention of my actual topic ("I'm an Ordinary Guy: Burning Down the House" for a paper on a play from Ancient Greece; notice how the title does not mention what text I was discussing.). As a professor, I have found that those two approaches remain popular with students. But while titles like that may be permissible for term papers that will be read only by your professors, they create bad habits for you as future professionals.

Titles need to be informative: readers need to have some idea of what your topic is going to be. This is especially true if you want your work to be found by other people through internet search engines. As academic scholarship has moved more and more online, the search engine has become more essential to locating relevant topics. Therefore, *titles need to be search-engine friendly* if they are going to show up in your colleagues' search results. We've all experienced the frustration of being unable to find the correct search terms for the topic we want; we have also all had the frustration of getting way too many irrelevant results. Searching for research articles is difficult enough without having to deal with titles that do not clue the search engine to their topic and therefore never make it to your computer screen.

Therefore, get in the habit *of crafting titles that give your readers a good sense of your topic and your approach*. Think about the key terms from your paper and include those. Think also about the subject headings that were useful to you in doing the background research—the closer your title comes to pre-existing subject headings, the more likely your paper will show up in related search results. Rather than trying to be clever, aim for recognition. You want other researchers to recognize that your topic matches their search. Consider which of these titles is more useful to someone trying to sort through a list of fifty to sixty possible papers: "Real Gossip Girls of L.A."? Or, "Assessing the Ways that Texting Affects How Gossip Is Spread among Teenage Women"? One may be catchier, but catchy is often not search-engine friendly.

10.2 ABSTRACT

The abstract is the first thing your readers will see—and if it comes up in a list of database search results, it may be the only part of your essay they will read. Yet it will probably be the last thing you write—or at least the last thing you edit. This is because the *abstract* contains a summary of your entire report. Therefore, you cannot complete it until you have finalized your research and the rest of your paper, i.e., until you are satisfied that you have analyzed your data thoroughly enough and that you have thought through your findings deeply enough to have completed your discussion section.

The purpose of the abstract is to give readers an overview of your paper so that they can decide if they need to read the entire thing. Even with the most up-to-date databases and with the best search engine designs, finding relevant articles on your topic still involves a lot of false leads. You rarely get a set of search results in which every article addresses your topic. Therefore, abstracts are tremendously helpful for weeding out off-topic articles. They are especially handy when the paper itself (or the journal it is published in) is unavailable both at your library and online;

they help researchers eliminate unfruitful loan requests, saving them time and saving the library money.

The tricky part of writing your abstract is figuring out how to distill the information from each section into one or two sentences. My students find that once they have written full versions of their reports, they are so connected to the details that they have trouble stepping back and extracting the main points. But what readers need first is *an overview of your project: what question you are asking, why you are asking it, how you tackled it, what your key findings are, and what those findings mean.* If you can summarize *each* of those in one or two sentences, you are on the right track. You might take an approach similar to the "elevator pitch" technique: can you state all the key elements of your paper in one minute—that is, quickly enough that you can share it with someone on a single elevator ride?

For help, *look at the abstracts of articles you read for class*: Always try to model your reports on publications in your field. When you are not sure how to phrase something, see if you can find a similar statement in an article; you aren't going to copy it word-for-word, since it is unlikely that the published statement would make sense for your research. But you are looking for clues about how to phrase your own sentence: How much background information does this author give in her abstract? How did she summarize her results? What sort of discussion comments does she make? When in doubt, ask your professor, but you will score points with the faculty if you show that you have been analyzing professional work as well.

Note that abstracts are common in both the sciences and in the humanities, but they are used in different ways. In some fields, they are included at the start of the published article and in the research databases, while in other fields they are used mostly when submitting your work to journals and conference panels but are not actually published with the article and perhaps not included in the article's database entry. Published abstracts serve as summaries of the full article, as discussed above, whereas unpublished abstracts may spend less time outlining the full contents and more time explaining how the research contributes something new to the field. As always, you need to find out how abstracts are used in your field and design yours accordingly.

10.2.a Key terms

After your abstract, you will want to include a short list of key terms. As with the title, choose search terms that will best help people find your paper.

10.3 INTRODUCTION

As with almost any formal presentation—including speeches—the Introduction is where you set up your project for your readers. It is how you get your reader up-to-speed on your topic, taking them from 0 to 60 mph in a few paragraphs. But whereas essays written for leisure reading might start with an anecdote that piques the readers' interest, research-focused papers (which include experimental reports) hook the readers by promising to solve an open question in the field.

Therefore, part of your job in the Introduction is not simply to set out your project, but also to explain why your project needs to be done at all: You must *justify your research*. Keep in mind that scientific research depends a great deal on external funding, which means that researchers must show that their work is relevant to open questions in the field and is not simply repeating what other scholars have already proven.

What this means for you is that your Introduction must set out the current state of the conversation about your topic: What has already been said and, most importantly, why is the question still open? We call this open question the *gap*: It is what is currently unknown about the topic—which is what you intend to uncover. Sometimes, the gap is that previous studies have given contradictory results; sometimes, that new data conflicts with previous research; sometimes, that other scholars have neglected to examine some aspect of the problem. *Whatever form the gap takes, it is your job to explain it to your readers in your Introduction in order to justify why your research is important.*

In presenting the gap, you present your *background research* on the topic: the current conversation as found in scholarly articles, books, news, etc. Usually, this means that you briefly mention what other studies have shown, summarizing their findings and often combining similar studies into one citation. It is common, for instance, to see citations grouped together like this:

> Recent studies have shown that the size of the Hellmouth has gotten bigger since it was first discovered by Whedon and Summers (Smith 2001; Toshi 2004; Ernst and Lubitsch 2008; Mendez 2010).

Your Introduction needs to prove to your readers—especially to experts in the field—that you have kept up with the research. In this way, a solid Introduction section also builds your ethos as a reliable scholar.

Notice that the sample sentence above doesn't actually quote the studies mentioned; it merely states whatever general finding is common to the group and relevant to your project. This is a key difference between scientific writing and humanities writing: *the sciences use far fewer quotes.* Whereas the subtle nuances of words can be crucial for scholars working with literary, historical, legal, philosophical, or religious texts, phrasing is less important in the sciences than the general facts that are being presented. In our example, the fact that the Hellmouth has gotten bigger is the key information, and it doesn't necessarily matter how any of the previous studies worded their findings.

This is not to say that wording is unimportant in the sciences: Terms must always be clearly defined, and your writing needs to be precise and unambiguous. If you are explaining a concept or presenting a theory, you might find yourself quoting scholars whose definitions have been influential, using their exact words instead of paraphrasing or summarizing them.

After you lay out the current conversation about your topic, you make your gap statement by showing what's missing, unknown, unresolved, puzzling, or absent from the discussion. Your readers need to see that your project is addressing a question or problem that is still in fact open. When you read lab-style reports in your classes, you should look for any statement that points out that *"previous research has done X but has not done Y,"* such as:

> Although several studies have explored the tensions between vampires and werewolves (Paquin 2006; Somerhalder and Hoechlin 2009; Skarsgard and Manganiello 2011), no in-depth research has been done on the few successful alliances between the two groups.

Make sure your statement remains respectful, even though you're pointing out a deficiency in the field; for instance, instead of saying *"scholars have failed to examine . . . "* you would write *"so far little research has been done on . . . "* As you move through your major, look at how published scholars phrase their gap statements and phrase yours accordingly.

Your response to the gap is known as your *intervention.* You are now inserting yourself into the conversation, pointing out the gap and then leading the way towards filling it with new, better, and/or more complete information. When you read reports in your classes, notice the intervention statements: If they are well-written, they should form logical counterparts to the gap statements. If the gap statement reads:

> Recent studies have examined the processes by which young wizards learn to control their wands (Rowling 2008; Dumbledore and Weasley 2010), but no one has yet explored whether having Muggle ancestry affects this process.

Then, the intervention statement might read:

> <u>Therefore, this study observed</u> a class of young wizards in their first year with their wands, <u>looking specifically for</u> differences between mixed- and full-blood wizards.

As you write your Introduction, remember your key tasks and present them in this order:

1) Set up a context that shows that the problem you are addressing is important.
2) Review the state of recent research on your topic.
3) Point out the gap in the current research.
4) Explain your project in a way that shows it as a direct intervention into the gap.

Remember to demonstrate your credibility, to show that you have done your homework regarding the current state of the topic; you will probably need to cite multiple studies. Remember also that you will not need to quote as much as you would in a humanities paper, but that using quotations to explain key theories or concepts might be useful.

Also, be careful not to narrate your research findings. I have seen many student introductions that include unnecessary statements like this one: *"As I was researching, I found this excellent source about . . . "* You do not need to narrate your background research. Present it as a simple fact:

> <u>Recent studies</u> (Anton 2008; Barnes 2009; Chang 2009) <u>have raised questions</u> about the validity of this model, but experiments have so far been inconclusive.

You really do not need to mention yourself much in this section, except perhaps at the end when you are laying out your intervention; notice how this sentence mentions the authors only once:

> In order to determine if having muggle-blood affects how students learn to use their wands, <u>we interviewed</u> 24 mixed-blood wizards.

For each section of your report, there are important phrases that you should get in the habit of using to help indicate the function of each paragraph. Hofmann calls these "signals"[43]; I will use the phrase **signal words**. Common signal words for the Introduction include (but are not limited to[44]):

- Unknown: " . . . is not known"; " . . . is unclear"; " . . . has not been determined"; "The question remains . . . "; etc.
- Question: "To determine . . . "; "To assess . . . "; "We hypothe-sized that . . . "; "We examined whether . . . "; etc.

10.4 METHODS

The function of your Methods section is to *explain the set-up of your experiment*, both so that readers can duplicate the experiment and so that they can evaluate the quality of your experimental design. After all, part of the scientific process is determining what kinds of experiments will correctly answer the question: There needs to be a clear connection between your research question and your experimental approach. Therefore, you want to explain your methodology well enough that your readers will believe that your approach measures what you intend it to. (If you are writing about a laboratory experiment, you will also describe the equipment and materials you used.)

Note that your Methods section will explain not what you plan to do, but what you *already did*—that is, *it is written in the past tense*. And unlike in the Introduction, there will be some narration (italicized here):

> <u>In order</u> to determine the risk for Kryptonite radiation in the food supply, *we placed* 14g of Kryptonite in a 50/50 water-sugar solution. *We then heated* the container with the solution and the Kryptonite to 350 degrees and *let it sit* for one hour. *We then tested* water-sugar solution <u>to see if</u> it had any traces of Kryptonite radioactivity.

Keep in mind, however, that you aren't simply telling a story; you are also explaining your choices. Therefore, the key moments in your experiment should include a bit of explanation, often in the form of an "in order to" statement, as in the single-underlined phrases in the above example.

One issue that may vary from professor to professor is the use of *passive voice* in this section. Scientific writing has long been known for its impersonal, even awkward style:

> *Beakers were filled* with 40ml of water and *were then placed* in the TARDIS for 24 hours, after which they *were removed and measured* for temperature change.

This use of the passive voice (*were filled, were placed,* etc.) makes sense given the idea that scientists are neutral observers who do not actively affect the experiments. But this idea has been challenged in recent years, and I am told by my colleagues that more scientists are using *active voice*:

We filled beakers with 40ml of water and then *placed* them . . .

The active voice reads better, but it runs the risk of repetition ("we did" X, and then "we did" Y). A related problem is that the "*we*" seems unnecessary, given that readers will assume you did the work: Since no one else was doing the experiment, the continual use of "*we*" feels like it adds unnecessary words. Therefore, you should *ask your professors which style they prefer* and adapt your writing style to their preferences.

Because the Methods section varies widely depending on the type of experiment you are performing—doing a long-term survey of people's attitudes requires a very different set of materials and procedures from measuring the results of a chemical reaction—there are not really any universal *signal words*. But you will want to make sure that those materials and procedures are described as clearly as possible.

10.5 RESULTS

The Results section is where you present your raw data: all the numbers, percentages, and other statistically relevant information that come out of your experiment. If you have read many experimental reports in your classes, you've probably realized that this section is often the most difficult to read, even when you're familiar with the subject matter. Your task is to present the most significant details from your data *and* to do so in an organized way so that readers do not feel overwhelmed by unconnected data. This section often includes the majority of your graphs, charts, tables, etc., and those need to be clearly labeled and placed near the paragraphs in which they are referenced so that readers can smoothly move from your text to the figure and back.

Besides being difficult to read, Results are difficult to write for several reasons. First, it is difficult to know which results to include. Some students include all their results, using what I call a "kitchen sink" approach to the section. For instance, whenever I have my students create and conduct a survey, I get several papers in which the Results section simply walks me through the responses to each question, starting with number one and going right down the list. This approach isn't useful because it makes it tough for readers to determine which data is most important. The data hasn't been organized for us, and we are left drowning in numbers. In her book, Hofmann recommends that you *start with the most important data and arrange your findings according to their importance*.[45] By the time you are writing your Results, you should have an idea of what your overall conclusion is, so select the findings that best lead to your conclusion and organize it in terms of relevance.

Be aware that although you are usually looking for clear trends and patterns in your data, you can also point out the absence of trends, which you might phrase as:

My results <u>found no correlation between</u> how long people have lived in Gotham City and their views on the legality of vigilante crime-fighting.

Similarly, students writing qualitative reports often include a lot of demographic data (age, gender, race, education level, etc.), without connecting it to the research question: they will tell me how many men and women were surveyed or their ages or their religious and political preferences, but they forget to connect that information back to the data. While it might be useful to know that you had a diverse sample pool for your surveys or interviews, it is even more useful to know how that diversity lines up with the surveys: Did women and men answer differently? Were certain ethnic groups more likely to respond a certain way than others? Were there distinct response patterns among gays or Christians or political independents? Breaking down your results according to demographics is an excellent approach to qualitative research, but you have to make those connections explicit in your report. Instead of:

Of the Hogwarts students who took our survey, most (56%) were Caucasian, with only 24% of African ancestry, 21% South Asian, 8% East Asian, and 1% other.

which tells us only the breakdown of respondents, present only those demographics that connect back to the main research question:

We found that <u>South Asians and East Asians were most likely</u> to study foreign languages at Hogwarts, with 18 of 21 (86%) South Asians and 6 of 8 (75%) East Asians <u>saying they either had taken or intended to take</u> a language, compared to only 23 of 56 (41%) Caucasian students and 10 of 24 (42%) African ancestry students.

A second difficulty is knowing how to present the numbers. It is important to remember that your raw data is not the results. Instead, results = data + context,[46] which my students have found a bit confusing).

157

The raw data might say that after 48 hours, there were 127 tribbles, but that number doesn't mean much by itself. What you need is some context:

> After 48 hours, the number of tribbles had increased from 40 to 127.

Or

> After 48 hours, the number of tribbles had tripled.

In a survey, the data might say that 57% of men and 19% of women said they would vote for Captain America for President. Those numbers by themselves do reveal some meaning, but the ratio is not immediately obvious to most readers: 57 and 19 are unusual numbers and not easy to work with. Don't make your readers search for their calculators! Add some context by explaining:

> Men were three times more likely than women to vote for Captain America.

A similar lack of context comes from using percentages only. Think of how difficult it is to decipher weather forecasts. It is unclear what it means to say that there is a 40% chance that we will be hit by a hurricane this season. Does that mean that 40% of hurricanes will hit us? That 40% of us will be hit by a hurricane? Or that (most likely), a hurricane hit us in 40% of years with similar weather conditions? Percentages are not only confusing; they can also be misleading. If you tell me that 50% of the men in your survey would rather be a muggle than a wizard, I'll want to know how many men were in the survey. There is a big difference between 50 out of 100 and 2 out of 4. They both make up 50% of the sample, but notice how differently the percentages change if one more man is added to each sample: the smaller the sample, the more volatile the percentages will be. Readers need to know that. For this reason, you should generally *present raw numbers first, followed by percentages in parentheses*[47]:

> Our results show that a slight majority of people prefer longer jail times for super-powered criminals, with 20 of 36 (55.6%) reporting that current jail times are too short, 10 (27.8%) saying that current jail times are sufficient, and 6 (16.7%) saying they are too long.

Another difficulty is in phrasing. In the Results, you do not need to narrate the order in which you analyzed the results (*first we looked for X; then we looked for Y*; etc.). It is rarely helpful to readers to know the sequence in which you uncovered your data. What is more helpful is to see the data presented in order of importance. The exception would be if your analysis shifted directions based on the results, as in this example:

> Results indicate that elves preferred the name brand elf food to generic elf food by a 3-to-1 margin. <u>With these results in mind,</u> <u>we focused our research</u> on the most popular generic elf food flavors to determine if there are any common denominators. We found that elves prefer generic brands that mix soft and crunchy textures.

In this example, one of the findings led researchers to narrow the focus of their analysis, and it makes sense that they narrated their work in this way. But in many situations, *you do not need to list your findings in chronological order; list them by importance.*

In order to avoid narration and to keep the focus on the actual results, use such as phrases *"Our results show that . . ."* or *"We found that . . . "* If you are doing a lab experiment in which your results are not quantifiable, such as noticing color change, odors, sounds, etc., you would state:

> We <u>observed his skin turn</u> from white to purple.

Or

> We <u>noticed a humming sound when</u> she stood within 6 feet of the stargate.

One remaining difficulty of the Results section is the temptation to add your conclusions, explanations, etc. The reasons for this temptation are simple: having finished both the experiment and the analysis, you have already mentally connected your data to your conclusions, and it feels odd to separate them in the paper. But remember: because of the standard structure of the lab report, people don't always read the entire thing. If your conclusions are buried in the Results, some readers will miss them, and your work will miss a potential audience. *Do not bleed your discussion into your Results!* Do not try to hypothesize why your results came out as they did or to draw conclusions to the overall research project. Save those for the Discussion section. (Similarly, make sure you aren't introducing new methods into your results section.)

The **signal words** for your Results[48] might include such phrases as:

- **Results:** "We found . . . "; "We observed . . . "; "We detected . . . "; "Our results indicate that . . . "; etc.
- **Context:** ", indicating that . . . "; ", consistent with . . . "; etc.

10.5.a Tables & Graphs

To help readers better interpret your results, it useful to have tables, figures, graphs, charts, or other visuals; these images can make the patterns in your data easier to see. But poorly designed graphics can frustrate your readers. Therefore, give your visuals with the same amount of attention you give to the rest of your paper. *Provide only the figures you need to support your argument, and use them only when they present the information more clearly than text alone.* Pick the type of figure that most quickly illustrates the patterns you want readers to see. Tables are most helpful when you need to provide precise numerical data; conversely, graphs are good for showing trends in data when exact numbers are not needed. And there are multiple types of graphs: pie graphs, line graphs, bar graphs, etc.; so be careful to pick the one that best suits your data.

When creating figures, *make sure they are labeled clearly enough that they can be interpreted even if the reader has not read the text.* Write a legend (it is like a caption) that clearly explains what the figure shows, then label your axes and provide a key for all the lines, colors, etc. in the image. If you create multiple images, make sure the designs have enough consistency to guide readers; for instance, if you have several graphs showing how people from different age groups feel about certain topics, use the same type of graph and make the colors the same for all of them. Don't go overboard with colors, patterns, line types, fonts, etc. *Keep the images as simple and uncluttered as possible.* Similarly, use the key words from your text, so that readers can quickly make the right connections. And remember to give a clear cue to the visual within the text (e.g., *"see Figure 2"*).

10.6 DISCUSSION

In some ways, the Discussion section is the most difficult to write, since it is the section that most requires you to show your skill at interpreting and explaining your data in a logically convincing manner. At the same time, it is the easiest section to organize, since there is a fairly common set of topics you need to cover. So let's address those topics in the order you would present them; as Hofmann notes,[49] you start narrow and gradually broaden:

10.6.a Opening Paragraphs

The most important element of the Discussion is that you *provide your final answer to your research question*—in a sense, it is here that you present your thesis statement. And remember, some of your readers may jump here first to find your conclusion, so make sure that you very clearly provide your solution to the question that guided your project, putting it right at the beginning of the Discussion. Where possible, use similar terms with the Introduction so that readers can easily see the connection between the question and your answer. If your research question is about which invisibility spell lasts longest, your Discussion statement should repeat the terms "invisibility," "spell," and "lasts longest." It may seem too obvious to state this, but you want to give your readers enough structural clues to make the connections clear on the first read.

After stating your overall conclusion, remind your readers (some of whom have not yet read the Results) of the *key information that supports your claim*—not in the same amount of detail, but in summary. This summary can be tricky to do; my students tell me that they have so many details swimming in their heads that it's difficult to figure out which data to include and how to summarize it. You might try the "phone home" technique: Imagine that you are describing your project to your parents on the phone; you won't tell them all your results, but which ones do they need to know to understand your answer?

Also, be careful not to include new results—or new methods!—in this section. Everything you mention here should have already been mentioned earlier.

10.6.b Middle Paragraphs

After you have stated your final answer to your research question and summarized the key evidence, there are several other important topics to consider. But now you have more freedom to decide how to arrange them. Your best bet is to arrange them from most to least important, in terms of how much they affect your final interpretation.

If you have *any other important findings beyond the original research question*, they belong here. Perhaps your study on whether people prefer hobbits to elves found no significant difference between age groups or between educational levels. Even though this information may not be the main focus of your research, it could be helpful for researchers doing similar work. Remember that this information should *also* be in the Results; do not add new results here.

Two other types of secondary results that should be discussed are any surprises and any discrepancies that came out of your data. *Surprises are important*, since they raise new questions that may lead to new projects for you or for your readers. Perhaps your study found that Jedi knights are disproportionately big fans of *Project Runway*. That's an important discovery that needs to be followed up to see if it holds true in general or is just a fluke in your study.

161

Results that seem to contradict other data—*discrepancies*—might also raise useful questions and should therefore be acknowledged as well. Perhaps your project found a general pattern of television viewing that holds true for almost all of the population—except for one small group. That result could just be a fluke of your project, or it could turn out to be accurate for that group nationwide. And if you decide to overlook this one exception when you present your conclusion, it is especially important to explain why you think this group does not contradict your final interpretation. Part of being a good scholar is creating a reliable *ethos*, showing that you are paying attention to all the data and not ignoring evidence that does not support your idea. Therefore, it is up to you to *explain why any discrepancies are not truly a problem for your final conclusion.*

Similarly, it is important to acknowledge the *limitations* of your project. Perhaps you discovered midway through analyzing your survey data that you should have asked a certain follow-up question or that your random sample of participants did not fully represent the population you are studying. Perhaps you were working with the data set from a previous study that did not ask certain questions. These problems may reasonably limit the reliability of your data, and it is important that you acknowledge them.

This middle section of the Discussion is also where you *compare and contrast your findings to other studies.* As in the Introduction, you will not try to give the full details of the previous studies; a general summary will do. However, if the other studies contradict your findings, you may need to provide more details about the other experiments so that you can explain the different results and show how they do not affect your conclusion. Notice how this example brings in other sources and gives just enough experimental detail to explain the different results:

Our study showed higher satisfaction with the quality of life in Gotham City than had previously been reported (Nolan 2009; Burton and Keaton 2011). However, those studies included data regarding the number of native residents who move away, whereas ours focused on natives who stayed and on current residents who moved here as adults.

Finally—for the middle paragraphs—this is the where you can *speculate about possible hypotheses or models* that would explain your findings. Make sure you clearly state that you are presenting a hypothesis; do not let your readers think your ideas have already been tested and confirmed. Moreover, you should provide readers with an example that illustrates how your model or hypothesis works. Don't assume that they will grasp your idea without a specific example.

10.6.c Closing Paragraphs

If the Discussion opens with the most direct statement of your answer, and if its middle paragraphs expand the scope to secondary results, possible problems, and other studies, then its final section is the broadest. Here you not only repeat your overall conclusion, but you also give the reader one last reminder of the "so what question," showing the significance of your work and *suggesting possible avenues for future research and/or practical uses for current issues*. For instance, a project on new trends in writing magic spells may lead you to suggest possible ways that spell-casting teachers can improve their teaching. Or perhaps your research raised new questions that need to be explored before the topic can be completely answered. Either way, this section moves your research out into the wider world, giving readers a clearer sense of what your work is contributing either to the field or to the culture at large.

Discussion *signal words* include[50]:

- *Main answer*: "Our study shows that . . . "; "Our findings demonstrate that . . . "; etc.

- *Summary*: "Taken together, . . . "; "We conclude that . . . "; "Overall, . . . "; "Finally, . . . "; etc.

- *Significance (from most certain to least certain)*: "Our findings can be used to . . . "; "We recommend that . . . "; "These findings imply that . . . "; "We propose that . . . "; etc.

- *Unexpected findings*: "To our surprise . . . "; " . . . was not expected,"; etc.

- *Conflicting results*: " . . . does not agree with . . . "; " . . . has also been reported . . . "; "However, other studies have found . . . "; etc.

- *Limitations*: " . . . could not be measured . . . "; " . . . was limited by . . . "; "Further observations are needed to . . . "; " . . . was not possible . . . "; etc.

- *Comparisons to other studies*: " . . . consistent with X,"; "Similar to . . . "; " . . . has also been observed by . . . "; etc.

- *Hypothesis*: "From these data we hypothesize that . . . "; "Our results lead us to conclude that . . . "; "We propose that . . . "; etc.

10.7 POSTERS

Finally, you should be prepared to turn your entire paper into a poster. It is common in scientific fields for researchers to create a visual summary of their project, which is then displayed in a hall for other scholars to browse. You can make yours by creating a single Power Point slide set to the appropriate size, for instance, 3 feet long and 2 feet high. *These posters have to be self-sufficient*; that is, since the researchers may not be able to stand next to the poster all day, the information must be thorough enough to explain the entire project to a viewer. However, you do not simply transfer your entire paper to the poster; you need to dramatically shorten your paragraphs, use bullet points where possible, eliminate all non-essential information, and rely on your charts and graphs. *Posters will present much less content through text than your paper*; Hofmann recommends using only 20% text, 40% images, and 40% white space.[51]

As with tables and figures, your poster needs to be easy for viewers to navigate. Your paper's title and the names of everyone on your research team are listed at the top. Beneath that, organize the material in a logical way, using columns and moving from left to right, either straight across the page or with top-to-bottom organization within each column. Present all the main sections of your paper: Introduction, Methods, Results, Discussion, and References. *Keep your design simple:* use colors, but choose only a few; if you use colors, bold and/or italics to make your subheadings stand out, give all the subheadings the same format. Text and background colors should be easy to separate—you don't want the words blending with the background—and avoid color combinations that are difficult for people with color-blindness to read. Fonts should be big enough to be readable from a few feet away. Imagine there are three people trying to read the same poster—they will not want to be huddled together like a football team trying to read your text and your graphs. Hofmann suggests using a sans serif font (such as Arial or Helvetica) at 22-28 point for the regular text, and with higher points for headings and titles.[52]

Summary

Overall, the way you write science papers has a lot in common with how you write humanities papers in terms of grammar, tone, and paragraph structure. The key differences in the lab report require that you work hard to understand what distinguishes the different sections and how to determine which information goes where. Make sure that you cover all the relevant material within each section and that you are not introducing new methods in your Results section, or new results in your Discussion, etc. Make sure your Introduction clearly lays out the problem/question to be solved and your Discussion clearly opens with your answer to that question. And make sure all your charts, graphs, tables, posters, etc. are visually clear, easy to interpret, and linked to the appropriate information in the text.

Finally, the best way to learn how to write reports in your field is to analyze professional publications in your field. In addition to analyzing papers you are reading for your class, hunt down journals in your subject and read them, noticing what writing techniques make the articles easy to read and which ones make it difficult. When you are stuck on how to write part of your essay, look over similar types of research reports and see how they solved that problem. Think of your degree as an apprenticeship: you learn to practice your subject by imitating the way your professors think, talk, and perform their scholarship. Do the same with professional writing: model your writing on the publications you find clear, easy to follow, and engaging. It is never too early to start treating yourself like a professional, and you never know what doors might open for you!

Themes for Writing

This chapter provides ideas for writing, including both content suggestions and themes by which that content might be fruitfully approached. These suggestions may be helpful both to instructors and to students as they seek topics for writing projects.

11.1 IDENTITY STEREOTYPES IN THE MEDIA, *Diana Edelman-Young*

One of the most fruitful topics in writing courses is personal identity. In order to concentrate on essential writing skills, students are often wisely advised to write about what they are familiar with or what they are personally interested in. Of all the things you can think of, what is most familiar to you? Yourself, of course! In addition, living in the United States, which thrives on mass culture and the media, you are likely familiar with a variety of sources for gathering information and being entertained—magazines, newspapers, television, radio, film, and the internet. When identity and the media come together, sometimes long-standing stereotypes are proliferated. Although stereotypes of all varieties certainly predate modern technology, the media has played an important role in both perpetuating and challenging identity stereotypes. Stereotypes can take many forms, but some of the most prevalent ones are based on **gender, race, class,** and **ethnicity.**

Given the vast number of cultures, races, classes, and genders represented in this country, it is difficult to cover them all. *The sections below address some of the most prevalent ones, but they are not intended to be exhaustive.* Feel free, in consultation with your instructor, to address any problems in the categories presented and to think critically about the reading and viewing material. You might even discuss with your instructor alternative essay questions that include different categories or address other relevant issues within that category, whether gender, race, class, or ethnicity. In addition, keep in mind that the stereotypes discussed here are just that—stereotypes. They are in no way intended to be taken as legitimate representations. The purpose here is to think critically about particular identity stereotypes, where they come from, and what effect those stereotypes have in the real world.

The readings and videos in each section discuss the stereotypes associated with gender, race, and class in American media. Although it might be easy to blame the media for negative images of a particular group, *the purpose of this section is not necessarily to place blame, but to think critically about these images and how they align (or do not) with the facts and our experiences.* When we think critically, we are more likely to understand ourselves and the world around us, which gives us more control over our own lives and choices, whether personal or political.

11.1.a Gender Stereotypes in the Media, *Diana Edelman-Young*

As we all know, the media are important forces that help shape our attitudes about the world. In fact, the media often contribute to our identity, our sense of who we are and how we fit into the world. One of the most powerful elements of our identity is our sex, a concept generally conflated with gender (the difference is explained more below). When a baby is born, we ask, "Is it a boy or girl?" Parents often look forward to a first ultrasound that will identify the baby as boy or a girl and even have "gender reveal" parties. If the baby is a boy, they will often choose more "masculine" colors for the room and decorate with sports or car themes. If the baby is a girl, they choose "softer" colors and decorate with dolls, flowers, or other "feminine" themes.

Ideally, sex should make no difference in how we think about and treat others; unfortunately, sometimes we make assumptions about people based on whether we see them as male or female. Example: Girls can't throw a ball. Boys shouldn't cry. How does this happen? When we see images of people in the media, even if they are fictionalized, we tend to take them for granted as accurate representations, particularly if we see the same representation over and over again. For example, if every image I see of a family includes a mom making dinner and dad coming home from work, I might tend to assume that a woman's primary role is in the home taking care of children while dad's job is to make money even if my own parents reverse or blur those roles in their day-to-day activities.

Gender stereotypes in the media also extend beyond male and female. Traditionally, American society has associated gender with biological sex, but increasingly, we have become aware that *sex and gender are two different concepts*. While sex is biological (male or female), **gender** is the cultural attitudes, behavior, and feeling associated with a sex. One's **gender identity** (male, female, transgender) can be formed regardless of biological characteristics. Gender identity should not be confused with sexual orientation, which will not be discussed here, but can be explored in other texts and courses. For many of you, your sex and gender are aligned, but for others they are not. *As stated in the introduction to this section, none of these three categories—gender, race, or class—are exhaustive.* This unit on gender begins with the two most recognizable concepts within gender—"masculine" and "feminine." This binary, however, is increasingly coming into question as the **LGBTQQIA** community finds a voice. LGBTQQIA stands for Lesbian, Gay, Bisexual, Transgender, Queer, Questioning, Intersex, and Ally Lesbian. This unit focuses on the concepts of **Masculinity** and **Femininity** in American culture, which is a place to start in discussing gender issues, but it is certainly not the end of the discussion. In fact, as you read, you will discover that even these fundamental concepts of maleness and femaleness are often socially and culturally constructed.

11.1.a(1) Exercises

The text and video in this section use some important terms such as "gender codes" and the "male gaze." As you read the article and/or view the video, jot down these and other terms and their definitions. Before answering any of the questions below, in groups (or on your own if the instructor prefers), identify key terms and develop your own definitions based on the reading, the video, and a basic internet search.

Your instructor may assign either the essay or the video or both. Your instructor will choose questions for the essay based on the material you cover in class or she/he may allow you to choose from the possible questions below. Before looking at the material, it is a good idea to read the questions to get a sense of what the content is and to have these ideas in mind before you start.

Texts

Craig, Steve. "Men's Men and Women's Women: How TV Commercials Portray Gender to Different Audiences." Originally printed in *Issues and Effects of Mass Communication: Other Voices* Ed. Robert Kemper. San Diego, CA: Capstone Publishers, 1992. 89-100. Print.
[This article is available online at https://humboldtcollege.wikispaces.com/file/view/mensmen.pdf.]

Films for the Humanities & Sciences. "Sexual Stereotypes in the Media."
Access Video On Demand. Films Media Group, 2008. Web. 7
Aug. 2014.
[This video is available through UNG's Films on Demand database at the UNG Libraries.]

11.1.b (2) Essay Questions

1) In his essay, Steve Craig describes four different character types that he noticed when watching commercials in the 1990s—men's men, men's women, women's men, and women's women. Choose a commercial that you believe includes one or two of these types. Usually, commercials geared towards men will include men's men and/or men's women. Commercials geared towards women will likely include women's men and/or women's women. For the commercial you have chosen, discuss in detail all the features of the ad that demonstrate that it fits Craig's pattern. If it deviates from that pattern, describe how it deviates and speculate about why that is (are gender codes changing, perhaps?).

2) Thinking about the categories that Steve Craig articulated, choose two or three advertisements that purposefully push the boundaries of traditional gender codes. Refer back to Craig's categories and then create your own category of character based on the advertisements you selected. Discuss all the features of these ads that contribute to your constructed category and this particular gender identity. You can use Craig's categories by way of contrast in order to assist you in your discussion of your new term. As you analyze the material, reflect on what this new category might mean about changing gender roles in society.

3) In this section, we have been discussing gender codes, the set of behaviors, characteristics, expectations, and traits associated with "masculinity" and "femininity" in American culture. Choose two recent commercials for the same product, one geared towards men and one geared towards women. Compare and contrast the commercials identifying how each targets its audience differently based on gender. Be sure to discuss in detail as many of the features of the commercial as you can—music, colors, characters, dialogue, text, time/date of airing, etc. As you analyze the advertisements, discuss the significance of these gender codes. In other words, why does this matter?

4) Choose a current commercial (within the last 5-10 years) and an older commercial (20 or more years ago) for the same product, geared towards either men or women. Compare and contrast the commercials in terms of how they target that gender. Be sure to discuss in detail as many of the features of the commercials as you can—music, colors, characters, dialogue, text, time/date of airing—identifying in particular anything that has changed since the older commercial. In other words, have gender codes changed since the first commercial? If so, how have they changed, and what do those changes suggest about the roles men and women play in society today?

5) View the documentary "Sexual Stereotypes in the Media" available for instant streaming via Films on Demand through the University of North Georgia Libraries. Around the 15-minute mark in the video, they discuss stereotypes of women and men. Girls are "sweet and pretty" whereas women are "soft and nurturing." The video states,

"[T]hese stereotypes don't appear hurtful or unkind, but they reflect gender bias that reinforces a harmful subtext. They tell women that you must please others before you can please yourself; that the closer you are to an idealized image of beauty, the happier you will be; that you are primarily an object of desire and sexual pleasure for men; and that an angry woman is hysterical or conniving."

Using some current print advertisements (magazines, billboards, or other ads), describe and analyze several examples of how these images are reinforced. Speculate about the effect these images might have on young girls and women.

6) According to the documentary, "for men, the message is different: showing emotion is a sign of weakness; you must be sexually potent to be successful; you are a failure if you don't accumulate wealth....You are defined by your car and other possessions...This idea of rugged masculinity, a term used by Teddy Roosevelt at the beginning of the century, translated into our modern idea of the buff, fit, young, clean shaven young man as the ideal man in American society." Using some current print advertisements (magazines, billboards, or other ads), describe and analyze several examples of how these images are reinforced. Speculate about the effect these images might have on young boys and women.

7) The video defines and discusses the following three terms: "stereotype threat," "agenda setting," and "mainstreaming." Think about whether you have experienced these phenomena. Then, interview some of your friends. In an essay, define these terms and then provide examples of when you and/or your friends have experienced these phenomena. As part of your thesis and as you discuss the examples, explain to what extent they have had a negative impact.

8) The documentary refers to John Berger's groundbreaking work Ways of Seeing in which he says, "men act and women appear." This is the theory of the "male gaze." Based on the video and some preliminary research, define the "male gaze." Then find several examples from magazines, billboards, or other advertisements that demonstrate this concept. As you discuss these examples, speculate about their effects on young girls and women.

9) Have you ever been in a situation where you were expected to act or think in a certain way based on your gender, but you did not? In an essay, narrate an experience or encounter in which you did not fit the "gender code," discussing what happened, how it made you feel, and how you responded.

10) In consultation with your instructor, feel free to choose a different selection, perhaps one that branches out beyond traditional gender categories and explores media representations of a group within the LGBTQQIA community. You and your instructor can devise a research question that addresses what interests you. Here is an example: Watch the television show Orange is the New Black on Netflix. After researching the word "lesbian" and identifying key terms and concepts associated with it (including the stereotypes), discuss the depiction of lesbians in the show. Do they fit the stereotypes? If not, what different characteristics do they demonstrate? Do you think the show reinforces or challenges lesbian stereotypes?

11.1.b Racial Stereotypes in the Media, *Diana Edelman-Young*

The previous section discussed gender stereotypes, what's "masculine" and "feminine" in American culture. As the introductory discussion demonstrated, even those basic distinctions are coming into question as a **gender spectrum** emerges. As the readings showed, much of what we take for granted as "male" and "female" is socially and culturally, not biologically, constructed. The same kinds of problems occur when dealing with racial identity; for although Latinos/Blacks/Asians/Immigrants/and all other race groups have, in actuality, as many different characteristics, personalities, class positions, jobs/careers as any other group, the media often presents stock images based primarily on limited (and limiting) stereotypes. Although there are many races one can discuss in this section, the selections focus on some of the most recurrent ones. Again, these selections are not meant to be exclusive, but to begin a conversation in which we come to understand the stereotypes proliferated in our culture. The critical thinking required here can be applied to any racial stereotype, even ones not specifically discussed.

The text in this section, by Michael Omi, uses some important terms such as "overt racism" and "inferential racism." As you read the article and watch the video, jot down these and other terms and their definitions. Just as before, prior to answering any of the questions, in groups (or on your own if the instructor prefers), identify key terms and develop your own definitions based on the reading, the video, and a basic internet search.

Your instructor may assign either the essay or the video or both (or something else altogether). Your instructor will choose questions for the essay based on the material you cover in class or she/he may allow you to choose from the possible questions below. Before looking at the material, it is a good idea to read the questions to get a sense of what the content is and to have these ideas in mind before you start.

Texts

Omi, Michael. "In Living Color: Race and American Culture." 14 May 2014. Web. 12 August 2014.
[This work is available as a PDF online at http://writeverse.files.wordpress.com/2013/04/inlivingcolor.pdf]

Films for the Humanities & Sciences. "Racial Stereotypes in the Media." *Access Video On Demand*. Films Media Group, 2008. Web. 12 Aug. 2014.
[This video is available through UNG's Films on Demand database at the UNG Libraries.]

11.1.b Essay Questions

1) According to Michael Omi, "overt racism" includes institutional policies and laws that exclude people of certain races whereas "inferential racism" is associated with the assumptions we make

about how certain races act, behave, dress, or think. Choose a particular race and identify the stereotypes associated with that race. Then, choose a film or television show that includes that race, discussing how the film or show perpetuates those stereotypes. In other words, find examples of inferential racism for that group in film and television. As you analyze the material, discuss the significance of these stereotypes for American culture and for the specific group represented.

2) Michael Omi claims that "popular culture has been an important realm within which racial ideologies have been created, reproduced, and sustained. Such ideologies provide a framework of symbols, concepts, and images through which we understand, interpret, and represent aspects of our 'racial' existence." Choose a particular race, and identify the stereotypes associated with that race. Thinking about the kinds of examples Omi gives in his article, choose 2-4 symbols or images from movies and television that you believe perpetuate the stereotypes associated with that race. Discuss in detail how these images represent the stereotype and what effect that has on American ideas about that particular race and on members of that race.

3) Watch the video "Racial Stereotypes in the Media" available in the Films on Demand database at the UNG Libraries. This video discusses stereotypes of Blacks, Latinos, Asians, Native Americans, and Arabs. Choose one of these groups and identify the stereotypes associated with each. Then, write an essay in which you provide several examples from recent films and television shows of these stereotypes. As you write this essay, speculate about the effects of those stereotypes on those groups and on others' attitudes towards them.

4) Watch a film or television show that features a particular race. Discuss how that race is portrayed in the film or show. Are the writers relying on a set of racial stereotypes? Are they breaking from a particular stereotype? Provide specific examples from the film or from various episodes of the television show. Speculate about why these portrayals are significant. If they reinforce stereotypes, how does that affect individuals in our culture? If they challenge the stereotype, what is the effect and why does it matter?

5) Have you ever been stereotyped? Write an essay in which you narrate an experience or encounter in which you were stereo-

typed. Give as much detail about the experience as possible so that your reader gets a sense of what happened and how it made you feel.

6) In consultation with your instructor, identify another reading or film (and/or another race not depicted above) and develop a new essay question topic.

11.1.c Stereotypes of Working Class Whites in the Media, *Diana Edelman-Young*

The previous two sections discussed gender stereotypes and ste-reotypes about minority cultures, such as Blacks, Latinos, and Asians, within the United States. Another rampant stereotype in American media is the working class white person. Although there are certainly a variety of races within the working class, one of the most ubiquitous stereo-types is the "redneck" or "white trash," which is often associated with the American South. Media images of "rednecks" and "white trash" are often accompanied by a Southern accent, but as you write about the characteristics associated with each, you will begin to see places where they might apply to other regions (and even socio-economic groups). As with the previous sections, this one narrows the focus to a particular stereotype that is immediately recognizable to most people. The readings and questions in this section are not meant to be exhaustive. Feel free, in consultation with your instructor, to identify another working-class stereotype represented in popular culture, perhaps one that addresses race and ethnicity as well.

The texts in this section use some important terms such as "redneck" and "white trash." As you read the articles, jot down these and other terms and their definitions. In groups (or on your own if the instructor prefers), before answering any of the questions, identify key terms and develop your own definitions based on the reading, the video, and a basic internet search.

Your instructor may assign one of the essays or both (or something else altogether). Your instructor will choose questions for the essay based on the material you cover in class or she/he may allow you to choose from the possible questions below. Before looking at the material, it is a good idea to read the questions to get a sense of what the content is and to have these ideas in mind before you start.

Texts

Heavner, Brent. "Redneck as a Slur in Print Media: A Cultural Analysis." *Conference Papers — International Communication Association* (2007): 1-29. *Communication & Mass Media Complete*. Web. 16 July 2014.
[This text is available as a PDF in Galileo through the UNG Libraries].

Price, Angeline F. "White Trash: The Construction of an American Scapegoat." University of Virginia. N.d., Web. 12 August 2014.
[This discussion is available at http://xroads.virginia.edu/~MA97/price/intro.htm]

11.1.c Essay Questions

1) On her web site, Angeline Price argues that "the hatred of the poor is an evil secret of America." Price then discusses two types of poor whites: "white trash" and "good country folk." Define these two terms, according to Price. Then, provide several examples from recent television shows or films that demonstrate the existence of these two types (or, with instructor permission, narrow your focus to one). As you do, consider the significance of these stereotypes. Why do they exist?

2) Using Angeline Price's "white trash" and "good country folk" definitions and examples, disagree with Price's analysis by providing examples of characters from film or television who do not fit these roles or who have traits of both. If the media presents characters who do not fit these roles, what does that mean for Price's argument? Does she overstate the case or are people's attitudes towards working-class whites changing?

3) In paragraph 3 of Brent Heavner's essay, he argues that the "redneck label works through four distinct but related discourses of space, race, class and culture." Choose one or two of these areas. Define what they are and how they function in American society, according to Heavner. Then, find multiple examples of this use of the redneck concept in the media. As you discuss these depictions, consider why these depictions exist and what effect they have on American attitudes towards race and class.

4) In recent years, reality television shows featuring real-life characters of working class whites, often Southerners, have emerged—Duck Dynasty, Moonshiners, Bayou Billionaires, Swamp People, and Here Comes Honey Boo Boo, to name a

few. Because these characters come from real life (and are not fictions drawn by Hollywood), it's more difficult to assess their roles in terms of American attitudes towards the working class. Write an essay in which you argue that shows like these either (a) reinforce class hatred/bias or (b) represent a positive shift in attitudes towards lower-class whites. You can, of course, argue that there are elements of both in these portrayals. As you write, speculate about the significance of these representations and the effect they have on the group's portrayed.

5) Watch a film or television show that features working class whites of different ethnicities than the ones presented from the South (e.g., the Irish dock worker in the classic film On the Waterfront starring Marlon Brando). In an essay, discuss how those working-class whites are portrayed. Using specific examples from the film or from episodes of the television show, analyze whether these characters are being stereotyped and whether they are being portrayed positively or negatively (or both). Discuss the significance of these portrayals in terms of attitudes towards the lower classes.

6) Have people ever made assumptions about you based on your class? Write an essay in which you narrate an experience or encounter in which someone wrongly assumed that you had certain traits or beliefs based on your socio-economic status. Give as much detail about the experience as possible so that your reader gets a sense of what happened and how it made you feel.

7) In consultation with your instructor, choose another reading that addresses another group within the working class that is not covered by the above readings and questions. Identify a film, television show, or other fictional representation of this group. Discuss how this group is stereotyped in the film or show. Where does this stereotype come from? What other media representations can you find of this group? Do these other representations reinforce or challenge the stereotype? What effect do you think this particular stereotype has?

11.2 DYSTOPIA, KAREN DODSON

A study of dystopia begins with an understanding of utopia, a word coined by Sir Thomas More in the title of his 1516 novella Utopia. More was embroiled in the political and religious intrigue of sixteenth-century England, when authors' works reflected the questions of authority in early modern society: Does the king speak for God? Who decides how human beings live? More's Utopia provided an image of a society in which all citizens work together for the good of the state; modern Marxists, therefore, eagerly appropriated More's idea of a commonwealth of shared responsibility, but no personal ownership of private property.

More's protagonist Raphael Hythloday relates his perception acquired in Utopia: "Unless private property is entirely done away with, there can be no fair or just distribution of goods, nor can the business of mortals be happily conducted" (36). Ironically, however, utopia means "no place," a name that suggests More believed such a country would never exist in this world.

Every dystopian society begins with utopia as its goal. In fact, dystopia (meaning "bad" place) can be defined as a utopian vision gone terribly wrong because the age-old question of authority arises when a perfectly functioning society must be closely controlled by someone or something in charge.

Dystopian works contain certain similarities:

- The purpose of a dystopian work is to warn contemporary readers of a horrific future that can be avoided only by current changes in the audience's own system.

- The setting is always futuristic and usually urban. Nature is considered a wild and forbidden place that cannot be monitored by the controlling powers.

- Historical information has been altered. A utopian experiment has led to a catastrophic event, the truth of which is only known by those in power.

- The protagonist is an anti-hero who begins as part of the system, comes to an epiphany about the truth of the dystopian situation, and rebels against it. Unfortunately, the protagonist's rebellion rarely overturns the system, and the narrative does not result in a happy ending.

- Dystopian societies are anti-motherhood and anti-family. Controlling powers seek to eliminate the familial bond and create beings who are loyal only to the state.

- Dystopian societies contain a caste system set up by those in power.

In a recent issue of Newsweek Global Alexander Nazaryan observes, "Utopia is illusory, but dystopia is all too real, a future more frightening even than the dreary present" (154). This frightening future can only be avoided with wise decisions of the present generation; unfortunately, history demonstrates, and dystopian novels illustrate, that concession in a present generation often proves easier than difficult decisions based on consequences for future generations. Utopia promises to give its citizens all they desire: dystopia forecasts the price for hubris and complacency.

Some critics dismissed dystopian novels in the twentieth century as "merely" science fiction fantasies, yet a recent wave of popular twenty-first century dystopian and post-apocalyptic works has emerged, suggesting that the implications of control in these works continue to concern modern audiences, and that these works thrive because of that concern. The new hero is one who stands up to resist the dystopian system or overcome the post-apocalyptic order.

11.6 Writing about Dystopia, *Karen Dodson*

When shaping a composition concerning dystopian literature, keep in mind that the themes are everywhere we look. Our favorite movies and television programs mirror the concerns taken up by authors for over 100 years. In the late twentieth-century and now in the twenty-first-century, writers have included post-apocalyptic visions, a look at the consequences of succumbing to the mind control inherent in dystopian works. Consider the popularity of The Hunger Games and The Walking Dead. The analysis of dystopian works of the past assists in understanding the popularity of modern stories with the same sinister themes.

11.6.a Exercises

1) Place your chosen dystopian work in historical context. Authors both reflect and influence the world in which they write.

2) Dystopian works are warnings to the general public about the consequences of absolute control. State the specific warnings in your chosen work.

3) Form an argument of the likelihood of these events coming to pass in our own culture. For example, Orwell's 1984 portends a society in which the political class keeps vigilant surveillance on its citizens, wherein "Big Brother is watching you." How does Orwell foreshadow the current debate in our country concerning liberty and security?

4) As you analyze the textual evidence in the work(s), consistently refer back to the author's intent. Answer the question for your reader: how and why did this utopian ideal go wrong?

11.7 Some Suggested Topics for Essays, *Karen Dodson*

1) Analysis of the work itself in the evolution of dystopian literature

2) Analysis of the work as foreshadowing the influence of media bias and propaganda

3) Analysis of the work's place in the history of censorship

4) Analysis of the work as a forewarning of educational mediocrity

5) Analysis of the work as foreshadowing political corruption

11.7.a Suggested (and Limited) List of Dystopian Authors and Works, *Karen Dodson*

(1895) H. G. Wells, *The Time Machine*
http://www.fourmilab.ch/etexts/www/wells/timemach/html/

(1921) Yevgeny Zamyatin, *We*
https://mises.org/books/we_zamiatin.pdf

(1932) Aldous Huxley, *Brave New World*
http://www.huxley.net/bnw/

(1945) Georgia Orwell, *Animal Farm*
http://www.george-orwell.org/animal_farm/index.html

(1949) George Orwell, *1984*
http://www.george-orwell.org/1984/

(1953) Ray Bradbury, *Fahrenheit 451*
http://kisi.deu.edu.tr/murat.goc/451.pdf

(1953) Arthur C. Clark, *Childhood's End*
(Not an open-access text)

(1954) William Golding, *Lord of the Flies*
http://gv.pl/pdf/lord_of_the_flies.pdf

(1984) William Gibson, *The Neuromancer*
(Not an open-access text)

(1986) Margaret Atwood, *Handmaid's Tale*
http://www.onread.com/book/The-Handmaid-s-Tale-191616/

(1992) P. D. James, *The Children of Men*
http://www.archive.org/stream/childrenmen00cogoog/children-men00cogoog_djvu.txt

(2009) Margaret Atwood, *The Year of the Flood*
(Not an open-access text)

(2013) David Eggers, *The Circle*
(Not an open-access text)

(2013) Chang-rae Lee, *On Such a Full Sea*
(Not an open-access text)

Grammar Handbook

Steven Brehe

In this chapter, we review basic terms and concepts of English grammar, terms that you will likely encounter in your English and Foreign Language courses, or in reference works like dictionaries. In the beginning, as we work with basic concepts, we'll keep examples simple, working up to more complex sentences as we go.

12.1 THE SUBJECT AND THE PREDICATE

We'll begin with **declarative sentences**, sentences that make a statement, instead of asking questions or giving orders. All of the examples you'll see in the next several sections are declarative sentences.

As we begin, it is helpful to know that declarative sentences in English usually follow this basic pattern:

Subject + Predicate

The subject comes first, and the predicate follows. The **subject** is the part of the sentence that names who or what the sentence is about. The **predicate** is the part that tells us something about the subject. Usually the predicate tells us what the subject is doing (or has done), or it describes the subject. These very simple sentences follow the simple **Subject + Predicate** pattern:

Subject	+	Predicate
Alice		fell.
Flowers		spoke.
Carroll		wrote.

As these sentences illustrate, the subject and the predicate can each be only one word, so it is possible to write a complete declarative sentence in just two words. In longer sentences, which we will see shortly, identifying the subjects and predicates of sentences becomes easy with practice.

12.1.a The Simple and the Complete

Every simple declarative sentence that we have seen contains a subject and a predicate, and usually the subject appears to the left of the predicate, at the beginning of the sentence or near it. In these cases the **complete subject** and the **complete predicate** are each just one word long. We can add more words to those subjects and predicates: We can add **modifiers**, words that describe the subject and the predicate:

Birds | *fly.*

Most *birds* native to the United States | *fly* well.

In this longer sentence, we call *birds* the **simple subject** and *fly* the **simple predicate**, we call *Most birds native to the United States* the complete subject, and we call *fly well* the complete predicate. That is, the simple subject with all its modifiers is the complete subject. And the simple predicate with all its modifiers is, of course, the complete predicate. (So, in *Birds fly*, the simple subject and the complete subject are identical, and so are the simple and complete predicates.)

Here are more examples, with the simple subjects and predicates in boldface:

A beautiful *day* like today | *is* a good time for a walk.

Mary's *cat* | *had* kittens yesterday.

A good *book* | *can make* a fine companion on a rainy day.

As the examples above show, some modifiers appear immediately before the word they modify: *A, beautiful, good, Mary's*. But modifiers can appear afterward, too, like: *today*.

In the next examples, we begin with the sentence *Irises grow*. In each example, the complete predicate is underlined; the rest of the sentence, the part not underlined, is the complete subject:

Irises | <u>*grow*</u>.

<u>Sometimes</u> *irises* | <u>*grow* well near the garage</u>.

<u>In the spring</u> *irises* | <u>*grow* well near the garage</u>.

Here again some modifiers of *grow* appear immediately before or after the word they modify: *well, near the garage*. And some modifiers of the predicate can even appear at some distance from *grow*: *Sometimes, In the spring*.

Here are some more pairs of sentences, with the simple subject and the simple predicate in *italics*. In each example, the complete predicate is <u>underlined</u>; the rest of the sentence, the part not underlined, is the complete subject:

Many *birds* in the U.S. | <u>*fly* south in the winter</u>.

<u>In the winter</u>, many *birds* in the U. S. | <u>*fly* south</u>.

Oscar Hammerstein | <u>*composed* songs rapidly in the winter of 1927</u>.

<u>In the winter of 1927</u>, *Oscar Hammerstein* | <u>*composed* songs rapidly</u>.

As you see in the second sentence of each pair, parts of the complete predicate can appear before the subject. This is a common sentence pattern, and we'll have more to say about it in later chapters.

12.1.b Transposed Order

In some sentences, it is possible to put the *entire* predicate before the subject; this is called **transposed order.** In the following sentences, the simple subjects and predicates are in *italics*, and the complete predicate is <u>underlined</u>:

<u>Softly *fell*</u> the *rain*.

<u>Gently *came*</u> the *dawn*.

<u>Into the quiet village *roared*</u> the *steam locomotive*.

Use transposed order with restraint, or it can become just a way of showing off with words.

In the next few chapters, we will learn more about subjects, predicates, and modifiers.

12.1.b Exercises

Answers to these exercises are in the back of the book. After you answer one set, check your answers before you go on—sometimes the answers will help you with the next set.

1) Write the definitions of the subject and the predicate.

2) In the following sentences, identify the simple subject and the simple predicate. Then identify the complete subject and the complete predicate. To help you, the simple predicate is <u>underlined</u>.

   a) Rain <u>falls</u>.

   b) Edward <u>knocked </u>at the door.

   c) In the morning, the family <u>ate </u>pancakes.

   d) In the morning, pancakes <u>seemed </u>like a good idea.

   e) Into the night, into the darkness, recklessly <u>rode</u> Rudolpho.

12.2 NOUNS AND VERBS

Nouns and verbs are two of the most basic and important concepts in grammar.

12.2.a Nouns

In the sentences we have seen, the simple subjects are all **nouns**. This traditional definition of nouns will serve our purpose: A *noun* is a word that names a person, place, thing, or idea.

- *Persons*: man, woman, child, children, student, teacher, Mr. Morton, Oscar Hammerstein.

- *Places*: kitchen, home, Main Street, St. Louis, Missouri, U.S.A., North America, Earth, solar system, Milky Way.

- *Things*: pen, ink, paper, printing press, telegraph, linotype, typewriter, computer, internet, cell phone.

- *Ideas*—that, is, abstractions: science, mathematics, truth, beauty, democracy, Platonism, Christianity, Catholicism, Scholasticism, Calvinism.

12.2.b Predicates and Verbs

In any sentence, the simple predicate is a **verb**—an indispensable part of English sentences. For our purposes, this definition will do: A *verb* is a word that names an action or indicates a state of being.

One kind of verb—an **action verb**—names actions. The great majority verbs in English are action verbs: *sit, stand, hit, run, hide, seek, say, sing, create, declare, pontificate, shout, cry, laugh,* and all the rest. Some action verbs name activities that are not actions in the usual sense: *pause, think, consider, wait.*

Gershwin <u>composed</u>.

George <u>loves</u> Ethel.

Pearl <u>painted</u> Mr. Morton's porch.

Another kind of verb names states of being. They appear in predicates that describe the subject. These verbs are called **linking verbs**.

Gershwin *was* a composer.

George *became* thoughtful.

Pearl *seems* busy.

There are relatively few linking verbs in English. The most common are the several forms of the verb *be*. *Be* has eight forms:

be	was
am	were
are	being
is	been

It is helpful to commit all the forms of *be* to memory, because you will need that information again and again throughout this chapter.

Here are some of the other linking verbs: *seem, become, remain.* Many linking verbs are related to our senses: *look, feel, smell, sound, taste, appear*:

> He *looked* angry.

> He *sounded* angry.

> He *felt* angry.

The examples of linking verbs may seem confusing because some verbs can be used as action verbs (*He appeared suddenly*) or as linking verbs (*He appeared ill*). To clarify the differences, consider the following pairs of sentences. The first sentence in each pair contains a linking verb in *italics*; the second contains an action verb underlined:

> Frank *felt* well.
> Frank felt the cold air.

> Marsha *looked* wonderful.
> Marsha looked out the window.

> The tomatoes *tasted* sweet.
> We tasted the tomatoes.

> Ed *remained* stubborn.
> Ed remained in his room.

In each pair, the first sentence, with the linking verb, describes the subject in some way, and the second, with the action verb, tells us what the subject did.

12.2.c Auxiliary Verbs and Main Verbs

Compare the verbs in these pairs of sentences:

> Mr. Morton broke the vase.
> Mr. Morton has broken another vase.

> Jeff sang an old Irish song.
> Jeff should have sung an old Lithuanian song.

Martha <u>won</u> the race.
Martha <u>should have been winning</u> all along.

In the second sentence of each pair, the simple predicate consists of more than one verb; in any sentence, the verb can be from one to four words long:

Mr. Morton <u>broke</u> the vase.
Mr. Morton <u>has broken</u> another vase.
Mr. Morton <u>has been breaking</u> vases all afternoon.
Mr. Morton <u>should</u> not <u>have been juggling</u> vases.

In any sentence with two or more words in the verb, the rightmost verb is called the **main verb**. (In the four sentences just above, *broke, broken, breaking,* and *juggling* are the main verbs.) All the other words in each verb are **auxiliary verbs** (sometimes called *helping verbs*). Together they make the *complete verb phrase*. Here is a list of the auxiliary verbs in English:

am	have	do	can	may
are	has	does	could	might
is	had	did	shall	must
was	having		should	ought (to)
were			will	
be			would	
been				
being				

You do not have to memorize this list, but you should refer to it often until you can recognize auxiliary verbs when you see them. The complete verb phrase is underlined. Remember that auxiliary verbs always come before the main verb. Also notice that *some* auxiliaries can be used as main verbs:

Rhianna <u>was planning</u> the party.   (*Was* is the auxiliary.)
Rhianna <u>was</u> early.   (*Was* is the main verb.)

The Browns <u>have purchased</u> the gift.   (*Have* is the auxiliary.)
The Browns <u>have</u> the receipt.   (*Have* is the main verb.)

The family <u>does like</u> to read.   (*Does* is the auxiliary.)

The family <u>does</u> the dishes every day.   (*Does* is the main verb.)

Still other auxiliaries in the list are used *only* as auxiliaries, as in these examples:

I *can* go	I *may* go.
I *could* go	I *must* go.
I *shall* go	I *might* go.
I *should* go	

Ought is an odd auxiliary, because it is always followed by a special form of the main verb called the *infinitive*, which usually begins with the word *to*. The entire verb phrase is underlined while the auxiliary and infinitive are italicized.

You *<u>ought to</u> <u>phone</u>*.
You *<u>ought to</u> <u>go</u>*.
You *<u>ought to</u> <u>leave</u>*.

We will spend more time on infinitives later, in section 12.14.

The auxiliary *do* is worth a bit of attention, because we use it in English for questions and for emphasis:

<u>Does</u> he <u>write</u> well?   *<u>Did</u>* he <u>arrive</u> early?

Yes, he *<u>does</u>* <u>write</u> well.   Yes, he *<u>did</u>* <u>arrive</u> early.

When you are learning another language and want to translate an English *do*-question or *do*-emphatic into your new language, you will find that other languages do not use their equivalent of *do* this way. Sometimes the complete verb phrase is interrupted by another word or two, and these usually appear after the first auxiliary verb:

Mr. Morton <u>has</u> actually <u>broken</u> another vase.

Mr. Morton <u>should</u> probably not <u>have been juggling</u> vases.

The Browns <u>will</u> definitely not <u>be inviting</u> Mr. Morton back.

The words that interrupt the verb phrase are always *adverbs*, which we will learn about shortly. And we will also return to the subject of verbs, which are often regarded as the most important part of the sentence.

12.2.d Exercises

In the sentences below, underline the complete predicates. Then enclose the simple subjects and simple predicates in brackets, like this:

[Sue] [did call] yesterday.

1) The family was having coffee.
2) Without warning, John entered the room.
3) John made an announcement.
4) The vases are gone.
5) The family became furious.
6) Mr. Morton had struck again.
7) Someday that man will regret taking vases.
8) Mr. Morton's reputation has been damaged by these allegations.
9) Everywhere people are hiding their vases.
10) Mr. Morton seems a little strange.

Now, in the sentences that you just examined, identify action verbs (with *A*) and linking verbs (with *L*), as in this example:

[Sue] [did call] yesterday. (A)

12.3 USEFUL, HELPFUL, DESCRIPTIVE—ADJECTIVES

12.3.a Modifiers and Phrases

As we saw in section 12.1, nouns and verbs often have **modifiers**, words that describe the noun, the verb, or other words. The following examples are not sentences, but only parts of sentences. Here *tree* is the noun; all the other words before and after *tree* are modifiers, and restrict the meaning of *tree* in some way:

The tree

The large tree *by the garage*

The beautiful tree, *tall and full*

As we have seen before, many modifiers appear immediately *before* the noun they modify: *large, beautiful.* But modifiers can appear afterward, too: *by the garage, tall and full.*

That brings us to a term that will be useful in this chapter: **phrase.** A phrase is *a word or group of words used as a single grammatical unit.* (This definition may not seem helpful yet, but it will.) The three examples above are **noun phrases.** They contain the noun *tree* and other words and phrases that modify *tree.* Each of those noun phrases could be used as a single grammatical unit—for example, as the subject of a sentence.

12.3.b Adjectives

Words like *large* and *beautiful* are **adjectives.** In the following phrases, all the underlined words are adjectives:

A great, big, beautiful doll
The silvery moon
The light brown hair

As these examples show, *adjectives modify nouns* (and sometimes pronouns) by describing the noun or placing limits on the word's range of reference. More simply, they describe nouns. Often the adjective names a quality of the noun: *tall, short, ripe, rotten, round, perfect, clean, dirty, blank, full, empty, old, new, ancient, medieval, modern,* and thousands more.

Color words are often adjectives: *a blue moon, green apples.* (But sometimes, in a different context, color words are nouns: *a dark blue, a vivid red.*). And numbers, particularly when they precede a noun, can be adjectives. But adjectives do not always have to precede a noun; they can appear immediately after it, as we have seen, or they can appear elsewhere in a sentence, as we will see in a later chapter.

12.3.c The Three Articles

There are only three **articles** in English: *a, an,* and *the,* always used to modify nouns. Some grammar books treat articles as if they are a separate class of words, but in this book we will consider them a small, special subset of adjectives. Articles are helpful in helping us recognize other adjectives. Consider this:

> *The* smaller child learned *the* simplest tasks.

When a word appears *between* an article and a noun, it is an adjective or another word functioning as an adjective.

There is some confusion about when to use *a* and *an*. Everyone knows that we use the article *a* before a word that begins with a consonant, and use *an* before a word that begins with a vowel, as in these noun phrases:

A child	An only child
A cheese omelet	An omelet

But readers are sometimes puzzled when they see *a* and *an* used in phrases like these:

> A union of concerned citizens
> An honor to serve you

So let's clarify the rules:

- Use *a* before a word beginning with a *consonant sound* (as in *a union* or *a child*).

- Use *an* before a word beginning with a *vowel sound* (as in *an honor* or *an only child*).

The important consideration is the first *sound* (not the first letter) in the word following the article.

Finally, *a* and *an* are called the **indefinite articles**, and *the* is the only **definite article**. This means that "the" can be used only when something has been specified or when only one exists.

> Give me the pencil he sharpened.
> The sun rises in the east.

12.3.d Comparisons of Adjectives

Some adjectives have three forms, which together make the *comparison* of the adjective:

Positive	**Comparative**	**Superlative**
hot	hotter	hottest
cold	colder	coldest
friendly	friendlier	friendliest
famous	more famous	most famous
suspicious	more suspicious	most suspicious
athletic	more athletic	most athletic

In any comparison of adjectives like these, there is a *positive* form of the adjective that simply names a quality the noun has: *hot, cold, friendly.* We use the *comparative* when we are comparing two—and *only two*—items, and we use the *superlative* when we are comparing *three or more*:

Positive: Susan is a *fast* runner.

Comparative: Susan is a *faster* runner than Alice.

Superlative: In fact, she's the *fastest* runner of all.

As we see in these sentences, when we are comparing one-syllable adjectives (and some two-syllable adjectives), we create the comparative and superlative forms by adding the suffixes *–er* and *–est.* (See the examples for *hot, cold,* and *friendly* in the table of comparisons above.) When we are comparing adjectives of three or more syllables (and some two-syllable adjectives), we create the comparative and superlative forms by placing the modifiers *more* and *most* before the adjectives. (See the examples for *famous, suspicious* and *athletic* in the table above.)

Some two-syllable adjectives, like those below, can take either kind of comparison:

happy, happier, happiest
happy, more happy, most happy.

often, oftener, oftenest
often, more often, most often

But many careful writers seem to prefer *happy, happier, happiest* and *often, more often, most often.* When in doubt about a comparison, turn to the dictionary. And never use both kinds of comparison on the same word:

INCORRECT: Ed is our <u>most hardest</u> working employee.

Some adjectives, those that describe absolute qualities, cannot be compared logically: We do not usually say *deader* or *deadest*, or *more pregnant* or *most pregnant*, unless we are kidding around. And it usually does not make sense to say *more full* or *more thorough*, or *most instant* or *most continuous*. But sometimes we ignore logic, especially in everyday conversation. *Unique* (meaning "one of a kind") is a well-known example. Logically, something is either unique or it is not, but people will still say things like this:

That tire swing in their living room is a *very unique* feature.

They mean that it is an *unusual* feature. But in everyday conversation (as opposed to professional writing), it seldom matters if you say *very unique* or *most unique*. And every now and then a careful writer will ignore all of these arguments and compare an absolute quality, and it works. The opening words of the Preamble of the United States Constitution are:

We, the People of the United States, in Order to form a *more perfect* Union. . . .

No one we know of has ever objected.

<u>12.3.e Points for Writers:</u>

1) A few adjectives have comparisons that do not follow the usual patterns: They are called **irregular adjectives**. They are some of the most commonly used adjectives, so you probably know most of them already:

Positive	**Comparative**	**Superlative**
bad	worse	worst
good	better	best
little	less	least
much (or many)	more	most
far	farther	farthest
	further	furthest

Far requires some attention: Traditionally *far, farther,* and *farthest* have been used to describe physical distance:

> He ran <u>farther</u> than I did.

Far, further, and *furthest* have been used in every other kind of situation:

> He went <u>further</u> in school than I did.

It is no surprise that many writers find this distinction unnecessarily complicated, especially because most Americans are not even aware of it. These writers argue that we need to settle on one set of comparisons for *far* and use it in all situations. But there is no clear consensus about this yet. We suggest that you observe this distinction in your professional writing unless an editor wants you to do something else.

2) Consider these sentences:

> I've heard Barbara and Stella sing.
>
> INCORRECT: Stella is the <u>best</u> singer.
>
> CORRECT: Stella is the <u>better</u> singer.

By the strict rules of usage, we should write *Stella is the <u>better</u> singer*, because we are only comparing two singers. Using the superlative form in a comparison of two is common in casual conversation, but avoid it in careful writing.

12.3.f Exercises

Give the comparative and superlative forms of these adjectives; use a dictionary when you need to. In some cases, there may be no comparative or superlative forms.

1) small
2) fast
3) bright
4) good

5) bad

6) curious

7) cheerful

8) happy

9) wrong

10) far (meaning anything except geographical distance)

12.4 INEVITABLY, ADVERBS

Adverbs are another important kind of modifier: Here is a definition that we'll refer to time and again: **Adverbs** are words that modify verbs, adjectives, and other adverbs. When adverbs modify verbs, they indicate *when, where, why, or how* the action was performed. (This is also a helpful definition to remember.)

Let's begin with the simple sentence *He ran. Ran* is a verb phrase, and we can expand the verb phrase by adding many adverbs:

He ran quickly.

Instead of *quickly*, we could use *slowly, clumsily, gracefully, erratically, fast, then, later,* and others. All the adverbs we can add to *He ran* answer this question: "When, where, why, or how did he run?" Common adverbs that modify verbs include *soon, later, now, then, before, after, here, there, forward, backward, badly, well, far, also, not*, and many others.

Remember the point we saw in an earlier chapter: When a word appears *between* an auxiliary verb and the main verb, it is an adverb that modifies the verb. When adverbs modify adjectives, they *modify the quality expressed* by the adjective:

The music seems very slow.

Instead of *very* (an overused adverb), we could write *quite, extremely, somewhat,* or *rather*. Here the adverbs answer the question, "How slow does the music seem?" When adverbs modify other adverbs, adverbs *modify the quality expressed* by the other adverb:

He ran quite quickly.

Instead of *quite*, we could write *somewhat, very, a bit, rather, more,* or *less*. Here adverbs answer the question, "How quickly did he run?"

Clearly adverbs are a diverse class of words; they have a wide range of uses and forms, as we will see.

12.4.a Comparisons of Adverbs

Some adverbs, like many adjectives, have three forms, which together make the *comparison* of the adverb:

Positive	Comparative	Superlative
close	closer	closest
fast	faster	fastest
early	earlier	earliest
warmly	more warmly	most warmly
generously	more generously	most generously
suspiciously	more suspiciously	most suspiciously

Here again, we use the positive when we are describing the action or quality of *one* thing, we use the comparative when we're comparing two (and only two), and we use the superlative when we are comparing three or more. A relatively small number of adverbs form comparisons with the *-er* and *-est* suffixes.

> Susan runs *fast*.

> Susan runs *faster* than Alice.

> In fact, she runs *fastest* of all.

The examples above show that some adverbs (like *fast*) resemble adjectives with little or no difference in spelling or pronunciation, but with the obvious difference in their use. This is obvious if we compare the three sentences above about Susan with the similar sentences we used in Chapter 3:

> Susan is a *fast* runner.

> Susan is a *faster* runner than Alice.

> In fact, she's the *fastest* runner of all.

With *fast* (and some words like it), the only feature that distinguishes the adverb *fast* from the adjective *fast* is the context. Most of the many adverbs that end with -*ly* use the *more* and *most* comparisons. Dictionaries can always help you find the right forms.

12.4.b Those Most Irregular Comparisons

There are also irregular adverbs—they do not follow the usual patterns. They are some of the most commonly used adverbs, so you know most of them already:

Positive	**Comparative**	**Superlative**
badly	worse	worst
well	better	best
little	less	least
much (or *many*)	more	most
far	farther	farthest
	further	furthest

The distinction between the two comparisons of *far*, the adjective, also apply to *far*, the adverb. (That word is far too troublesome.)

12.4.c Points for Writers

1) Adverbs that modify verbs are often moveable; they can be placed in several places in the sentence without changing the meaning:

Example 1	**Example 2**
Quickly Phil called the police.	Quietly the children hurried home.
Phil quickly called the police.	The children quietly hurried home.
Phil called the police quickly.	The children hurried home quietly.

Both underlined adverbs, *quickly* and *quietly*, obviously work in several places in the sentence. But moving *some* adverbs can change the meaning:

Only Mr. Morton broke the vase.
(Mr. Morton broke it by himself.)

Mr. Morton only broke the vase.
(He didn't do anything else to it.)
Mr. Morton broke only the vase.
(He didn't break anything else—yet.)

2) Writing for publication or other professional reasons, you must observe the distinction between good and well:

He is a good writer.
He writes well. (Never write *He writes good.*)

Good is an adjective. *Well* is sometimes an adverb and sometimes an adjective, depending on context. (It can be an adjective meaning *healthy*, as sentences like this: *Finally my son is well.*) It's hard to use *well* well.

Probably every American has confused *good* and *well* in casual conversation at one time or another, and it seldom matters. But readers and editors may assume you are a careless writer—that you do not write *good* (meaning *well*)—if you confuse them in your professional writing.

12.4.d Exercises

These exercises refer to matters you have read about in the last two sections. Do not hesitate to turn back to Section 12.3 if you need to review.

In the following sentences, mark the underlined words to classify them as adjectives (*ADJ*) or adverbs (*ADV*). Count the articles *a, an,* and *the* as adjectives. The adverbs here modify verbs only. Here are examples to help:

ADJ
This is <u>a pleasant</u> day.
ADJ   ADV
<u>The small</u> child runs <u>quickly.</u>
ADJ   ADV
<u>The other</u> child runs <u>faster.</u>

199

1) The child learns eagerly.

2) John almost had an answer to the difficult question.

3) Father always encourages realistic thinking.

4) The furious family did not wait to see the busy manager.

5) A thick, wet snow fell softly.

6) Silently, a strange man in a black cape stood in the shadows.

12.4.d (2) Exercises

Write the comparative and superlative forms of these adverbs; use a dictionary when you need to.

1) fast

2) quickly

3) slowly

4) angrily

5) carefully

6) well

7) badly

8) early

9) far (referring to geographical distance)

10) often

12.5 THE PERSONAL PRONOUNS

We have seen that nouns can be the simple subjects in sentences. There is another kind of word that can be a simple subject (and can play other roles in a sentence). It is the **pronoun**: a word that *takes the place of a noun that appeared earlier* in the context. Common English pronouns include *he, she, it, him, her, his, hers, its*, and others.

When a pronoun takes the place of a noun, the noun replaced is called the *antecedent* of the pronoun. The antecedent usually appears before (*ante-*) its pronoun. In the sentences that follow, the pronouns are underlined. Not all of them are subjects:

Gershwin composed.
He composed.

Gershwin is the antecedent of *He*.

George loves Ethel.   *George* is the antecedent of *He*.
He loves her.   *Ethel* is the antecedent of *her*.

Pearl painted Mr. Morton's porch.   *Pearl* is the antecedent of *She*.
She painted his porch.   *Mr. Morton's* is the antecedent of *his*.
She painted it.   *Porch* is the antecedent of *it*.

There are thousands of nouns in English, but only a few dozen pronouns, and those we use most are called the **personal pronouns.** All of the pronouns in the sentences above, and all that we discuss in this chapter, are personal pronouns—pronouns that indicate *person, gender, number* and *case.*

The following tables contain all of the personal pronouns in English, organized according to their several characteristics:

12.5.a Singular Personal Pronouns

	Nominative	Objective	Possessive
First Person	I	me	my, mine
Second Person	you	you	your, yours
Third Person	he, she, it	him, her, its	his, her, hers, its

Notice that in the third-person, these singular pronouns also have gender: *he, she,* or *it.*

12.5.b Plural Personal Pronouns

	Nominative	Objective	Possessive
First Person	we	us	our, ours
Second Person	you	you	your, yours
Third Person	they	them	their, theirs

Notice that most of the personal pronouns, singular and plural, have two forms in the possessive case. One possessive form goes before nouns (*my vase*, *your vase*). The other form is used in place of nouns (*Mine* is the best. No, *hers* is the best). The forms used in place of nouns all end with *–s* (except *mine.*)

The tables also show us that all personal pronouns are classified by *number*. They are either singular or plural.

All personal pronouns are also classified by *person*. If you're referring to *yourself* with pronouns, you use **first-person** pronouns: *I, me, my,* and *mine,* or the plural forms *we, us, our(s)*. If you are referring to the person you are speaking with, you use **second-person** pronouns: *you* and *your(s)*. The plural forms are the same, *you* and *your(s)*. Lastly, if you are referring to another person outside the conversation, you use **third-person** pronouns:

> *he, she, it;*
> *him, her, it;* and
> *his, her, its* (or the plurals *they, them, their,* and *theirs*)

The third-person singular pronouns are also classified by gender: **masculine, feminine, and neuter.**

Finally, we classify personal pronouns by cases: the **nominative case**, the **objective case**, and the **possessive case**. These terms are used all the time in discussions of language, so it is helpful to understand them. They refer to the forms of the pronouns that we use in certain positions in a sentence.

The pronouns in the **nominative case** are the ones we use as subjects:

> I talked to Mr. Morton.
> You talked to Mr. Morton.
> He talked to Mr. Morton.
> She talked to Mr. Morton.
> We talked to Mr. Morton.
> They talked to Mr. Morton, too, but he is still juggling vases.

The pronouns in the **possessive case** are used to indicate possession, and most of the possessive pronouns have two forms:

> Hey, that's my vase. (Or, That vase is mine.)
> Hey, that's your vase. (Or, That vase is yours.)
> Hey, that's his vase. (That vase is his.)

Hey, that's <u>her</u> vase. (Or, That vase is <u>hers</u>.)
Hey, that's <u>our</u> vase. (Or, That vase is <u>ours</u>.)
Hey, that's <u>their</u> vase. (Or, That vase is <u>theirs</u>.)

Notice that there are no apostrophes in the *–s* possessives. This rule frequently confuses inexperienced writers.

The pronouns in the **objective case** are used for almost every other purpose in a sentence, purposes we will study later:

Give <u>me</u> that vase. Give it to <u>me</u>.
Give <u>her</u> that vase. Give it to <u>her</u>.
Give <u>him</u> that vase. Give it to <u>him</u>.
Give <u>us</u> that vase. Give it to <u>us</u>.
Give <u>them</u> that vase. Give it to <u>them</u>.

If we are native speakers of English, we typically use the correct cases naturally, out of habit. But, if you need it, you can learn this simple test sentence to help you remember the three cases of pronouns:

N took *O* to *P's* house.

Here, *N, O,* and *P* stand for the three cases: nominative, objective, and possessive. Insert the right pronoun in each position, and you will know the case of the pronouns in question:

He took *her* to *their* house.
They took *us* to *her* house.
We took *them* to *his* house.

The personal pronouns are the most important pronouns in English. We will examine other kinds later.

12.5.c Points for Writers

1) Use pronoun gender carefully: The third-person singular pronouns (*he, she, it,* and the others) can be troublesome. Consider this passage:

Each physician should submit *his* credentials to the hospital's human resources department. Each nurse must submit *her* credentials, too.

In the past, these sentences may have been completely acceptable to most readers and editors. As you know, they are *not* acceptable today. Most readers and editors object to the apparent assumption that all physicians are men and all nurses are women. Today the usual way to avoid this problem, and the way we recommend in most cases, is to make the sentence plural:

> <u>All physicians and nurses</u> must submit <u>their</u> credentials to the hospital's human resources department.

> Or the pronoun can be deleted altogether:

> <u>All physicians and nurses</u> must submit credentials to the hospital's human resources department.

Other ways, like the use of *his or her* or *his/her*, are possible, but some editors disapprove of them.

2) Avoid pronoun ambiguity: Used carelessly, pronouns can be confusing.

> CONFUSING: The speaker discussed the causes of the recession, but I didn't understand <u>it</u> at all.

> BETTER: In his speech, <u>the speaker</u> discussed the causes of the recession, but I didn't understand <u>him</u> at all.

> Or

> BETTER: The speaker discussed the causes of the recession in his <u>speech,</u> but I didn't understand <u>it</u> at all.

These three sentences demonstrate the importance of selecting the right pronouns for your context. This is called **pronoun agreement**. When writers neglect pronoun agreement, they often confuse their readers.

Here are two more examples of pronoun ambiguity: In these sentences, what is the antecedent of *she*?

Sally's mother has collected dolls since *she* was twelve years old.

Sally told her mother that *she* was too old to play with dolls.

In both sentences, *she* could be referring to Sally or Sally's mother. The reader should not have to guess. It is usually easy to rewrite the sentences to avoid ambiguity:

Since the age of twelve, Mrs. Sue, Sally's mother, has collected dolls.

Thinking that her mother was too old to play with dolls, Sally told her so.

(Sally is asking for trouble.)

3) Maintain a consistent point of view. That is, do not change pronouns unnecessarily: Consider the confusing point of view in this paragraph:

When *you* have worked with adolescents for a few months, *we* know what to expect. People who work with adolescents quickly learn what problems *they* will encounter in most situations. *You* get to know how *they* think.

Do not shift point of view without a good reason. In general, use third person or, when reasonable, first person, or a careful combination of first and third. Here is an improved version of the same paragraph:

After *you* have worked with adolescents for a few months, *you* will know what to expect. *You* will quickly learn what problems *you* will encounter in most situations. *You* will get to know how *they* think.

In general, avoid second-person pronouns (*you* and *your*) except in personal communications like letters and emails, or in instructions like the passage above.

4) Some pronouns are overused. Using *they, you,* and *it* vaguely can be a symptom of careless writing:

FLAWED: *They* don't allow *you* to build fires in the city park.

CORRECT: *The city* doesn't allow *anyone* to build fires in the city park.

FLAWED: *It* says in the letter from the City Council that *your* band, Noise Pollution, is banned from performing in the city limits.

CORRECT: *The City Council's letter* says that *your* band, Noise Pollution, is banned from performing in the city limits.

12.5.d Exercises

In this exercise, you need to write five versions of the same short sentence. Each version will use a different pronoun.

First read the pronouns in the parentheses after each sentence. Then, for each pronoun, find the correct case to insert into the blank. Consult the pronoun tables in this chapter if you need to.

Example:

Give the book to _____. (I, he, we, they, she)

Give the book to <u>me</u>.
Give the book to <u>him.</u>
Give the book to <u>us</u>.
Give the book to <u>them.</u>
Give the book to <u>her</u>.

As you can see, to complete the sentence, you needed the *objective case* for each of the requested pronouns (*I, he, we, they, she*).

Use the *objective* case in these sentences:
1) You can go with _____. (I, he, we, they, she)
2) We will take _____ to the mall. (he, she, they, you)

Use the *nominative* case in this sentence:

    3)   _____ can go with me. (him, her, you, them, us)

Use the *possessive* case in these sentences:

    4)   That book isn't yours. It is _____. (I, he, we, they, she)

    5)   We won't go to your place. We'll go to _____ place. (I, he, we, they, she)

Write the pronoun that is specified by the terms. Usually only one pronoun is possible for each exercise. Consult the pronoun tables when you need to.

Example:

> First-person nominative singular: *I*
> Second-person possessive: *your, yours*
> Masculine third-person objective singular: *him*

1) First-person objective singular:

2) First-person objective plural:

3) Second-person nominative singular (or plural):

4) Feminine third-person nominative singular:

5) Third-person nominative plural:

6) Third-person objective singular:

7) Third-person objective plural (masculine):

8) First-person nominative plural:

9) First-person possessive singular:

10) Neuter third-person nominative singular:

12.6 PREPOSITIONS

Prepositions are short, simple, and remarkably useful words. We use prepositions to create modifying phrases called **prepositional phrases**.

With prepositions we can connect a noun phrase or a pronoun—called the **object of the preposition**—to another word in a sentence. The preposition and its object together make the prepositional phrase. A prepositional phrase usually modifies a noun or verb, but it can also modify an adjective or adverb.

Here are some examples of prepositional phrases. The prepositions are underlined, and the rest of the words in each phrase are the objects of the prepositions:

beside our house	*to* our house
on the roof	from the roof
in the room	*by* the room
on the screen	*after* dinner
for your birthday	*with* her

As you can see, prepositions usually *precede* their objects—they are *pre-positioned* before the objects.

When pronouns are the objects of prepositions, they are always in the objective case—and any native English speaker usually uses the objective case intuitively in a prepositional phrase:

I gave the book to Julie. I gave it to *her*.

Mike said that I can ride with *him*.

There are relatively few prepositions in English (about sixty or so). If you read over this list a few times, it will be easier to recognize prepositional phrases:

aboard	before	except	over
about	behind	for	past
above	below	from	per
across	beneath	in	regarding
after	beside	into	since
against	between	like	through
along	beyond	near	throughout
amid	but	of	till
among	by	off (but not *off of*)	to
around	concerning	on	toward
as	despite	onto	upon
at	down	out	under
atop	during	outside	underneath

until	upon	within
up	with	without

Some of the words in this list can serve other functions, as we'll see. Usually prepositional phrases are used as adjectives or adverbs—that is, they are used *adjectivally or adverbially*. Adjectival prepositional phrases usually follow the nouns they modify. The following sentences contain adjectival prepositional phrases, which are italicized:

> The dog *in the yard* barked loudly.
> I read the first *of three volumes.*
> This is my letter *to the principal.*

In each of the sentences above, the prepositional phrase modifies the noun it follows.

In these sentences, the **adverbial** prepositional phrases are italicized:

> I arrived *at noon.*
> I drove *into the garage.*
> I walked *for exercise.*
> I walked *at a fast pace.*

As adverbs, these prepositional phrases tell us *when, where, why, or how* the action of the verb was performed.

We learned earlier that adverbs modifying verbs are often movable. In the sentences below, we see that some of the italicized adverbial prepositional phrases are also movable:

> The dog barked loudly *in the yard.*
> *In the yard*, the dog barked loudly.

> Little Ruthie practiced the violin *for two hours.*
> *For two hours*, little Ruthie practiced the violin.

> Mr. Lochenhocher would rather listen *to the dog.*
> I've heard Ruthie play, and I'm *with Lochenhocher.*

Notice that we cannot move the adverbial prepositional phrase in the last two sentences. Sometimes the guidelines for discerning adverbial and adjectival phrases don't work as well as we would like. Here is another example:

We drove the car *into* the garage.

"Into the garage" follows *car*, but the phrase obviously does not modify *car*. Here the prepositional phrase is *adverbial*; it answers the question, "Where did you drive the car?" But this adverbial phrase is *not* moveable: We probably would not write

Into the garage, we drove the car.

When we are trying to identify the function of the prepositional phrase, the most important point to consider is the meaning of the phrase: Is it describing the noun or is it describing the action?

12.6.a Two-Word Prepositions

Two-word prepositions consist of (can you guess?) two words used as a one-word preposition. (Some grammar books call these *phrasal prepositions*.) In these prepositional phrases, the two-word prepositions are underlined:

except for me	according to the Bible	out of flour
as for me	because of her	instead of coffee
up to me	owing to the weather	

Some grammar books mistakenly identify the following phrases as prepositions:

ahead of	next to	contrary to
together with	alongside of	

In fact, *ahead, next, contrary,* and the others are adjectives or adverbs (depending on context) followed by one-word prepositions. Here the prepositional phrases are adverbial, modifying the adjectives and adverbs:

We are ahead of them.
We are next to them.
Events were contrary to expectations.
We went together with Anne.
We pulled alongside of the truck.

Some books classify the following three-word phrases (and a few others) as prepositions:

> by means of   in back of   in case of
> in charge of   in front of   in search of

But these are better analyzed as a series of two prepositional phrases, as in these examples:

> She is *in* front | *of* the audience.

> Call me *in* case | *of* an emergency.

So we will claim that *prepositions are never more than two words long.* But do not be surprised if you encounter other grammar books that recognize some three-word phrases as "phrasal prepositions" or "compound prepositions."

12.6.b Points for Writers

1) Use objective-case pronouns as objects: Sometimes you see nominative-case pronouns used as objects of the prepositions:

   INCORRECT: Between he and I, we'll get the job done.

   INCORRECT: Give the responsibility to her and I.

   But the nominative case is never right in this position. Always use the objective case as the object of the preposition:

   Between him and me, we'll get the job done.

   Give the responsibility to her and me.

   In both sentences, the plural pronoun *us* would usually work better, but sometimes we need to use both pronouns.

   By the way, there is no *grammatical* reason to put *me* or *I* last in the sentences above; it is a matter of courtesy.

2) Should you end a sentence with a preposition? One of the best known rules of prescriptive grammar insists that we must never end sentences with prepositions. But in fact, good professional writers do it all the time.

But you should be aware that, in formal contexts, some writers and editors regard sentences like the following as too informal or just plain wrong:

He is the person <u>who</u> I want you to give this <u>to</u>.

This sentence is troubling for at least three reasons: First, the preposition *to* is no longer before its object, *who*. Second, the preposition and its object are widely separated. Third, by the strictest rules of grammar, *who* should be *whom*. Some editors and supervisors of writers would prefer this version of the sentence:

He is the person <u>to whom</u> I want you to give this.

Because of the use of *whom*, other editors might find this version excessively formal for some contexts and readers. Usually we can rewrite the entire sentence to eliminate the problem:

Give this to him.

or

He is the person who should get this.

12.6.c Exercises

In the following sentences <u>underline</u> the prepositional phrases and <u>double-underline</u> the preposition. Some sentences contain more than one prepositional phrase. If you need to, refer to the lists of prepositions in this chapter.

1) In the morning, I drink coffee with cream.
2) As a rule, I never put sugar in it.
3) Amid cars and trucks, Edwina ran across the street.
4) I am looking for the owner of this dog.

5) Do you mean the dog that is attached to your leg?

6) Throughout the book, the author emphasizes the influence of history upon our perception of events.

7) Like Arthur, I walked down the hall and paid no attention to the noise within the office.

8) According to Arthur, the noise out of the office was because of an argument between Ed and Grace.

9) Arthur should not have been left in charge of the office during the summer.

10) In case of further conflicts, we should make plans regarding appropriate training for all employees.

12.7 CONJUNCTIONS AND COMPOUNDS

Like prepositions, conjunctions are connecting words. Broadly defined, conjunctions join one word or group of words with a similar word or group of words. There are two kinds.

12.7.a Coordinating Conjunctions

Coordinating conjunctions *create compound structures*: They connect two or more *grammatically equivalent* units of language: a word with a word, a phrase with a phrase, and one sentence with another sentence.

I gave him time *and* money.	(noun *and* noun)
I gave promptly *and* generously.	(adverb *and* adverb)
The white *and* blue car is there.	(adjective *and* adjective)
I saw Bill *and* told him the news.	(predicate *and* predicate)

Here are a few sentences with **compound subjects**; the conjunctions (*and* and *or*) are in italicized, and one of the sentences contains a three-part compound subject:

You *or* I have to clean up this mess.

Mark Twain, Damon Runyon, *and* J.R.R. Tolkien are three of Sam's favorite authors.

All the king's horses *and* all the king's men are having egg sandwiches.

These sentences contain compound verbs:

We <u>hiked, swam *and* sailed</u> until dark.

You <u>can behave *or* leave</u>.

I will <u>sit *and* think *and* write</u> all afternoon.

Here are sentences with compound prepositional phrases:

We can't find the dog <u>in the house *or* in the yard</u>.

<u>In the spring, through the summer, *and* into the fall</u>, we work in the garden.

All the compound structures above depend on just two coordinating conjunctions: *and* and *or*. In fact, there are only seven coordinating conjunctions in English, so it is convenient to memorize them:

for	but
and	or
nor	yet
so	

There is a well-known mnemonic (a memory aid) for remembering these conjunctions: The first letters of these seven words spell the word *FANBOYS*. Also remember that the *FANBOYS conjunctions*, the coordinating conjunctions, are words that create compound structures by joining two or more grammatically equal parts.

12.7.b The Compound Sentence and the Clause

These seven conjunctions can also join two or more sentences together to create a **compound sentence**, and for that larger sentence we select the conjunction that best communicates the relationship between the two parts that we are connecting.

Each of the two original sentences can also be called a **clause** (see Section 12.9 for a definition of *clause*). Each of the following is complete sentences, and each contains only one clause:

You will have to behave yourself.
You will have to leave.

With a coordinating conjunction, we can combine these two sentences into a single sentence that contains two clauses:

You will have to behave yourself, *or* you will have to leave.

The following are more compound sentences containing two clauses (the last one contains three), all joined by coordinating conjunctions.

You have to leave, *for* you are not behaving yourself.

You are not behaving yourself, *so* you will have to leave.

Now you're behaving yourself, *but* you have to leave anyway.

You're behaving yourself now, *yet* you have to leave, *and* you can't come back.

The coordinating conjunction *nor,* when used to construct a compound sentence, is a bit unusual, because it often requires a special word order: In the second clause, *nor* makes an **auxiliary verb** move to a position *before* the subject:

We do not want you to stay, nor *do* we want you to return.

You may not stay, nor *may* you return.

In these examples, *nor* makes the auxiliaries *do* and *may* shift to the left of the subjects (*we* and *you*).

12.7.c Correlative Coordinating Conjunctions

Correlatives are a special subclass of coordinating conjunctions. There are just four:

  either . . . or
  neither . . . nor
  both . . . and
  not only . . . but also

As you see, these correlative coordinating conjunctions consist of two parts, and the second part always contains one of the *FANBOYS conjunctions*: *or, nor, and,* and *but.* You have probably used them many times:

> *Either* Fred *or* George should clean up their mess.

> *Neither* Fred *nor* George cleaned up their mess.

> *Both* Fred *and* George are jerks.

> Fred and George are *not only* jerks, *but also* idiots.

(Correlative conjunctions are *very* useful.)

Use *not only . . . but also* carefully. Some inexperienced writers use the structure too often, or in ways that seem to imply that the first element of the compound structure is less important than the second portion:

> She is not only a physician, but also a classical violinist.

> He is not only a Lutheran minister, but he is also a professional wrestler.

If we do not want to minimize the importance of being a physician or a minister, we should rewrite these sentences and leave out the *not only* part:

> She is both a physician and a classical violinist.

> He is a Lutheran minister, and he is also a professional wrestler.

In the second sentence, *and also* is simply a coordinating conjunction accompanied by the adverb *also*.

12.7.d Subordinating Conjunctions

Subordinating conjunctions are the largest group of conjunctions; there are about thirty or so. These conjunctions are used *only* to connect one sentence to another to make a single longer sentence with two (or more) clauses. And the new sentence has qualities that we do not find in the compound sentences created by the coordinating conjunctions.

The subordinating conjunction always appears at the beginning of one of the clauses, and the clause begun this way is a **subordinate clause**.

Lists of the subordinating conjunctions vary a bit from one reference book to another, but the following list is reasonably complete. These are the one-word subordinating conjunctions:

after	that
although	though
as	till
because	unless
before	until
if	when
lest	whenever
once	whereas
since	whether
than	while

Here are sentences that each contain one subordinate clause, which is underlined, with the conjunction in italicized:

He left *because* he wanted to leave.
I'll go *when* I'm ready.
We'll let you know *if* she calls.

Subordinate clauses are adverbial, so many of them can be moved to another part of the sentence, and they often appear at either the beginning or the end of the sentence:

Because he wanted to leave, he left.
When I'm ready, I'll go.
If she calls, we'll let you know.

Notice that you cannot do the same thing with clauses joined by *coordinating* conjunctions. You can certainly use a coordinator to join two coordinate clauses:

He was ready to leave, *so* he left.

But you cannot move the second clause, with the conjunction, to the beginning of the sentence:

INCORRECT: *So* he left, he was ready to leave.

The movability of subordinate clauses is a helpful feature: It helps us identify subordinate clauses, and it gives writers more options in arranging sentences.

The following are **correlative subordinating conjunctions**, pairs of words that work together for the same purpose as one-word subordinating conjunctions:

> as . . . as
> so . . . that
> the . . . the

We use the correlative subordinators like this:

> I'll be there *as* soon *as* I can.
> He was *so* impatient *that* he slammed the door.
> *The* more he does that, *the* less I like him.

Some subordinating conjunctions are more than one word: *as if, as though.*

> You should act as if you know what you're doing.
> You should study as long as you need to study.

We will discuss subordinate clauses more in the next chapter.

12.7.e A Note about Conjunctive Adverbs

The following words appear often in our reading, writing, and speaking:

therefore	however
moreover	nevertheless
thus	hence
indeed	in fact

These words (and others like them: *consequently, furthermore, instead, meanwhile,* and more) indicate some connection between the clauses they appear in and previous clauses:

> He has been late three times this week; *therefore,* I don't consider him reliable.

> She has been late three times this week; *however,* she is usually reliable.

218

These are **conjunctive adverbs,** sometimes called *transitional adverbs*, are *adverbs that vaguely resemble conjunctions,* because they indicate a relationship between the *ideas* of *two clauses.*

But they are *not* conjunctions: They cannot—by themselves—join the two clauses into a compound or complex sentence. (That is, the connection indicated by conjunctive adverbs is one of ideas, not grammatical structure.) This condition affects punctuation. Notice the use of semi-colons—not commas—above.

In each example, we could use periods instead of semi-colons. We can tell that these words are adverbs and not conjunctions because they are moveable in many contexts:

> She has been late three times this week; *however,* she is usually reliable.

> She has been late three times this week; she is, *however,* usually reliable.

We typically cannot move a true conjunction around in its clause, as we can move these conjunctive adverbs. If *however* were a subordinating conjunction, it would have to remain at the beginning of the clause it introduces.

Notice, too, that in the second sentence, the placement of *however* after *is* creates a pause that emphasizes the following words *usually reliable.*

In other words, conjunctive adverbs have at least two rhetorical uses: to indicate transition from one idea to the next, and (in some cases) to emphasis words that follow the adverbs.

Sometimes *however* is used in ways that are not conjunctive, to modify adjectives or adverbs:

> You must pay the fee, <u>however</u> unreasonable.
> School children, <u>however</u> young, can learn responsibility.

12.7.f Points for Writers

1) **Variations on Compound Structures:** Sometimes writers choose to omit the conjunction (usually *and*) from compound structures. Carefully used, this unusual practice can make the compound structures more emphatic. Consider these series of compound phrases:

   > This project will require *hard work, unwavering attention, total dedication.*

"... government *of the people, by the people, for the people,* shall not perish from the earth."

Be warned: If you use this variation several times in a single short work, it ceases to be effective and simply becomes distracting or annoying.

Another variation is to use the conjunction *and* to join each part of a compound structure with the next part, to emphasize that all the parts are of equal importance:

This project will require hard work *and* unwavering attention *and* total dedication.

Again, do not overuse this pattern.

Sometimes, when we have several compound sentences, we can improve sentence variety by omitting the conjunction in a two-clause sentence and replacing it with a *semicolon*:

Edward excels at school, for he devotes hours every week to studying.

Edward excels at school; he devotes hours every week to studying.

You have probably noticed in your reading that that just one coordinating conjunction can create a compound sentence of three, four, or more parts:

A coordinating conjunction can join a sentence of two clauses, it can create a sentence of three or four clauses, *and* in rare cases it can be used in a sentence of even five clauses.

2) **Compound Subjects and their Verbs:** Compound subjects take singular or plural verbs, depending on the conjunction or, in some cases, the right-most subject. Look at these three examples:

Bob *and* Ray *are* assisting.
Either Bob *or* Ray *is* your assistant.
Either Bob *or* the <u>twins</u> *are* your assistants.

The *and* in the first example means that the subject, *Bob and Ray*, is plural, so you need a plural verb: *are*.

The *or* in the second example means that the subject, *Bob or Ray*, is singular, so you need the plural verb: *is*.

In the third example, the plural subject, *twins*, is the subject closest to the verb. In this case, you need the plural verb, *are*. If the compound subject were reversed—*either the twins **or** Bob*—the verb would be singular: *is*.

So the third example is grammatically correct, but it sounds awkward to many readers. We can usually improve an awkward sentence like this by rewriting it:

BETTER: Either Bob or the twins will assist you.

12.7.g Exercises

1) Try to write, from memory, the seven coordinating conjunctions. (A hint: Remember *FANBOYS*.) Check your answers with the list in this chapter.

2) Try to write, from memory, the four correlative coordinating conjunctions. Check your answers with the list in this chapter.

12.7.g (1) Exercises

In the following sentences, underline and classify the conjunctions as coordinating (c) or subordinating (s), and put brackets around any prepositions. Refer to the lists in this chapter and the previous chapter if you need to. Classify correlative conjunctions as coordinating. Here is an example:

[In] the following sentences, underline <u>and</u> (c) classify the conjunctions [as] coordinating <u>or</u> (c) subordinating, <u>and</u> (c) put brackets [around] any prepositions.

1) The film was not only boring, but also offensive, so we asked for a refund and went home.

2) In the morning and again in the evening, Ruthie practices her violin until her mother can't stand it anymore.

3) We went to the diner for lunch, for we were expected back soon.

4) Because I am tired, I'll take a short break before I continue studying.

5) Fred and George have been gone since Friday night, since they took a "short break" from studying.

6) After I finish this project, we can meet after work and discuss the project.

7) Frank and George are neither punctual nor organized, yet they somehow do their work well.

8) He was so confident that he underestimated his opponent.

9) The room looked as if it had not been occupied in some time, but it had been occupied for days or weeks.

12.8 VERBS AND COMPLEMENTS

In many sentences, **complements** are an important part of the predicate: They are called complements because they *complete* the verb. For example, all these sentences are obviously incomplete:

> Ralph seemed.
> Alice gave.
> Ed is.

The verbs here (*seemed, gave,* and *is*) need another word (or more) to complete their meanings, and that is where complements come in. For example:

> Ralph seemed impatient.
> Alice gave him his present.
> Ed is the neighbor.

The underlined words are complements—nouns, pronouns, or adjectives that complete the verb in some way.

12.8.a Predicate Adjectives

Earlier we discussed two kinds of verbs: *linking verbs* and *action verbs*. We said that the relatively small number of linking verbs in English include *seem, become, appear, looked, felt*, and forms of the verb *to be*.

All linking verbs require complements. In these sentences, the complements are underlined:

> Ben is <u>kind</u>.
> The staff appears <u>efficient</u>.
> All of his sisters are <u>musical</u>.

Notice that each of these underlined words is an adjective that follows the verb, and each describes the subject of the sentence. Such a complement is called a **predicate adjective**. Here are some more sentences with predicate adjectives:

> This chapter looks <u>easy</u>.
> He seems <u>friendly</u>.
> They became <u>calm and quiet</u>.

(The last sentence above contains a compound predicate adjective.)

12.8.b Predicate Nominatives

Predicate nominatives are nouns or pronouns that follow linking verbs and describe the subject. In these examples, the predicate nominatives are underlined:

> George became <u>President</u>.
> Helen was <u>a teacher</u>.
> We are also <u>teachers</u>.

In each sentence, the noun phrase following the linking verb identifies the subject of the sentence. Here are more examples:

> Ralph became <u>president of our club</u>.
> Norton is <u>a menace</u>.
> The Browns are <u>good neighbors and good citizens</u>.

(The last sentence before contains a compound predicate nominative.)

Some grammar books combine predicate adjectives and predicate nominatives into a single category called the **subject complement**.

12.8.c Direct Objects

We have discussed action verbs before, but here we learn a bit more about them. There are two kinds of action verbs, **transitive** *and* **intransitive verbs.** *Transitive* verbs *have* complements; *intransitive* verbs *do not need* them. The sentences that follow contain intransitive verbs— no complement is present:

> The accountant disappeared.
> It rained today.
> Rain fell all day.

Some intransitive verbs, like *disappeared,* typically do not take complements in any context.

Transitive verbs *always* take one or more complements, and the most common kind of complement is a **direct object**, a noun or pronoun that typically follows the verb and in some way is the object of the verb's action:

> Susan <u>saw *them*</u> at the mall.
> June <u>addressed *the audience*</u>.
> Ed <u>baked *the cake*</u> yesterday.

Here are more examples:

> Ed <u>wrote *the article*</u>.
> The newspaper <u>published *the article and Ed's photos*</u>.
> Mr. Lochenhocher <u>wants *peace and quiet*</u>.

Many verbs can be transitive or intransitive: That is, they can be used with or without direct objects:

> Intransitive: I'll run to the store.
>   She read for two hours.
>   He laughed.
>   She sang.

> Transitive: I run <u>the store</u>.
>   She read <u>the book</u>.

He laughed <u>a hearty laugh</u>.
She sang <u>an Irish song</u>.

12.8.d Indirect Objects

Indirect objects appear only in sentences with direct objects, and then they appear *between* the verb and the direct object. They name a person or thing that *receives* the direct object in some way. In the following sentences, the indirect objects are <u>underlined</u> and the direct object is *a note*:

Bailey *wrote* <u>me</u> *a note*.
Ed *wrote* <u>her</u> *a note*.
We *wrote* <u>Bailey and Ed</u> *a note*.

Here are more sentences with indirect objects followed by direct objects:

Mr. Redden *taught* <u>me</u> *history*.
Last night I *read* <u>my daughter</u> *a book*.
We *bought* <u>Ruthie</u> *an accordion*.

Remember that the indirect object *always* appears between the verb and the direct object.

There is a test for the indirect object: The indirect object can be turned into a prepositional phrase beginning with the preposition *to* or *for* without changing the meaning of the sentence. The prepositional phrase then appears *after* the direct object:

Mr. Redden taught history <u>to me</u>.
Last night I read a book <u>to my daughter</u>.
We bought an accordion <u>for Ruthie</u>.

But please notice the important difference: This sentence has an indirect object:

Mr. Redden taught <u>me</u> history.

The next sentence has *no* indirect object; *to me* is a prepositional phrase:

Mr. Redden taught history to me.

Some transitive verbs can take direct objects but cannot take indirect objects, as in these sentences:

Ned ate the cake.

Julie wanted cake.

Mr. Lochenhocher hates the accordion.

12.8.e Object Complements

The **object complement** is the fifth and last kind of complement for a transitive verb. Here are some examples:

We elected Bernice <u>president</u>.

We made Bob <u>treasurer</u>.

The news made Mr. Lochenhocher <u>angry</u>.

Object complements are nouns or adjectives that *follow* the direct object and *describe* the direct object, in the same way that a predicate adjective or predicate nominative describes the subject. We do not distinguish between the adjectives and the nouns that describe the direct object—they are all object complements if they appear after the direct object and describe it. Here are more examples:

She made her room <u>beautiful</u>.

We made Bill <u>president</u>.

We made the essay <u>better</u>.

Only a small number of transitive verbs can take object complements, and a sentence can never contain both an indirect object and an object complement.

It is important to distinguish object complements from other complements. In the following pairs of sentences, the first sentence contains an object complement and the second contains a different structure that is identified in the bracketed comments:

They found Will <u>irritable</u>.

They found Will in the dining hall.

[*In the dining hall* is a prepositional phrase]

They made Bill <u>an officer</u>.

They made Bill a cake.

[Here *Bill* is the indirect object; *cake* is a direct object.]

<u>12.8.f Exercises</u>

In the following sentences, fill in the blanks with one word: *always, never,* or *sometimes.*

1) Sentences with action verbs _____ have a complement.
2) Sentences with linking verbs _____ have a complement.
3) Sentences with intransitive verbs _____ have a complement.
4) Sentences with transitive verbs _____ have a complement.

<u>12.8.f (2) Exercises</u>

In the sentences below, identify the complements and classify them as a direct object, an indirect object, a predicate adjective, a predicate nominative, or an object complement. Remember that some sentences will have two complements, but never more than two. In the first six sentences, the complements are underlined.

1) My daughter made <u>me proud</u>.
2) My aunt brought <u>me a souvenir</u>.
3) My sister is <u>late</u>.
4) Both my sisters are <u>teachers</u>.
5) Alice became <u>upset</u>.
6) Six hours a day, Ruthie practices <u>the accordion</u>.
7) We sent Bill and Sue a gift.
8) They were kind and grateful.
9) I will address that issue at another time.
10) That fellow became our assistant.
11) Bonnie bought Ed that painting.
12) Edward and Phil are reckless.

Now go back through the sentences above and identify the verbs as linking, transitive, or intransitive.

12.9 CLAUSES AND SENTENCES

Previously we learned about conjunctions that join one clause to another. Now we can finally define some of the most important terms in grammar: the independent clause, the dependent clause, and the sentence.

A **clause** is a unit of language that contains *at least one subject and at least one predicate*. There are two general kinds of clauses in English.

An independent clause contains at least one subject and at least one predicate, *and it contains no word* (like a subordinating conjunction) *that makes the clause dependent on another clause* to be complete. (That is, it contains no word like a subordinating conjunction.) It is grammatically complete by itself, without the addition of other clauses.

A dependent clause contains at least one subject and at least one predicate, *and it is not grammatically complete by itself.* In most sentences, it functions as part of an independent clause. Dependent clauses include the subordinate clause (which contains a subordinating conjunction), and other kinds of dependent clauses that we will learn about soon.

According to these definitions, this is an independent clause:

We went to the museum.

But if we add a subordinating conjunction to it, it is a dependent clause that needs to be connected to part of a larger sentence:

After we went to the museum. . . .

A subordinate clause is a type of dependent clause: It contains at least one subject and one predicate and it's connected to an independent clause *by a subordinating conjunction*. The clause above ("After we went to the museum . . .") is a subordinate clause.

Notice the difference between dependent clauses and subordinate clauses: A subordinate clause is one kind of dependent clause. This is a distinction that some grammar books and foreign language textbooks do not make.

Finally, this is the definition of a **sentence**: *A sentence is a unit of language that contains at least one independent clause.* It may also contain one or more dependent clauses. (Like most definitions of a sentence, this one would not satisfy most linguists, who are a notoriously argumentative bunch, but it will do for our purposes.)

With these definitions, we can go on to this well-known four-part classification of sentences, based on their structures:

Simple
Compound
Complex
Compound-Complex

You have probably encountered them before:

Simple: A simple sentence *contains just one independent clause*:

I went to the garage.

A simple sentence can have a compound subject, a compound predicate, or other compound structures. The following sentence contains compound structures, but it is only one independent clause:

Alphonse and I went to the garage, found his car, and drove it home.

Compound: A compound sentence *contains two or more independent clauses joined by one or more coordinating conjunctions* (which are italicized in the examples that follow):

I went to the garage, *and* I found my bike.

Complex: A complex sentence *contains one independent clause and one or more dependent clauses*. Here the dependent clause is joined to the rest of the sentence by a subordinating conjunction (also italicized):

I went to the garage *because* I needed my bike.

Compound-Complex: A compound-complex sentence *contains two or more independent clauses joined by one or more coordinating conjunctions, and one or more dependent clauses*. Here, the dependent clause is joined to the independent clause by a subordinating conjunction:

I went to the garage *because* I needed my bike, *and* I found it.

There is a fifth kind of sentence that is not really a sentence at all: It is a **fragment sentence**, *a structurally incomplete sentence*, and there are many ways to write them. Here is one:

I went to the garage *and* I found my bike. *Because* I needed it.

The second sentence is a fragment; it is simply a subordinate clause that is punctuated like a sentence. We use such fragments all the time in conversation, and usually no one objects.

But in careful writing; we should avoid fragments unless we are deliberately using them for emphasis. And, even then, we should use them with restraint. What if we combine two fragments? The following consists of two subordinate clauses, punctuated like a complete sentence:

When he finally arrives, if the plane is on time.

Combining two (or three or more) dependent clauses still make a fragment sentence, and this kind of fragment is never acceptable.

12.9.a Another Classification

There is another way to classify sentences: according to their purposes. Even in these classifications, sentence structure and punctuation are important. As we have seen, **declarative sentences** make a statement. They usually have the *subject* + *predicate* structure we have examined (subject first, predicate second), and they usually end with a period:

I am in trouble.

Interrogative sentences ask a question; they may begin with a question word (*Who? What? When? Where? Why? How?*) or with a verb. They typically end with a question mark:

Why do these things always happen to me?
Do things like this ever happen to you?

Sometimes, especially in conversation and written dialogue, interrogatives are just a word or two that make sense in context (we hope):

What? Why?
Who, me?

Interrogatives can also be statements that end in tag questions:

You forgot your books, didn't you?
I won't need them, will I?

An imperative sentence is a command, and it may end with a period or an exclamation mark, and it may be missing a subject:

Get out of here!
Go!
Scram!
Get lost!

Often the missing subject in an imperative sentence is an implied second-person pronoun, *you*:

[You] Get out of here!
[You] Stop that!

Commands can be phrased more politely, but they are still imperatives:

Please don't do that.

Exclamatory sentences express strong emotion. They have no distinctive structure or end punctuation. They are often incomplete sentences, or just a word or phrase:

No!
Don't!
Oh, that's just *great*.
What the heck?

(Someone is having a bad day.)

12.9.b Reflecting on Sentence Types

The four classifications we have just examined illustrate how inadequate simple terms and concepts are to analyze what language can do. In some cases, because language is capable of explicit and implicit meanings, sentences don't clearly fit in any single category; they may have meanings quite different from their explicit purpose.

Suppose a teacher in a classroom says to a student,

You look puzzled.

In that context, this declarative sentence may contain an implicit interrogative: *Do you have a question?*

Or suppose the teacher says to a student in the back row,

"I'm watching you."

That could be an implicit imperative, meaning *Stop what you're doing! Behave yourself!* The teacher might imply the same imperative idea with a question: *Did you have something to say?*

12.9.c Points for Writers

1) **Beginning Sentences with Conjunctions:** You may have learned in school that writers should not begin a sentence with the subordinating conjunction *because*, like this:

Because Linda was late for school, she left home hastily.

In fact, this is a perfectly good complex sentence. But you should not do this:

INCORRECT: Because Linda was late for school. She left home hastily.

As we saw earlier, a subordinate clause has to be connected to an independent clause unless you are deliberately writing a fragment.

You can also begin sentences with coordinating conjunctions, but do not overdo it. We have done it twice elsewhere in this chapter.

But you should not do this.
And, even then, we should use them with restraint.

The initial conjunction connects the idea of the sentence to the preceding sentences—it helps to create **paragraph coherence**. It also contributes to a somewhat less formal tone, which is desirable in some contexts.

A sentence that begins with a coordinating conjunction is *not* a fragment sentence. It *is* a stylistic variation that should be used with restraint.

232

2) Commas in Compound Structures: When a sentence contains a compound phrase of two parts, commas are usually not necessary:

My brother and your sister are planning a party.

When there are three or more parts in the compound structure, we typically use only one conjunction to join them all, and commas separate the parts:

My brother, your sister, and their friends are planning a party.

The second comma in the sentence above is often referred to as the "Oxford comma." Some writers prefer to omit this last comma in a series; just be sure that if you do so, you are not leaving your sentence's meaning open to confusion.

As you may have noticed in the examples earlier in this chapter, in compound sentences we use a comma to mark the end of every independent clause except the last:

Now you're behaving yourself, *but* you have to leave anyway. You're behaving yourself now, *yet* you have to leave, *and* you can't come back.

When the two clauses are short and simple, we can omit the comma:

I am angry and I am leaving.

When the clauses are long and complex, the commas separating the clauses become more important; they help the reader understand where one clause begins and another ends.

When a subordinate clause begins the sentence, the comma separates the subordinate clause from the independent clause, unless the subordinate clause is brief and the sentence is unambiguous without the comma:

Because I could not stop for Death, I hid behind a tree. (Emily Dickinson, improved.)

The sentences below challenge our comprehension (at least a little) because they each need a comma to mark the end of a subordinate clause. Read these sentences and decide where the commas should go:

> Because you've already eaten dinner at our house tonight will be postponed.
> After you've eaten the dog should be fed right away.

Yes, we *deliberately* wrote these sentences to be difficult without the comma. But such sentences do occur in our everyday writing. Commas in these cases are important because they clarify the structure of the sentence for the reader. (If you have not worked it out, both of those last two examples needs a comma after *eaten*.)

12.9.d Exercises

Go back to the beginning pages of this chapter and reread the definitions of an independent clause, a dependent clause, and a sentence. Then try to write the three definitions from memory, and use the book to check your work.

Classify the following sentences according to their structures: Each sentence will be simple, compound, complex, or compound-complex. Refer to the definitions in this chapter when you need to. Here are a few points to help you:

- Pay attention to punctuation, which often helps.
- Watch for conjunctions of all kinds; don't confuse prepositions with conjunctions.
- Remember that a compound phrase of some sort (like a compound subject or compound direct object) may be in a sentence that does not have compound structure.
- Finally, there is at least one fragment sentence here that cannot be classified any other way. Classify every incomplete sentence you find as a fragment.

1) My family owned a cocker spaniel when I was young.
2) Before the meeting, we will set up the room, and you should prepare the refreshments.

3) Before the meeting begins, we will set up the room, and you should prepare the refreshments.

4) He has done well since graduation, and he credits his success to the university.

5) As if he is the supervisor.

6) Since graduation, when he began working here, while Arthur was the supervisor of both departments.

7) Louise and Sharon went to the garage and found their car.

8) Either we find a way to solve this problem ourselves, or we must seek help.

9) Both spring and fall are their favorite seasons for camping in the mountains and fishing.

10) We sat nervously as we waited for our interviews.

11) During our interviews, we occasionally answered poorly, but in general we did well.

12) After we left the office, we returned, for Louise had forgotten her portfolio.

12.10 RELATIVE CLAUSES

In this chapter we learn about another kind of dependent clause, the **relative clause**. There are two kinds of relative clauses, and the first kind we'll examine is based on the relative pronouns.

12.10.a Relative Pronouns

These are the **relative pronouns**:

who
whom
whose
which
that

Whom is the objective form of *who*, and *whose* is the possessive form of *who*. Committing these five relative pronouns to memory will help you recognize relative clauses.

As you will see in the examples below, relative pronouns begin relative clauses. The relative clauses are underlined:

The man <u>who spoke to you</u> is my uncle.
My uncle is the man <u>whom you saw</u>.
The woman <u>whose car you hit</u> is my neighbor.
The car, <u>which is a total wreck</u>, is a Chevrolet.
The car <u>that you hit</u> is a Chevrolet.

Relative clauses *modify nouns* in a sentence. They cannot be shifted around like subordinate clauses, but always appear immediately after the nouns they modify.

Relative pronouns play two roles in a sentence. First, relative pronouns *connect their own clause to another clause*, which is usually independent. Second, as pronouns, they *stand in for nouns*: That is, the relative pronoun appears in the relative clause, and the antecedent of the pronoun is in the independent clause. The antecedent is always the noun modified by the relative pronoun.

Let's begin with two brief independent clauses:

1) You want the job.

2) The job is part-time.

With a relative pronoun, we can replace the words *the job* in Sentence 1 with a relative pronoun, creating a relative clause. Then, after changing the word order, we can embed that clause into the middle of Sentence 2:

The job *that* you want is part-time.

The words *that you want* make up the relative clause, which we have made part of Sentence 2, which is an independent clause.

As you have just seen, with relative pronouns we can combine two independent clauses into one sentence. The resulting sentence has one independent clause and one relative clause embedded inside the independent clause. (And, of course, the sentence can contain more than two clauses.)

As the example above shows, the relative clause is adjectival; the relative clause modifies *job*. Relative clauses are *always* adjectival and always follow the nouns they modify.

Here's another example, using *who*. (To review use of *who* and *whom*, or the principles of *nominative* and *objective* case, see Section 12.5.) We will begin with two independent clauses:

1) That man is my uncle.
2) That man talked to you.

Now we use *who* to replace *that man* in Sentence 2; then we embed the resulting relative clause into the middle of Sentence 1:

That man <u>*who* talked to you</u> is my uncle.

Here is another example, using *whom*:

1) The man is my uncle.
2) You saw the man.

Again we replace *the man* in Sentence 2 with *whom* and combine the clauses:

The man <u>*whom* you saw</u> is my uncle.

Here are some more sentences with relative clauses. The relative clauses are underlined and the relative pronouns are in bold:

I got the job, <u>*which* is part-time</u>.
I borrowed the broom from the woman <u>*whose* house I rent</u>.

Relative pronouns can also be the objects of prepositions. In that case, the relative pronoun appears just after prepositions in the relative clause:

There is the man <u>to *whom* you must speak</u>.

In all of these examples, and any others we might find, we see the same features of the relative clause built with relative pronouns:

1) The relative pronoun appears at or near the beginning of the relative clause.
2) The relative pronoun stands in for the modified noun, which is always the antecedent of the relative pronoun.
3) The relative clause follows the antecedent—that is, it follows the noun it modifies. (This means that relative clauses *cannot* appear at the beginning of a sentence, as subordinate clauses can, but only in the middle or at the end.)

4) The relative pronoun must be in the correct case for the function it performs in the relative clause.

12.10.b Relative Adverbs

There are just two relative adverbs, *when* and *where*, and, like the relative pronouns, they help us form relative clauses that are adjectival. (Yes, it seems odd that an adverb is the basis of an adjectival clause, but wait and see.)

The relative adverbs *when* and *where* are like relative pronouns in other ways: They seem to refer back to a noun earlier in the sentence, and they begin the clause they introduce. We use *when* to begin a relative clause that modifies a word related to *time*:

> I have to finish this paper by noon, <u>*when* it is due.</u>
> The year 1929, <u>*when* the stock market crashed,</u> is the subject of this new book.

In each case, the relative clauses are underlined, and *when* is an adverb in the relative clause. *When* refers to the time word (*week*, *1929*) that is modified by the relative clause.

We use *where* to create a relative clause that modifies words that have to do with *places*:

> Her favorite city is Atlanta, <u>*where* she was born.</u>
> Marshfield, Missouri, <u>*where* astronomer Edwin Hubble grew up,</u> is a pleasant small town.

In each sentence, the relative clause modifies the place word (*Atlanta* and *Marshfield, Missouri*) that precedes the relative adverb.

Here are some more examples:

> This is a month <u>*when* temperatures are low.</u>
> I know a store <u>*where* we will find that book.</u>
> This is the time of year <u>*when* days get shorter.</u>
> I know a spooky old house <u>*where* ghosts, werewolves, and my old high school teachers have been seen.</u>

In this section, all the sentences containing relative clauses are complex sentences, with one independent clause and one dependent clause.

12.10.c Points for Writers

1) **Omitted relative adverbs:** Sometimes, in casual writing and conversation, the relative adverbs *when* and *where* are left out:

> This is the time of year <u>days get shorter.</u>
> This is the month <u>temperatures are low.</u>
> I know a place <u>we can find that new book.</u>
> Don't do this in formal writing.

2) **Troublesome relatives:** Some grammar books include *why* among the relative adverbs:

> I know the reason <u>*why* he left.</u>

But sentences like this are considered redundant, because we can usually delete the modified noun (*reason*, above) without losing any information:

> I know <u>*why* he left.</u>

In this new sentence, *why he left* is not a relative clause, but a different kind of dependent clause that we'll learn about soon.

3) **More troublesome relatives:** (You know, it's *difficult* to get rid of troublesome relatives.) Notice the ambiguous use of *which* in this sentence:

> The senator said he believed that the general will resign, and the newspaper published an editorial agreeing with what the senator said, <u>*which* disappointed me.</u>

Using pronouns of any kind in long sentences often confuses the reader, who often cannot tell what the precise antecedent is. (In the example above, what does *which* refer to? It is impossible to be certain.) This is an important point of usage because clarity is always important.

4) Who and that: Compare these two sentences:

I'll speak with the man <u>who</u> runs this place.
I'll speak with the man <u>that</u> runs this place.

We use both versions in informal communication. In formal writing, however, some writers and editors prefer to use only *who* to refer to people. It is a simple rule to remember and follow, so why not follow it?

12.10.d Exercises

Underline the relative clauses in the following sentences. Double-underline the relative pronouns. Locate the nouns modified by each relative clause and enclose them in square brackets, as in this example:

We took that bin of recyclables to the [agency] <u>that collects them.</u>

Remember that some uses of *that* are not relative pronouns. You will see an example here.

1) The house that is being renovated was my grandmother's home.
2) Please get the book, which I left in my office.
3) You can give that letter to the man who is waiting outside.
4) The woman whose car you dented wants to speak to you.
5) The man who is waiting already has that letter that you left in your office.
6) The customer whom you phoned is waiting in the office.
7) I know the man to whom they spoke.

12.10.d (1) Exercises

Underline the relative clauses in the following sentences. Double-underline the relative adverbs. Locate the nouns modified by each relative clause and enclose them in square brackets, as in this example:

Yesterday my father drove by the [house] <u>where he was born.</u>

1) The house where he was born is on Fifth Street.

2) In April 1943, when he was born, his parents were living and working in the city.

3) Spring is the season when I am happiest, and home is the place where all of us are most comfortable.

4) Marceline, where Walt Disney grew up, is a small town in north-ern Missouri.

5) Disney left Marceline in 1917, when his family moved to Chicago.

12.11 MORE ON VERBS

We return to verbs to learn more about these important words.

12.11.a Tense: The Simple Tenses

One of the many pieces of information verbs can communicate has to do with time: In the right context, verbs communicate that the action took place in the present, past, or future:

SIMPLE PRESENT:	Today I <u>phone</u> my mother.
SIMPLE PAST:	Yesterday I <u>phoned</u> my mother.
SIMPLE FUTURE:	Tomorrow I <u>will phone</u> my mother.

This quality of communicating information about time is called **verb tense**, and English has *three* **simple tenses** (shown above): the simple present, simple past, and simple future. Here are more examples of sim-ple tenses:

SIMPLE PRESENT:	Today I <u>talk</u>.
SIMPLE PAST:	Yesterday I <u>talked</u>.
SIMPLE FUTURE:	Tomorrow I <u>will talk</u>.

SIMPLE PRESENT:	Today I <u>build</u>.
SIMPLE PAST:	Yesterday I <u>built</u>.
SIMPLE FUTURE:	Tomorrow I <u>will build</u>.

As these examples illustrate, in the great majority of English verbs, the simple past tense is created by adding -*d* (as in *phone*) or -*ed* to the pres-ent form—or in a few cases, -*t* (as in *built*).

In absolutely all verbs, the simple future is created with the auxiliary verb *will*.

12.11.b Tense: The Perfect Tenses

English sentences are capable of containing four different tenses, and the perfect tenses are the next set we'll examine.

The **perfect tenses** refer to an action that has been completed (that is, *perfected*) or will be completed by a particular point in time. Verbs in the perfect tenses always take the auxiliary verb *have* or its variants (*has* or *had*). The future perfect tense also has the auxiliary *will*. Here are some examples:

PRESENT PERFECT: Today I have walked.
PAST PERFECT: Yesterday I already had walked.
FUTURE PERFECT: By this time tomorrow I will have walked.

PRESENT PERFECT: Today I have built.
PAST PERFECT: Yesterday I already had built.
FUTURE PERFECT: By this time tomorrow I will have built.

If you compare the main verbs in these perfect tense sentences with the main verbs in the simple past, you will see that they are exactly the same words. This is an important point that we will return to when we discuss regular and irregular verbs.

12.11.c Tense: The Progressive Tenses

The **simple progressive tenses** refer to an action that is in progress at a particular point in time. The main verbs in the progressive tenses always end in *–ing*, and they always take an auxiliary verb that is a form of the verb *be*. The future progressive tense always begins with the auxiliary *will*. Here are some examples:

PRESENT PROGRESSIVE: Today I am phoning.
PAST PROGRESSIVE: Yesterday I was phoning.
FUTURE PROGRESSIVE: Tomorrow I will be phoning.

PRESENT PROGRESSIVE: Today I am hunting.
PAST PROGRESSIVE: Yesterday I was hunting.
FUTURE PROGRESSIVE: Tomorrow I will be hunting.

PRESENT PROGRESSIVE: Today I am building.
PAST PROGRESSIVE: Yesterday I was building.
FUTURE PROGRESSIVE: Tomorrow I will be building.

Notice that we drop the final *–e* in *phone* and other verbs ending in *–e* when we add *–ing*.

In the **perfect progressive tense**, the last tense we will examine, the main verb is still an *–ing* form, and it always contains *both* a form of *have* and a form of *be*. (And, of course, the future perfect progressive contains *will*.)

PRESENT PROGRESSIVE:	Today I <u>have been phoning</u>.
PAST PROGRESSIVE:	Yesterday I <u>had been phoning</u>.
FUTURE PROGRESSIVE:	Tomorrow I <u>will have been phoning</u>.
PRESENT PROGRESSIVE:	Today I <u>have been hunting</u>.
PAST PROGRESSIVE:	Yesterday I <u>had been hunting</u>.
FUTURE PROGRESSIVE:	Tomorrow I <u>will have been hunting</u>.
PRESENT PROGRESSIVE:	Today I <u>have been building</u>.
PAST PROGRESSIVE:	Yesterday I <u>had been building</u>.
FUTURE PROGRESSIVE:	Tomorrow I <u>will have been building</u>.

12.11.d The Three Principal Parts

Most English verbs have highly consistent verb forms that we use to create the four tenses we have just examined. These are called the **regular verbs** because the form to create the past tense and perfect tenses are identical.

That is, in both the simple past tense and the perfect tenses, we add *–d*, *–ed*, or (in a few cases) *–t* to the verb. No other change in spelling or pronunciation happens.

So we speak of *three principal parts* of the verb: the **present**, the **past**, and the **past participle** (the form used with *have* for perfect tenses). These are usually presented in a table like this:

present	**past**	**past participle**
I talk	I talked	I have talked
I hunt	I hunted	I have hunted
I phone	I phoned	I have phoned
I build	I built	I have built

Notice the relatively new verb *to phone*. Newly created English verbs are nearly always regular: *fax, faxed; text, texted; friend, friended.* (But there is an exception: *We hung out at the mall.*)

When we speak of a *fourth* principal part, it is always the **present participle**, the *–ing* form used for progressive tenses: *talking, hunting, phoning, building.*

Irregular verbs are less consistent in their past and past participle forms, and although there are only several dozen of them in English, they are among the most commonly used verbs. Here are some of them:

present	**past**	**past participle**
I begin	I began	I have begun
I break	I broke	I have broken
I bring	I brought	I have brought
I drink	I drank	I have drunk
I fly	I flew	I have flown
I know	I knew	I have known
I ride	I rode	I have ridden
I ring	I rang	I have rung
I see	I saw	I have seen
I speak	I spoke	I have spoken
I swim	I swam	I have swum
I swing	I swung	I have swung

All of us make errors now and then with some of the irregular verbs, and it is a good idea to identify those that give you the most trouble and study them. The table above gives you some of the most troublesome irregulars, and you can find complete lists in many grammar books and on the Internet. A dictionary can always help you with particular verbs. Here are a few verbs that require special attention.

The verb *dive* is not necessarily irregular:

I dive	I dived	I have dived

(Note that *dove* is correct also and employs the irregular version of this verb. Both the regular and the irregular versions of this verb are correct.)

The verb *burst* is super-regular. It doesn't change at all:

I burst	I burst	I have burst

There are three pairs of verbs that are often confusing:

I <u>sit</u> down.	I <u>set</u> the books down.
I <u>lie</u> down.	I <u>lay</u> the books down.
I <u>rise</u> up.	I <u>raise</u> the books up.

In the left column, the verbs indicate the way you are positioning *yourself.* In the right column, the verbs indicate the way you are positioning the books (or anything else separate from you).

It is easy to keep these verbs straight: The verbs on the left all have the letter *i* as their first vowel. Remember that "the *i*-verbs indicate what *I* do with my position."

Let's take a look at the principal parts of these six verbs. You probably know these already:

present	**past**	**past participle**
I sit	I sat	I have sat
I set	I set	I have set

You may also know these:

present	**past**	**past participle**
I rise	I rose	I have risen
I raise	I raised	I have raised

Perhaps the most difficult of all irregular verbs are *lie* and *lay*:

present	**past**	**past participle**
I lie	I lay	I have lain
I lay	I laid	I have laid

Lay, as you see, is a regular verb, but it complicates our use of *lie*. *Lie* (meaning *to recline*) is irregular, and it is confusing because its past form, *I lay*, is identical to the present form of *lay*. It is probably accurate to say that many Americans, perhaps most Americans, do not use *lie* correctly, but you can master it in a few moments and remember it with a little review now and then.

Even with irregular verbs, the past participle is **always** used with the auxiliary *have* (or its other forms *has* or *had*) to create perfect tenses, and forms of the verb *be* are used with the *–ing* form, the present participle, to create progressive tenses.

<u>12.11.d (1) To Be:</u>

Because the verb *to be* is the most frequently used verb in English, and because it is also the most irregular verb, let's look at it in detail:

To Be: The Simple Tenses

<u>Singular</u>	<u>Present</u>	<u>Past</u>	<u>Future</u>
1st person	I am	I was	I will be
2nd person	You are	You were	You will be
3rd person	He is	He was	He will be

<u>Plural</u>	<u>Present</u>	<u>Past</u>	<u>Future</u>
1st person	We are	We were	We will be
2nd person	You are	You were	You will be
3rd person	They are	They were	They will be

Notice that the second-person forms are identical in the singular and plural. Notice too that there is great variety in the singular (which uses six different forms of *be*), but the plurals are far more consistent. For that reason, we will look only at the singular in the remaining tenses.

To Be: The Perfect Tenses

<u>Singular</u>	<u>Present</u>	<u>Past</u>	<u>Future</u>
1st person	I have been	I had been	I will have been
2nd person	You have been	You had been	You will have been
3rd person	She has been	He had been	She will have been

Notice in this table that the main verb is always the past participle, *been,* and the auxiliaries *have, had,* or *has* show tense and number in every tense but the future.

To Be: The Progressive Tenses

Singular	Present	Past	Future
1st person	I am being	I was being	I will be being
2nd person	You are being	You were being	You will be being
3rd person	He is being	He was being	He will be being

Notice here and in the perfect progressive tense that the main verb is always *being*. The first auxiliary verb, *am, are, is, was,* or *were,* show tense and person.

To Be: The Perfect Progressive Tenses

Singular	Present	Past	Future
1st person	I have been being	I had been being	I will have been being
2nd person	You have been being	You had been being	You will have been being
3rd person	He has been being	He had been being	He will have been being

As you can see, as we go from the simple tenses to the tenses that require more auxiliaries, there is less variety among the persons and tenses.

With the four tables above, you can construct a verb phrase from any English verb by simply replacing the main verb. The auxiliaries will always be the same.

12.11.e Active and Passive Voices

In the chapter on complements, we discussed two classes of verbs called transitive and intransitive:

INTRANSITIVE:	He sang.
TRANSITIVE:	He sang a song.
INTRANSITIVE:	She ran.
TRANSITIVE:	She ran a mile.

Linking verbs are never transitive.

Transitive verbs—and only transitives—are capable of two voices: active and passive.

With **active voice verbs**, the subject is the performer of the action and the direct object is the receiver of the action.

247

The boy <u>hit</u> the ball.

In **passive voice verbs**, the receiver of the action is the subject, and the performer is either deleted from the sentence, or it is shifted to the end of the sentence in a prepositional phrase:

The ball <u>was hit</u>.
The ball <u>was hit</u> by the boy.

Passives always take an auxiliary that is a form of *to be*:

You <u>were made</u> chairman.
She <u>has been</u> elected chairwoman.
She <u>is elected</u> captain every time.

12.11.f The Moods of Verbs

Mood is another quality of verbs, related to the content and purpose of the sentence.

Indicative mood describes a verb in a sentence that makes a statement about facts or asks questions about facts; most of the sentences we write and speak are in the indicative mood.

Subjunctive mood appears in statements about supposed or possible situations: suggestions, wishes, prayers, recommendations, and speculations. Usually the verb is the same as in the indicative mood, but in some cases, especially using the verb *to be*, the verb is different:

<u>May</u> the Force <u>be</u> with you!
Blessed <u>be</u> the name of the Lord!
If I <u>were</u> rich, I'd leave this job.
<u>Be</u> that as it may, let's continue.
If he <u>weren't</u> so lazy, he'd be a millionaire.
I move that this meeting <u>be</u> adjourned.
I insist that Bill <u>consult</u> a doctor.

Increasingly in present-day English, we do not use special subjunctive verbs. Instead we rely on context to express the hypothetical nature of these ideas (as in *Bill should consult a doctor*).

As the examples above indicate, we have preserved distinct subjunctive forms chiefly in traditional and conventional expressions (*If I were you . . .*; *Blessed be the name of the Lord!*), or in sentences that imitate them (*May the Force be with you!*).

Conditional mood expresses a conditional statement, a sentence about a possibility or necessity. In English, these are often expressed by using certain auxiliary verbs in sentences:

> I <u>may juggle</u> vases.
> You <u>could drop</u> the vases.
> I <u>should have been</u> more careful.
> Now you <u>must leave</u>.

Imperative mood expresses a command:

> Leave!
> Don't go.
> Be quiet!
> Make me!

Modal Auxiliaries: Often the imperative omits a subject and an auxiliary, as in three of the sentences above. Notice the difference between the conditional and the imperative:

> You must leave.
> Leave!

Some auxiliary verbs contribute to creating verbs of a particular mood:

> Present-tense: will, shall, can, may, must, ought to
> Past-tense: would, should, could, might

12.11.g Phrasal Verbs

Phrasal verbs are two-word verbs used as one word. The second word, called a **particle**, always looks like a preposition, but without an object:

> I'll <u>look up</u> the word.
> I'll <u>write out</u> a check.
> We'll <u>wait out</u> the storm.
> She <u>looked in</u> on the kids
> We <u>signed up</u> for a class.

Phrasal verbs have an informal tone, and the particle cannot be the beginning of a prepositional phrase. Notice the differences:

I'll <u>look up</u> the word.
I'll <u>look up</u> the chimney.
Despite disappointment, they <u>went on</u>.
They <u>went on</u> the train.

Sometimes the particle is separated from the first word in the verb:

I'll <u>look</u> the word <u>up</u>.
I'll <u>write</u> the check <u>out</u>.

12.11.h Exercises

Complete the following tables for the simple tenses of the verb *to be* and check your answers against the tables in this chapter. Some subjects have been provided.

Simple tenses:

Singular	**Present**	**Past**	**Future**
1st person	I		
2nd person	You		
3rd person			

Plural	**Present**	**Past**	**Future**
1st person	I		
2nd person	You		
3rd person			

Complete the following table for the perfect tenses of the verb *to be* and check your answers against the tables in this chapter.

Singular	Present	Past	Future
1st person			
2nd person			
3rd person			

Complete the following tables for the progressive and perfect progressive tenses of the verb *to be* and check your answers against the tables in this chapter.

Perfect tenses:

Singular	Present	Past	Future
1st person			
2nd person			
3rd person			

Perfect progressive tenses:

Singular	Present	Past	Future
1st person			
2nd person			
3rd person			

In the following sentences, label the verb as transitive, intransitive, or linking. You will need to label some verbs *transitive* and *passive*. Refer to the chapter if you need to.

1) I saw the accident.
2) The accident occurred this morning.
3) That street sign will cause an accident.
4) He sang an old song.
5) The meteor shower was witnessed by millions.
6) He sang in the shower.
7) We are old friends.
8) We are going to the movies.
9) We attended a movie.
10) The guest will be introduced by Julie.

12.12 INTERJECTIONS AND THE PARTS OF SPEECH

The **interjection** is a common grammatical category and a simple one: Any word or group of words that we use to express shock, surprise, pain, joy, admiration, and a wide range of other feelings and responses is an interjection. Interjections are used by themselves or as part of a sentence:

Good grief!
Cool!
Oh, no!
My!
What now?

Interjections have no distinctive form: They can be phrases or sentences; they can end with periods, question marks or exclamation marks:

What the heck?
Well, that's just *great*.
Just look at this mess!

Some interjections serve social purposes: greetings (*Hello, Goodbye*), agreement or disagreement (*yes, no, yeah, nah, maybe*), politeness (*please, thanks*), or rudeness (*Says you! Baloney! Yeah, right!*). Some interjections are not even actual words in the usual sense, but merely sounds that have become conventional reactions: *Ouch! Yikes! Sheesh! Oof! Oops! Whoopee!* They are generally easy to recognize.

The most important thing to know about interjections is that, although they are useful for self-expression or social interaction, they play no *grammatical* role in the sentence. In analyzing a sentence that contains interjections, you can disregard them.

Some grammar books classify some of these words as adverbs, though they do not clearly modify verbs, adjectives, or other adverbs. For our purposes, calling them interjections is sufficient.

12.12.a The Eight Parts of Speech

We are ready now to speak of the **eight parts of speech**, eight categories in conventional grammar study that account for all the words in English.

Three of the parts of speech are nouns or words associated with nouns:

- **Nouns:** Words that stand for persons, places, things, or ideas.
- **Pronouns:** Words that take the place of nouns.
- **Adjectives:** Words that modify nouns or pronouns.

Two of the parts of speech are verbs and adverbs:

- **Verbs:** Words that indicate an action or a state of being.
- **Adverbs:** Words that modify verbs, adjectives, or other adverbs.

Two of the parts of speech are connecting words:

- **Conjunctions:** Words that connect phrases and clauses to each other and indicate the grammatical relationship between the connected units.
- **Prepositions:** Words that connect nouns or pronouns (the objects of the preposition) with other words in the sentence to modify those other words.

And the eighth part of speech is *interjections*.

An important part of analyzing the grammar of any sentence is to classify every word according to the eight parts of speech. That's not always easy.

12.12.b A Form and Its Function

It is important to distinguish between *form* and *function* in grammar:

The **form** can be a part of speech, like a noun or a verb. It can also be a larger unit constructed upon a part of speech, like a verb phrase or a prepositional phrase.

The **function** is the grammatical job the form does in a particular sentence. Nouns can perform functions that include subjects or direct objects; nouns can also be indirect objects, predicate nominatives, objects of a preposition, and more. Prepositional phrases can be adjectival or adverbial.

A number of forms (nouns, verbs, modifiers) assembled together can build larger forms—clauses, for instance. A relative clause has an adjectival function in a larger sentence; a subordinate clause has an adverbial function.

The forms and functions are therefore typically defined by context. Often you cannot look at a single word in isolation and define its form, and you can never define its function. (There are exceptions: It is usually safe to say that *the* is an article and an adjective. But in that last sentence, *the* was used as a noun, as the subject of a clause: "*The* is an article.")

Consider this word: *bill*. Is it a noun or a verb? To answer, we need context:

> I will bring your monthly <u>bills</u>.
> We will <u>bill</u> you later.

In the first sentence, the form of *bill* is a noun, and it functions as a direct object. In the second, *bill* is a transitive verb; it functions as the main verb of the sentence.

This matter of form and function becomes particularly important as we move on to later sections.

12.12.c Exercises

In the following sentences, use context to identify the form and function of the underlined words.

1) In the increasingly chaotic country, university students are <u>revolting</u>.
2) I don't care how much you defend them, I'm tired of these <u>revolting</u> students.
3) We were <u>jogging</u> around the block.
4) All of us enjoy <u>jogging</u>.

5) He will replace the <u>shattered</u> lamp.

6) He <u>shattered</u> it accidentally.

7) This rose bud is <u>for</u> you.

8) I gave you a rose bud <u>for</u> I care about you.

9) I wanted to get you more, <u>but</u> I couldn't afford it.

10) I bought you nothing <u>but</u> this rose bud.

12.13 NOMINAL CLAUSES

A nominal clause can fill noun positions in a sentence. Nominal clauses give us the powerful ability to embed the clause within a larger sentence, in order to make some statement or judgment about the nominal clause.

There are two kinds, distinguished by the word that begins the clause.

12.13.a Question-Word Nominals

These nominal clauses begin with the question words *who, what, when, where, why,* and *how.*

Let's begin with a question: *Who did that?* We can embed that question within a declarative sentence, as a direct object. Here the nominal clause is underlined:

I know *who* did that.

We can also create direct objects with other clauses that begin with question words:

I learned *what* they did.
I discovered *when* they did that.
I saw *where* they did that.
I will ask *why* he did that.
I show you *how* he did that.

Notice that most of these nominal clauses are not complete sentences by modern standards, nor do they have normal word order. Consider the example:

I will ask *why* he did that.

Compound pronouns (a class of pronouns that contain the word *ever*) can also begin nominal clauses:

> We will use <u>*whatever* we find</u>.
> We will hire <u>*whoever* applies for this job</u>.

As the examples above illustrate, nominal clauses are often the direct objects of transitive verbs like *know, see,* and *learn*.
Nominal clauses can also be subjects:

> <u>*Where* these people went</u> is not yet known.
> <u>*Why* they came here</u> is a mystery.

These clauses can also be objects of a preposition:

> The professor is writing a book about <u>*how* people can improve their writing.</u>
> Mr. Chayle has time for <u>*whoever* needs help.</u>

12.13.b Nominals with *that, if,* or *whether*

The three words *that, if,* and *whether* (sometimes called **nominalizers**) can also make independent clauses into nominal clauses that fill noun positions. Here are nominal clauses functioning as direct objects:

> I wonder <u>*if* she arrives today.</u>
> I learned <u>*that* she arrives today.</u>
> I don't know <u>*whether* [or not] she will arrive today.</u>
> He demanded <u>*that* we serve him immediately.</u>
> We doubt <u>*if* he will cooperate.</u>

The sentences above demonstrate that these nominal clauses can be direct objects of the verbs *know, see,* and *learn,* as well as *demand, ask, inquire, imagine, doubt,* and others. These verbs denote an intellectual process being performed upon the idea in the nominal clause.
These clauses can perform almost every other function of a noun. They can be subjects or appositives:

> <u>*That* the sun is at the center of our solar system</u> is beyond all question.

The physicist's idea, **that** <u>multiple universes exist</u>, baffles me.

These clauses can also perform other nominal functions, including those of predicate nominatives, objects of prepositions, or indirect objects:

The main complaint about the car was *that* <u>it was too expensive</u>.
We know nothing about him except *that* <u>he arrived yesterday</u>.
You can give *whoever* <u>applies</u> the job.

12.13.c Exercises

In the following sentences, underline the nominal clauses and then identify their functions in each sentence.

1) We were taught that anything worth doing is worth doing well.

2) That statement summarizes what he is trying to say.

3) We will learn if tickets are still available.

4) When we will meet is the next topic for discussion.

5) There is no question about who broke the equipment.

6) I will tell whoever is interested about the news.

7) I don't know why he left.

8) His claim, that he was abducted by aliens, is preposterous.

9) His wife made him what he is today. I don't think that we should blame that on his wife.

12.14 VERBALS

A **verbal** is a verb in *form* with a different *function*, *a verb used as another part of speech*. A verbal is used as a noun, an adjective, or an adverb.

While verbals are used as other parts of speech, they retain some of the qualities of verbs. For example, they can take direct objects and indirect objects and other complements, and they can be modified by adverbs.

Verbals are therefore quite useful, and they appear frequently in our sentences. There are only three kinds.

12.14.a Gerunds: Verbs as Nouns

A gerund appears *only* in the present participle form—the *–ing* form—and it is *always* used as a noun

I enjoy <u>baking</u>.
I enjoy <u>hiking</u>.
I enjoy <u>reading</u>.

In all the sentences above, the gerund (underlined) functions as a direct object. Some gerunds, created from transitive verbs, can also take their own direct objects. In both the following sentences, the underlined portion includes the gerund and its direct object.

I enjoy <u>baking cakes</u>.
I enjoy <u>reading books</u>.

Gerunds can also take indirect objects:

I enjoy <u>reading my child books</u>.

Notice that the last example is, in a way, a combination of two clauses:

I enjoy reading.
I read my child books.

We *reduced* the second sentence above into a gerund phrase: *I enjoy reading my child books.* That is why gerund phrases (and verbal phrases of all kinds) are sometimes referred to as "reduced clauses."
We can also use transitive verbs with object complements:

We regret <u>making Albert angry</u>.

Verbals created from linking verbs can be used with predicate nominatives and predicate adjectives:

Stanley enjoys <u>being a comedian</u>.
Oliver enjoys <u>being funny</u>.

Verbals can perform any function in a sentence that nouns perform: They can be subjects, appositives, and objects of prepositions, and they can perform the other functions shown above.

12.14.b Participles: Verbs as Adjectives

The **present participles** of verbs (the *–ing* forms) and the **past par-**

ticiples of verbs (the forms used with *have*) are used to create adjectival phrases that *precede* the noun. In some sentence structures, they can also follow the noun:

Walking quickly to the door, the detective threw it open.
The detective, walking quickly to the door, threw it open.

We watched the snow falling softly.
We watched the softly falling snow.

Shaken from his fall, the old man sat for a moment.
The old man, shaken from his fall, sat for a moment.

Heard across the street, the scream disturbed the neighbors.
The scream, heard across the street, disturbed the neighbors.

12.14.c Infinitives: Verbs as Nouns, Adjectives, and Adverbs

Infinitives are the most complex of the verbals. Most of the time, an infinitive is the form of a verb beginning with *to*: *to laugh, to be, to help, to break*. They can be in the present or perfect form, and can be active or passive. They can be used *nominally, adjectivally, and adverbally*.

They can be used *nominally*:
To quit now would be a mistake. [a subject]
He likes to run. [a direct object]
His goal, to explain the book, is reasonable. [an appositive]
Our goal is to win. [a predicate nominative]
To know her is to trust her. [a subject *and* a predicate nominative]

Infinitives can be used as *adjectives, following* a noun or a linking verb:

I need a book to read. [a modifier of *book*]
An opportunity to succeed is a wonderful thing. [a modifier of *book*]
He appears to have some money. [a predicate adjective]
He seems to be a jerk. [a predicate adjective]

And infinitives can be used as *adverbs*, modifying verbs or adjectives. Modifying verbs, the infinitive can appear before or after the verb:

She plays to win. [How does she play?]

<u>To succeed</u>, he studies every day. [Why does he study?]

Modifying adjectives, the infinitive appears after the adjective:

He was ready <u>to study</u>. [How was he ready?]
I'm happy <u>to help</u>. [In what way are you happy?]
Eager <u>to please</u>, the new employees arrived early. [In what way were they eager?]

In a few cases, infinitives are used without the *to* particle:

I want <u>him *to win* the race</u>.
I saw <u>him *win* the race</u>.
I allowed <u>him *to win* the race</u>.
I let <u>him *win* the race</u>.
I'll ask <u>him *to go*</u>.
I'll have <u>him *go*</u>.
I'll force <u>him *to leave*</u>.
I'll make <u>him *leave*</u>.

The absence of the *to* particle is determined by the verb that precedes the infinitive phrase: A small number of verbs make the *to* in infinitives unnecessary. (In the exercises in this book, however, we will always use the *to* particle.)

Like verbs, infinitives can be used with direct and indirect objects, with adverbs, and with other grammatical entities associated with the verb.

Infinitives can even have subjects:

I like *Kelly* <u>to enjoy these nightly readings</u>. [Kelly is the subject of the infinitive verb.]
I like *my children* <u>to read every day</u>.
I need *you* <u>to go to the store today</u>.
I want *her* <u>to enjoy reading</u>.

12.14.d Points for Writers

Dangling Participles: We usually put participles very close to the nouns they modify, either before or after. Avoid the infamous **dangling participle**, a carelessly used participial phrase that does not apply logically to a nearby noun. Nonsense often results:

Rowing across the river, the boat struck the ice.
Dancing to the jazz, the orchestra played its closing number.
Falling softly, we watched the snow.

12.14.e Exercises

In the following pairs of sentences, read the first sentence and then analyze the underlined verbal phrase in the second, using the first sentence as a clue:

1) He likes mystery novels.
   He likes to read mystery novels.

2) He reads them before school.
   He likes reading them before school.

3) She is quite ready.
   She is ready to sing.

4) She is very happy.
   She is happy to sing.

5) He sings the aria loudly.
   Singing the aria loudly, the opera star took center stage.

6) He sings arias at 6 am.
   His singing arias at 6 am annoys us.

Identify the underlined verbals as gerunds, participles, and infinitives. Then identify the function that the verbal performs in each sentence.

12.14.e (2) Exercises

Identify the underlined verbals as gerunds, participles, and infinitives. Then identify the function that the verbal performs in each sentence.

1) He likes to read.

2) He likes reading novels.

3) Running quickly, he soon arrived at home.

4) His singing annoyed us.

5) Known to the entire community, the mayor is respected.

6) Seen but never recognized, the silent film star lived in our neighborhood.

7) He wants to earn money.

8) He writes <u>to learn</u>.

9) They were prepared <u>to fight</u>.

10) <u>To succeed</u>, you must be prepared to work hard.

12.15 MORE ON NOUNS

In this section we will discuss more of the basics of nouns and a few of the more difficult points.

12.15.a The Common and the Proper

You may already know about common and proper nouns: **common nouns** are words like *man, woman, child, city, state*. They name general, nonspecific persons or things. **Proper nouns** name particular persons or things, and those names are capitalized: *Henry, Annie, Herbert, St. Louis, Missouri*.

Usually it is easy to know when to capitalize a noun, but there can be uncertainly about words that may—or may not—be official titles:

I spoke with Doctor Smith yesterday.
I spoke with my doctor yesterday.

The president of the club lives in a white house.
The President lives in the White House.

Dictionaries often have helpful information about making the distinction.

12.15.b Plural Nouns

As you know, we make most nouns plural by simply adding *–s* to the end. If a word ends with *s, x, z, sh,* or *ch,* we add *–es*: basses, boxes, dishes, churches, and others. But there are quite a few exceptions—irregular plurals—and for these you may need to refer to a dictionary. The easiest irregular plurals are those that are identical to the singular forms: *sheep, deer, moose*.

Still other familiar irregulars change a vowel within the word (*mice, men, teeth, feet*) or add *–en*: *oxen, children*. With a noun that ends with a consonant and *o*, we usually use *–es* for the plural: *heroes, zeroes, potatoes*. But there are other nouns that end with a consonant and *o* that take only *-s*. Some of these are musical terms from Italian: *pianos, cellos, solos*. A noun that ends with a vowel followed by *o* takes only *–s* for the plural: *patios, radios, rodeos, zoos*.

With some nouns that end with *f* or *fe*, follow the familiar rule: change the *f* to *v* and add *–es*: *calves, halves, knives, wives*. But other plurals that end with *f* or *fe* take only *–s*: *roofs, proofs, handkerchiefs, beliefs*. And you probably recall that in nouns that end with a consonant and *y*, we change *y* to *i* and add *–es*: *armies, ladies, rallies*. But when a vowel precedes *y*, we add only *–s*: *bays, boys, alleys, valleys*.

And then there are a number of words from Latin or Greek that retain their original plural forms (or something similar to them). In the context of English, these plurals seem quite irregular:

alumnae	phenomena
alumni	radii
criteria	stimuli
media	theses
nebulae	vertebrae

We will remind you again that a dictionary always helps with problems like these. Most writers will seldom use most of these unusual plurals, but we all need to remember a few, including, probably, these:

- *medium* (the singular) and *media* (the plural), as in *the medium of television*, or *the media of radio, television, and internet*

- *criterion* and *criteria*

- *phenomenon* and *phenomena*

Almost every professional field has its special terms that include certain irregular plurals, and it is a good idea to learn them as soon as possible for your professional writing.

It is also helpful to know that almost no one uses *memorandum* and *memoranda* anymore; we simply write *memo* and *memos*. And for most purposes today, *data* and *statistics* are accepted as both singulars and plurals, depending on context.

12.15.c Possession

It is usually easy to indicate possession in English nouns; with singular nouns, we add an apostrophe and *–s*: *man's, woman's, child's, Oliver's, Stanley's*. With plurals, we add a lone apostrophe after the final *–s*: *friends', students', teachers'*.

But English sometimes makes things a bit harder. When a plural does not end in *–s*, we make the possessive form with the apostrophe first, then *–s*, like the regular singular possessive: *men's, women's, children's.*

Now comes the frustrating part. Suppose a singular noun ends in *–s*, like *boss* or *Ross, Charles* or *Bess*? Do we add only an apostrophe? Or do we add an apostrophe and *–s*?

The sad truth is that American English has no universally accepted way of marking possession in these cases. Some authorities insist on one way, some on the other. When you are writing for school or your career, you must find out which way is preferred and stick to it. If your organization has no standard way to deal with plural possessives, persuade your leaders to adopt one of the standard style guides to answer such questions.

In this book, we will create possessives with *– 's* after singulars ending in *s*, like this:

> The boss's desk
> Ross's desk
> Bess's desk

12.15.d The Expletive *There*

The expletive *there* takes the place of the subject, postponing the appearance of the subject, a noun or a pronoun, *until after the verb*. The expletive is never the actual subject:

> <u>A picture</u> was on the walls.
> There was <u>a picture</u> on the walls.
>
> <u>Stray dogs</u> were in our yard.
> There were <u>stray dogs</u> in our yard.

The expletive *there*, like the expletive *it* (which we'll see in a moment) has no grammatical function in the sentence: It has only a stylistic function, to stand in for the true subject, postponing it until later in the sentence.

In modern English, expletive constructions are the usual way to say certain things:

> <u>There</u> will now be a short intermission.

We can't say, *A short intermission will now be.*

> Somewhere <u>there</u> is a place for us.

We cannot say, *Somewhere a place for us is.*

Do not confuse the expletive *there* with the adverb of place *there*. Here is a useful test: Can you replace the word with *here* and retain the original general sense of the sentence?

> ADVERB: Your keys are over <u>there</u>. (Compare: *Your keys are over here*.)
>
> ADVERB: <u>There</u> are your keys. (Compare: *Here are your keys*.)
>
> EXPLETIVE: <u>There</u> are keys all over the place.

(We would not say, *Here are keys all over the place*.)

All the sentences we have used so far contain linking verbs. Action verbs, transitive and intransitive, are also possible in expletive constructions, and the subject is postponed to a point between auxiliaries and the main verbs:

> <u>A dog</u> is growling in the yard
> There is <u>a dog</u> growling in the yard.
>
> <u>A boy</u> is building something on the porch.
> There is <u>a boy</u> building something on the porch.

12.15.e Appositives

An **appositive** is *a noun or pronoun that usually appears immediately after another noun to rename the noun and provide additional information about it.* The appositive is usually enclosed in a pair of commas, although we may sometimes use dashes or parentheses, depending on our desired style, tone, or emphasis.

More than one appositive is possible, and sometimes the appositive has modifiers of its own:

> My boss, <u>Mr. Smith</u>, was talking to my parents.
>
> Mr. Smith, <u>my wonderful boss</u>, was talking to my parents.
>
> My boss—<u>that bore, that ogre, that man whom I hate more than any other person living, with the possible exception of my English teacher</u>—was talking to my parents.

In the sentences above, the appositives all rename the subject (*My boss* or *Mr. Smith*), and for that reason they are considered part of the subject. In the third example, the dashes are helpful to mark the beginning and end of the long appositive phrase, which contains three commas.

Pronouns used as appositives should be in the case that matches the function of the nouns they rename. In the example below, the appositives rename the object (*judges*) of a preposition, so the pronoun is in the objective case:

> The photos were given to the judges, <u>Eric and me</u>.

In the next example, the appositives rename the subject (*judges*), so the pronoun is in the nominative case:

> The judges, <u>Eric and I,</u> will study the photos.

Sometimes we use the conjunction *or* before the appositive, to indicate a synonym:

> The common dog, or *Canis lupus familiaris,* belongs to the <u>*Canidae* </u>family.

> Mergenthaler's type-setting machine (or *Linotype,* as he called it) was invented in 1884.

Do not confuse the appositive with adjectives that appear after the noun they modify:

> The children, <u>thrilled and excited</u>, dashed through the living room.

Restrictive and Non-restrictive Appositives: Sometimes the pair of commas is not used, depending on the larger context. In the first example below, the writer has more than one daughter; in the second, he has only one:

> My daughter <u>Mary</u> plays the tuba.
> My daughter, <u>Mary,</u> plays the tuba.

In the first example, *Mary* is a **restrictive** appositive: it restricts or limits the meaning of *daughter*. In the second example, the **non-restrictive** appositive *Mary* simply provides supplementary information. As the commas indicate, it is added information, and omitting it does not change the meaning of the sentence. However, a restrictive appositive leaves the meaning ambiguous.

Here are more examples of restrictive appositives, followed by non-restrictive examples. In both cases the restrictive appositive, without the commas, is used to identify a specific person:

My cousin <u>Bob</u> plays the harmonica.
My cousin, <u>Bob</u>, plays the harmonica.

Our custodian <u>Mr. Halley</u> does good work.
Our custodian, <u>Mr. Halley</u>, does good work.

12.15.f Nouns of Direct Address

In written dialogue and letters, as in daily conversation, we sometimes use the names of the people we are addressing. These names are called nouns of direct address:

I don't like to be disappointed, and you, <u>Renfru</u>, disappoint me.
<u>Mr. Smith</u>, I'd like to speak with you, please.

Sometimes nouns of direct address are common nouns that apply to one person or an entire audience:

<u>My friend</u>, I hope you will take my advice.
This news, <u>my friends</u>, should comfort us all.

The noun of direct address is always enclosed by a pair of commas, and it has no grammatical function in the sentence. That is, it is not considered part of the subject or the predicate; it is simply there to get the attention of the people addressed, or to clarify who is being addressed.

Sometimes, if the context doesn't resolve ambiguities, readers may confuse nouns of address and appositives:

Your supervisor, <u>Mr. Watley</u>, told you to finish that project.

Is *Mr. Watley* the supervisor or the person being addressed? We usually depend on the larger context to clarify this.

12.15.g Exercises

In the following sentences, identify the sentences that contain nouns of address, appositives, and expletives. In sentences with expletives, identify the subject of the sentence. A sentence may contain more than one of these structures.

Examples:

- My brother Ed has left. *Appositive*
- Ed, see if my brother has left. *Noun of address*
- There are no printer cartridges in the supply closet. *Expletive, and "no printer cartridges" is the subject.*

1) Dr. Kildare, you can speak with my assistant.
2) June, speak with my physician, Dr. Kildare.
3) Your brother is odd, Alice.
4) There is rain forecast for tomorrow.
5) It is clear that Ed is a menace.

12.16 A BRIEF REVIEW OF PUNCTUATION

By now many of the basic rules of punctuation are probably second nature to you. But here are a few reminders. If you need help with some of the grammatical terms, those are explained elsewhere in this book.

12.16.a Commas

Put a *pair* of commas where you could put parentheses. That is, put a pair of commas around an appositive:

> Mr. Smith (the principal) went to talk to the Addams family.
> Mr. Smith, the principal, has never returned.

Put a pair of commas around a parenthetical comment (one that interrupts the sentence):

> That Addams boy (whom I've pointed out before) is a strange kid.
> That Addams boy, the one I mentioned previously, has been staring at me.

Place commas around states (in city-state patterns) and years (in dates):

> Salem, Massachusetts, is my favorite city.
> October 31, 1938, is the day the Martians landed in Grovers Mill, New Jersey, to abduct Orson Welles.

Use a comma *after* a coordinating conjunction that joins two independent clauses:

>He got the job at the book store, <u>and</u> he means to keep it.
>He intended to keep the job, <u>but</u> then he found a better one.

In a sentence that begins with a subordinate conjunction and a subordinate clause, add a comma *before* the independent clause:

>Because Mortimer was late, the boss docked his pay.
>After he docked Mortimer's pay, the boss spoke with him.

When we rewrite the sentences above with the independent clause first, no comma is necessary because the subordinate clause comes *after*, not *before*, the main clause:

>The boss docked Mortimer's pay <u>because he was late</u>.
>The boss spoke with Mortimer <u>after he docked his pay</u>.

Never place *just one* comma between the subject and verb of the sentence:

>INCORRECT: Nancy, is the best treasurer we've ever had.
>(*Nancy* is the subject, so no comma needed.)

>INCORRECT: Nancy, the treasurer is not here today.
>(Two commas are needed around *the treasurer*, which is an appositive.)

>CORRECT: Ed, did you know that Nancy is the treasurer?
>(This is correct, because *Ed* is a noun of direct address, not the subject.)

We have one more point on commas: We all know that we use commas to separate items in a series:

>His favorite tie contains <u>blue, green, red, and gray</u>.

But there is disagreement about that last comma (the one before *and*), which is known as the *serial comma*. Some authorities leave it out unless it's necessary for clarity. Find out which style your teacher prefers and use it consistently.

12.16.b Semi-colons

Use a semi-colon—and no coordinating conjunction—to join two independent clauses into one sentence:

> Jill likes the human anatomy class; she doesn't need it for her major, however.

Use the semi-colon to join two or more groups of words that contain commas:

> Your supervisor, Mr. Smith, will be here Tuesday; Ms. Jones, his assistant, will be here Wednesday; and you, Bob, should be here every day.

> The hideous creature had fangs, tentacles, and a drooling maw; wings, claws, and piercing eyes; and blond wavy hair.

12.16.c Colons

Use a colon *after a complete sentence* to introduce a list, a clause, or a quotation:

> Successful students have certain traits: patience, determination, ambition.

> Successful students have certain habits: they plan their work, they organize carefully, and they look for ways to improve their plans and organization.

> Steve quoted Mark Twain on golf: "Golf is a good walk spoiled."

A colon *never* follows words like *include, such as,* or *like*:

> INCORRECT: A successful student's qualities include: patience, determination, ambition.
> CORRECT: A successful student's qualities include patience, determination, ambition.

> INCORRECT: I want to take courses such as: biology, astronomy, and physics.
> CORRECT: I want to take courses such as biology, astronomy, and physics.

A colon should also appear at the end of a sentence that introduces a block quotation. (See the example at the end of this section.)

12.16.d Apostrophes

Apostrophes show *possession* with nouns, and *contraction* with personal pronouns and verbs:

> Heather's car—it's gone, isn't it?

Possessive pronouns (like *his, hers, its, yours,* and *theirs*) **never** contain apostrophes.

Plural possessives that end in *–s* take an apostrophe and no additional *–s*: *supervisors', librarians', soldiers'.* Plurals that don't end in *–s* take both the apostrophe and *–s* to show possession: *media's, criteria's.*

There is no consensus on punctuating some possessives. Some authorities (like the Modern Language Association and Strunk and White) call for - *'s* after *all* singular nouns to form possessives, including nouns that end in *-s*: *Clemens's, Dickens's, Jesus's.* Other authorities (like the *Associated Press Stylebook* and the American Psychological Association) omit the final *–s* in those possessives: *Clemens', Dickens', Jesus'.* Find out which style your teacher prefers and use it consistently.

Similarly, some authorities call for apostrophes to make certain unusual plurals:

> He wants to earn all <u>A's and B's</u> this semester.
> He prefers the jazz from the <u>1940's</u>.

Other authorities would omit the apostrophes here. Follow your teachers' (or supervisors') preferences on these, too.

12.16.e Quotation Marks

Use quotation marks around titles of *short* works (short stories and poems, articles, songs, or a web page within a larger site): "The Raven."

Titles of long works (books, newspapers, magazines, movies, plays, or entire websites) should be underlined or in italics: *The Lord of the Rings.*

Commas and periods go to the left of quotation marks— ," ."—and *never* to the immediate right.

12.16.f Ellipses and Square Brackets

We are permitted to *delete* words from direct quotations if we use *ellipses* (three spaced periods) to tell our readers (1) that words have been deleted and (2) where they were deleted.

Similarly, we can *add* words to quotations by enclosing the additions in square brackets.

The following sentence, which contains a quotation, uses both ellipses and brackets:

> In his book *The Great Movies*, film critic Roger Ebert writes that *The Maltese Falcon* is "[a]mong the movies we not only love but treasure. . . " (279).

In the original text by Ebert, the quoted words were at the beginning of a sentence, so the writer has used brackets to make the first letter of *among* lowercase.

Also notice that after the ellipsis marks there is (eventually) a *fourth* period to end the sentence.

Here's a second example, using a block quotation from Garry Wills's book *Certain Trumpets: The Nature of Leadership.* Here the writer, having introduced the quotation, has deleted words with ellipses and inserted a comment in square brackets:

> Wills explains why radicals of the 1930's and 1940's objected to moderate leaders like Eleanor Roosevelt:

> Those who reject the moderate leader because only a radical protest is "authentic" [a term for protest radicals believe to be sincere and effective] will never understand the need more ordinary people have for help to meet life's daily problems. Nor do they see how moderates alter power by making it more responsible . . . Eleanor Roosevelt was "naïve" in the eyes of ideologues . . . who did not understand her extraordinary appeal. (Wills 66)

With the explanation added in brackets, the student has clarified the meaning of authentic (as Wills uses it); with the ellipses, the student has improved the focus of the quotation so that it more clearly supports the student's argument.

When in Doubt . . .

As you work with sources and quotations, and as you work on college (and professional) writing projects in which complex sentences are sometimes necessary, you'll find yourself dealing more and more with the finer points of punctuation. When you're uncertain about punctuating a sentence, consult this handbook, ask your instructor, or use one of the many internet sources on punctuation. One excellent on-line source is *The Punctuation Guide* at thepunctuationguide.com.

Appendix

3.2.d Exercise: Possible Answers

1) College is a time when <u>many</u> young people can explore their interests and form their own values before officially entering the "adult world."

2) With its emphasis on standardized testing, public schools are <u>not doing enough to develop</u> students' critical thinking or creative problem-solving skills.

3) To prevent antibiotics' decreased effectiveness in treating adult infections, parents should <u>consider carefully before</u> giving their children these medicines.

4.5.a Exercise

Charlotte Gilman's use of Gothic elements in <u>her</u> short story "The Yellow Wallpaper"[58] helps produce a powerful impression of the subconscious battle many of <u>us</u> face in trying to fulfill <u>our</u> personal desires while simultaneously conforming to society's often rigid expectations. For example, the story is set at an old estate, <u>which</u> the narrator refers to as a "haunted house," with "hedges and walls and gates that lock." The post-partum narrator describes the room <u>she</u> shares with her doctor husband as having windows that are "barred" and wallpaper that somehow disturbs <u>her</u>: "It is dull enough to confuse the eye in following, pronounced enough to constantly irritate and provoke study, and when <u>you</u> follow the lame uncertain curves for a little distance <u>they</u> suddenly commit suicide—plunge off at outrageous angles, destroy

274

themselves in unheard of contradictions." Her description of the summer place's features, together generating
the tone of Gothic horror, reflect not only the restrictions
she feels as a result of society's standards for women,
but also the psychological fragmentation caused by her
struggles with those standards, ultimately breaking down
her "stable" social self.

- Transition words: For example
- Repeated key words: Gothic, society, narrator
- Pronouns/antecedents: her/Gilman, us/readers, our/readers',
  which/estate, she/narrator, her/narrator, you/narrator or reader,
  they/curves, themselves/curves, Her/narrator's, she/narrator, her/
  narrators', her/narrators'
- Groups of words with common or **linked** meanings: Gothic—old
  estate, haunted house, horror; subconscious—personal desires,
  psychological fragmentation; rigid social rules (or traps)—rigid
  expectations, lock, barred, restrictions, standards

5.6.a Exercise: Test Your Knowledge & Discuss the Results

1) c
2) a
3) b
4) d
5) c
6) e

12.1.b Exercise

The **subject** is the part of the sentence that names who or what the sentence is about. The **predicate** is the part that says something about the subject.

	Simple subject	Simple predicate
a)	Rain	falls
b)	Edward	knocked
c)	family	ate
d)	pancakes	seemed
e)	Rudolpho	rode

12.2.d Exercise

    1) The [family] [was having] coffee. - A

    2) Without warning, [John] [entered] the room. - A

    3) [John] [made] an announcement. - A

    4) [All] of our vases [are] gone. - L

    5) The [family] [became] furious. - L

    6) [Mr. Morton] [had struck] again. - A

    7) Someday that [man] [will regret] taking vases. - A

    8) Mr. Morton's [reputation] [has been damaged] by these allegations. - A

    9) All over town, [people] [are hiding] their vases. - A

    10) [Mr. Morton] [seems] a little strange. - L

12.3.f Exercise

    1) Small, smaller, smallest

    2) Fast, faster, fastest

    3) Bright, brighter, brightest

    4) Good, better, best

    5) Bad, worse, worst

    6) Curious, more curious, most curious

    7) Cheerful, more cheerful, most cheerful

    8) Happy, happier, happiest

    9) Wrong: There are no comparative or superlative forms for *wrong*.

    10) Far, further, furthest

12.4.d Exercise

	ADJ	ADV	
1.	The child learns	eagerly.	

	ADV	ADJ	ADJ
2.	John almost had	an answer to	the difficult question.

```
         ADV              ADJ
3. Father always  encourages    realistic      thinking.


       ADJ               ADV              ADJ
4. The furious family   did not wait  to see   the busy manager.


      ADJ              ADV
5. A thick, wet snow       fell     softly.


      ADV     ADJ              ADJ              ADJ
6. Silently,  a strange man in  a black cape stood in   the
      shadows
```

12.4.d (2) Exercises

1) Fast, faster, fastest
2) Quickly, more quickly, most quickly
3) Slowly, more slowly, most slowly
4) Angrily, more angrily, most angrily
5) Carefully, more carefully, most carefully
6) Well, better, best
7) Badly, worse, worst
8) Early, earlier, earliest
9) Far, farther, farthest
10) Often, more often, most often

12.5.d Exercise

1) 1. *me, him, us, them, her*
2) 2. *him, her, them, you*
3) 3. *He, She, You, They, We*
4) 4. *mine, his, ours, theirs, hers*
5) 5. *my, his, our, their, her*

1) First-person objective singular: *me*
2) First-person objective plural: *us*

3) Second-person nominative singular (or plural): *you*

4) Feminine third-person nominative singular: *she*

5) Third-person nominative plural: *they*

6) Third-person objective singular: *him, her,* or *it.*

7) Third-person objective plural: *them*

8) First-person nominative plural: *we*

9) First-person possessive singular: *My* or *mine*

10) Neuter third-person nominative singular: *it*

12.6.c Exercise

1) In the morning, I drink coffee with cream.

2) As a rule, I never put sugar in it.

3) Amid cars and trucks, Edwina ran across the street.

4) I am looking for the owner of this dog.

5) Do you mean the dog that is attached to your leg?

6) Throughout the book, the author emphasizes the influence of history upon our perception of events.

7) Like Arthur, I walked down the hall and paid no attention to the noise within the office.

8) According to Arthur, the noise out of the office was because of an argument between Ed and Grace.

9) Arthur should not have been left in charge of the office during the summer.

10) In case of further conflicts, we should make plans regarding appropriate training for all employees.

12.7.g Exercise

For, And, Nor, But, Or, Yet, So.

Either . . . or; neither . . . nor; not only . . . but also; both . . . and.

1) The film was not only (c) boring, but also (c) offensive, so (c) we asked [for] a refund and (c) went home.

2) [In] the morning and (c) again [in] the evening, Ruthie practices

her violin <u>until</u> (s) her mother can't stand it anymore.

3) We went [to] the diner [for] lunch, <u>for</u> (c) we were expected back soon.

4) <u>Because</u> (s) I am tired, I'll take a short break <u>before</u> (s) I continue studying.

5) Fred <u>and</u> (c) George have been gone [since] Friday night, <u>since</u> (s) they took a "short break" [from] studying.

6) <u>After</u> (s) I finish this project, we can meet [after] work <u>and</u> (c) discuss the project.

7) Frank <u>and</u> (c) George are <u>neither</u> (c) punctual <u>nor</u> (c) organized, <u>yet</u> (c) they somehow do their work well.

8) He was <u>so</u> confident <u>that</u> (s) he underestimated his opponent.

9) The room looked <u>as if</u> (s) it had not been occupied [in] some time, <u>but</u> (c) it had been occupied [for] days <u>or</u> (c) weeks.

12.8.f Exercise

1) Sentences with action verbs *sometimes* have a complement.

2) Sentences with linking verbs *always* have a complement.

3) Sentences with intransitive verbs *never* have a complement.

4) Sentences with transitive verbs *always* have a complement.

12.8.f (2) Exercise

1) My daughter made <u>me</u> <u>proud</u>. *Direct object, object complement*

2) My aunt brought <u>me</u> <u>a souvenir</u>. *Indirect object, direct object*

3) My sister is <u>late</u>. *Predicate adjective*

4) Both my sisters are <u>teachers</u>. *Predicate nominative*

5) Alice became <u>upset</u>. *Predicate adjective*

6) Six hours a day, Ruthie practices <u>the accordion</u>. *Direct object*

7) We sent <u>Bill and Sue</u> <u>a gift</u>. *Indirect object, direct object*

8) They were <u>kind and grateful</u>. *Compound predicate adjective*

9) I will address <u>that issue</u> at another time. *Direct object*

10) That fellow became <u>our assistant</u>. *Predicate nominative*

11) Bonnie bought <u>Ed</u> <u>that painting</u>. *Indirect object, direct object*

12) Edward and Phil are <u>reckless</u>. *Predicate adjective*

1) Transitive

2) Transitive

3) Linking

4) Linking

5) Linking

6) Transitive

7) Transitive

8) Linking

9) Transitive

10) Linking

11) Transitive

12) Linking

12.9.d Exercise

An independent clause contains at least one subject and at least one predicate, and it contains no word (like a subordinating conjunction) that makes the clause dependent on another clause to be complete.

A dependent clause contains at least one subject and at least one predicate, and it is not grammatically complete by itself.

A sentence is a unit of language that contains at least one independent clause. It may also contain one or more dependent clauses.

1) My family owned a cocker spaniel when I was young. *Complex*
2) Before the meeting, we will set up the room, and you should prepare the refreshments. *Compound*
3) Before the meeting begins, we will set up the room, and you should prepare the refreshments. *Compound-complex*
4) He has done well since graduation, and he credits his success to the university. *Compound*
5) As if he is the supervisor. *Fragment*
6) Since graduation, when he began working here, while Arthur was the supervisor of both departments. *Fragment*
7) Louise and Sharon went to the garage and found their car. *Simple*
8) Either we find a way to solve this problem ourselves, or we must seek help. *Compound*

9) Both spring and fall are their favorite seasons for camping in the mountains and fishing. *Simple*

10) We sat nervously as we waited for our interviews. *Complex*

11) During our interviews, we occasionally answered poorly, but in general we did well. *Compound*

12) After we left the office, we returned, for Louise had forgotten her portfolio. *Compound-complex*

12.10.d Exercise

1) The [house] that is being renovated was my grandmother's home.

2) Please get the [book], which I left in my office.

3) You can give that letter to the [man] who is waiting outside.

4) The [woman] whose car you dented wants to speak to you.

5) The [man] who is waiting already has that letter that you left in your office.

6) The [customer] whom you phoned is waiting in the office.

7) I know the [man] to whom they spoke.

1) The [house] where he was born is on Fifth Street.

2) In [April 1943], when he was born, his parents were living and working in the city.

3) Spring is the [season] when I am happiest, and home is the [place] where all of us are most comfortable.

4) [Marceline], where Walt Disney grew up, is a small town in northern Missouri.

5) Disney left Marceline in [1917], when his family moved to Chicago.

12.11.h Exercise

For all the tenses of *to be*, consult the tables in the section in page 241.

1) I saw the accident. *Transitive*

2) The accident occurred this morning. *Intransitive*

3) That street sign will cause an accident. *Transitive*

4) He sang an old song. *Transitive*

5) The meteor shower was witnessed by millions. *Transitive (and passive)*

6) He sang in the shower. *Intransitive*

7) We are old friends. *Linking*

8) We are going to the movies. *Intransitive*

9) We attended a movie. *Transitive*

10) The guest will be introduced by Julie. *Transitive (and passive)*

12.12.c Exercise

1) In the increasingly chaotic country, university students are <u>re-volting</u>. *Form and function, verb*

2) I don't care how much you defend them, I'm tired of these <u>revolting</u> students. *Form, verb; function, adjective modifying "students"*

3) We were <u>jogging</u> around the block. *Form and function, verb*

4) All of us enjoy <u>jogging</u>. *Form, verb; function, noun*

5) He will replace the <u>shattered</u> lamp. *Form, verb; function, adjective*

6) He <u>shattered</u> it accidentally. *Form and function, verb*

7) This rose bud is <u>for</u> you. *Form and function, preposition*

8) I gave you a rose bud <u>for</u> I care about you. *Form and function, conjunction*

9) I wanted to get you more, <u>but</u> I couldn't afford it. *Form and function, conjunction*

10) I bought you nothing <u>except</u> this rose bud. *Form and function, preposition*

12.13.c Exercise

1) We were taught <u>that anything worth doing is worth doing well</u>. *Direct object*

2) That statement summarizes <u>what he is trying to say</u>. *Direct object*

3) We will learn <u>if tickets are still available</u>. *Direct object*

4) <u>When we will meet</u> is the next topic for discussion. *Subject*

5) There is no question about <u>who broke the equipment</u>. *Object of the preposition*

6) I will tell <u>whoever is interested</u> about the news. *Direct object*

7) I don't know <u>why he left</u>. *Direct object*

8) His claim, <u>that he was abducted by aliens</u>, is preposterous. *Appositive*

9) His wife made him <u>what he is today</u>. *Object complement.*

10) I don't think <u>that we should blame that on his wife</u>. *Direct object*

12.14.e Exercise

1) He likes mystery novels.
   He likes <u>to read mystery novels</u>. *Nominal infinitive, direct object*

2) He reads them before school.
   He likes <u>reading them before school</u>. *Gerund, direct object*

3) She is quite ready.
   She is ready <u>to sing</u>. *Adverbial infinitive, modifying "ready"*

4) She is very happy.
   She is happy <u>to sing</u>. *Adverbial infinitive, modifying "happy"*

5) He sings the aria loudly.
   <u>Singing the aria loudly</u>, the opera star took center stage. *Participle, modifying "opera star"*

6) He sings arias at 6 am.
   <u>His singing arias at 6 am</u> annoys us. *Gerund, the subject.*

12.14.e (2) Exercises

1) He likes <u>to read</u>. *Infinitive, direct object.*

2) He likes <u>reading novels</u>. *Gerund, direct object.*

3) <u>Running quickly</u>, he soon arrived at home. *Participle, modifying "he"*

4) His <u>singing</u> annoyed us. *Gerund, subject*

5) <u>Known to the entire community</u>, the mayor is respected. *Participle, modifying "mayor"*

6) <u>Seen but never recognized</u>, the silent film star lived in our neighborhood. *Participles, modifying "film star"*

7) He wants <u>to earn money</u>. *Infinitive, direct object*

8) He writes <u>to learn</u>. *Infinitive, modifying "writes"*

9) They were prepared <u>to fight</u>. *Infinitive, modifying "were prepared"*

10) <u>To succeed</u>, you must work hard. *Infinitive, modifying "must work"*

<u>12.15.g Exercise</u>

1) Dr. Kildare, you can speak with my assistant. *Noun of address*

2) June, speak with my physician, Dr. Kildare. *Noun of address, and appositive*

3) Your brother is odd, Alice. *Noun of address*

4) There is rain forecast for tomorrow. *Expletive, and "rain" is the subject*

5) It is clear that Ed is a menace. *Expletive, and the nominal clause "that Ed is a menace" is the subject.*

Glossary

action verb: a verb that indicates action: run, walk, speak, read, fly, and sail are all action verbs. Some action verbs are not actions in the usual sense: pause, consider, think, hesitate. See Linking Verbs

active verb: a transitive verb in the active voice, in which the subject is performing an action upon a direct object: The explosion shattered the windows. See Passive Verb.

adjectival: a term for any word that functions like an adjective

adverbial: a term for any word that functions like an adverb

adverb: a word that modifies a verb, an adjective, or another adverb. Also, one of the Eight Parts of Speech.

appositive: a noun phrase that renames or provides supplemental information about another noun phrase; the appositive usually appears immediately after the renamed noun phrase.

argument: a case made for a particular position or perspective

articles: class of adjectives, the three words: a, an, and the

auxiliary verb: When a simple predicate contains more than one verb, the words before the main verb are auxiliary verbs: In I can juggle, the auxiliary is can.

case: a quality (or inflection) of pronouns that indicates the function of the pronoun in a sentence. English pronouns can be in the nominative, objective, or possessive case.

charged language or diction: words or phrases carrying emotional weight, either negative or positive; language considered to be inherently *biased*

chronological order: arrangement of items in the order in which they occurred in time (Also, see *reverse chronological order.*)

cite: to mention or reference in a research project (as you might a secondary article)

clause: a unit of language that contains a subject and a predicate. See Dependent Clause and Independent Clause

class: societal category based on perceived economic or social grade

coherence: the quality of overall unity/connectedness around a central idea

cohesion: the quality of connectedness among items near each other, such as sentences in a paragraph

common noun: a noun that indicates a general class of persons, places, or things instead of a particular member of a class. Common nouns are typically not capitalized. See Proper Noun

comparison: a quality of some adjectives and adverbs that permit the word to be inflected by three degrees of comparison: small, smaller, smallest; good, better, best

complement: the noun or adjective that follows a transitive verb or a linking verb. See Direct Object, Indirect Object, Object Complement, Predicate Adjective, and Predicate Nominative

complete predicate:the verb of a clause, with all its complements and modifiers

complete subject: the simple subject of a sentence, with all its modifiers and associated words (like appositives)

compoumd semtemce: a sentence consisting of two or more independent clauses, joined by coordinating conjunctions

compound structure: a grammatical structure consisting of two or more grammatically equivalent units of language, joined by coordinating conjunctions: Jim and Ed have arrived

compound-complex sentence: a sentence consisting of two or more independent clauses, joined by coordinating conjunctions, and one or more dependent clauses

conditional mood: one of the moods of verbs, it expresses (by means of modal auxiliaries) necessary, possible, or permitted actions to be performed in the future

conjunction: words (including coordinating conjunctions and subordinating conjunctions) that connect one unit of language with another. One of the Eight Parts of Speech

conjunctive adverb: an adverb that signals a relationship between the idea of its own clause and the idea of a preceding clause: e.g., therefore, thus, on the contrar.Also included among transitional phrases used to create paragraph coherence.

coordinating: joining items of equal value

coordinating conjuction: also called the FANBOYS conjunctions, a class of conjunctions that join one unit of language with an equivalent unit; e.g. for, and, nor, but, or, yet, so: You can go or you can stay

correlative coordinating conjunction: a class of conjunctions, just four phrases, each consisting of two to four words, that function like coordinating conjunctions: either/or, neither/nor, both/and, and not only/but also

dangling participle: a participle that does not clearly or logically modify a nearby noun: Honking wildly, Jonathan watched the car careen by

declarative sentence: a sentence that makes a statement of fact, as contrasted with sentences that ask questions, give commands, or make speculations

deductive reasoning: drawing a conclusion based on logical equation; see *syllogism* and *enthymeme*

definite article: the article the, used to indicate a definite noun phrase that is already known to the listener: Give me the book. See Indefinite Article

dependent clause: a unit of language that contains a subject and a predicate but cannot stand by itself as a complete sentence; includes the nominal clause, the relative clause, and the subordinate clause

diction: word choice

direct object: a complement that follows a transitive verb and receives the action of the verb: I read <u>the book</u>

emphatic order: arrangement of items in the order of importance (or emphasis), such as least important to most important or most important to least important

enthymeme: A logical statement missing the *warrant* or major premise; thus, "Cynthia is mortal because she is a woman." That she is a woman is the *minor premise*, and the *claim* or conclusion is that she is mortal. What is missing is the *warrant*, that "All women are mortal." See *syllogism*.

ethos: the appeal to ethics, or a reader's trust in the author/speaker

ethnicity: one's ethnic qualities, meaning one's cultural or religious affiliations associated with one's lineage

femininity: qualities traditionally pertaining to the female sex

form: a word that may perform any of several functions in a sentence: e.g., a noun (a form) can perform the function of a subject, direct object, indirect object, or other functions

function: the role that a word plays in a sentence: e.g., a noun (a form) can perform the function of a subject, direct object, indirect object, or other functions

gender: the cultural attitudes, behavior, and feeling associated with a sex

gender (grammar): the inflection of pronouns that indicates the sex of the antecedent of the pronoun: In English, the three genders of pronouns are *masculine, feminine,* and *neuter*

gender codes: a set of culturally constructed rules pertaining to the behavior of genders and how these genders interact with each other

gender identity: how one identifies one's personal gender

gender spectrum: unlike a gender binary (male and female), a gender spectrum represents gender in varying degrees, encompassing biological factors, gender expression, gender identity, and more

genre: type or category of literature, such as autobiography, application letter, or proposal

gerund: a verbal: A present participle that is used as a noun, as in, Juggling is his hobby

imperative sentence: A sentence that makes a command: Stop that!

imperative mood: the mood of the verb in imperative sentences, in which the subject and auxiliaries are often implicit: Stop that!

in-text citation: source reference information inserted in the essay itself immediately following the reference (includes parenthetical citation, footnote, and endnote)

indefinite articles: the articles a B73 an, used to introduce a nonspecific noun phrase: Give me a book. See Definite Article

independent clause: a clause that contains a subject and predicate and that can stand by itself as a complete sentence. It does not contain a word (like a subordinating conjunction) that makes the clause depend on another clause to be a complete sentence

indicative mood: the mood of a verb used in declarative sentences

indirect object: an object of a transitive verb that appears between the verb and the direct object and in some sense receives the direct object: He lent me the money

inductive reasoning: forming conclusions based on samples

infinitive verb: basic form of a verb, a verbal, typically preceded by the particle to: e.g., to strive, to seek, to find. Infinitives can be used nominally, adjectivally, or adverbially

inflections: changes in a word's spelling or pronunciation (or both) that alter the grammatical role of the word: The different endings in walk, walks, walked,and walking are inflections

interjection: a phrase that expresses an emotion or serves some social purpose (e.g., greetings, politeness, agreement, or disagreement), but serves no grammatical role in a sentence. One of the Eight Parts of Speech

interrogative sentence: a sentence that asks a question: Has he stopped?

intransitive verb: an action verb that does not have a direct object: The child slept soundly

irregular verb: a verb whose principal parts do not conform to the pattern of regular verbs: lie, lay, lain are the principal parts of the irregular verb to lie (meaning to recline)

jargon: specialized language used by experts in a field

lead: the opening of an essay or other piece of writing which draws in the reader

LGBTQQIA: stands for Lesbian, Gay, Bisexual, Transgender, Queer, Questioning, Intersex, and Ally Lesbian

linking verbs: verbs appearing in predicates that describe the subject; they include seem, become, appear, and all forms of be, and take predicate adjectives and predicate nominatives as complements: The child was sleepy.

logical fallacy: conclusion drawn from faulty reasoning

logos: the appeal to intellect or logic

main verb: the last verb in the simple predicate, and the word that specifies the action: I can juggle. See Auxiliary Verb

masculinity: qualities traditionally pertaining to the male sex

modal auxiliary: auxiliary verbs used to create the conditional mood: can, could, shall, should, will, would, must, might, and may

modifiers: words that modify the meanings of other words: Adjectives modify the meanings of nouns, as adverbs modify the meaning of verbs

mood: the qualities of verbs that are appropriate for declarations, questions, commands, necessity or possibility, and speculations. See Conditional, Imperative, Indicative, and Subjunctive Mood

nominal: a word, phrase, or sentence that can perform the function of a noun

nominalizers: the words if, that, and whether when used to create a nominal clause

nominative case: a quality of pronouns used as the subject of a clause: I, we, he, she, and they are all in the nominative case

noun: a word that indicates a person, place, thing, or idea. Nouns can usually be singular or plural and are modified by adjectives. See Common Noun and Proper Noun

noun phrase: a noun and all its modifiers

objective case: a quality of pronouns used as a direct or indirect object or an object of a preposition: me, us, him, her, and them are all in the objective case

object of a preposition: the noun phrase or pronoun that typically follows a preposition in a prepositional phrase

paragraph coherence: the quality of paragraphs that are unified and cohesive in subject, language, and organization: Properly used, pronouns and antecedents, conjunctive adverbs, and sentence structure contribute to coherence

paraphrase: restatement of a passage in one's own words; the retelling is roughly the same length as the original.

participle: a verbal: The past participle or present participle form of a verb, used adjectivally: The child,sleeping, was quiet at last.

passive verb: a transitive verb in the passive voice, in which the subject is receiving the action of the verb: The windows were shattered by the explosion. See Active Verb

past: the second of the three principal parts of any verb, used to create the past tense: e.g., knew, rang, rose

past participle: the third of the three principal parts of any verb, used with the auxiliary have to create perfect tenses: have read, had read, will have read

pathos: the appeal to a reader's emotions

peer reviewed source: a researched article or book that has been reviewed and evaluated by experts in the same field before being approved for publication

perfect tenses: the tenses created with the past participle of a verb, preceded by some form of the auxiliary have: e.g., have known, had known, will have known

person: the quality of personal pronouns that indicates whether a pronoun refers to the speaker (e.g., I, we), the audience (you), or a third party (he, she, they)

personal pronoun: a group of pronouns that show number, case, person, and gender: e.g., I, my, me; you, yours; she, her, hers.

phrasal verb: a verb consisting of two words, the second of which (called a particle) resembles a preposition: call in (to telephone), make up (to reconcile), take off (to leave).

phrase: a word or series of words used as a single grammatical unit: e.g., a noun phrase or a prepositional phrase.

plagiarism: the use of another person's ideas or language, presented either as the borrower's own work or without proper citation so that credit is no clearly attributed to the original author

popular source: an article, book, newspaper, blog, website, or other source written for and marketed to the common reader, rather than to experts on the subject

possessive case: a quality of pronouns used to indicate ownership, also known as the genitive case: my, mine; his, hers; your, yours; and their, theirs are all in the possessive case.

predicate: that portion of any clause that provides information about the subject, describing it or indicating the subject's actions. See Complete Predicate and Predicate

predicate adjective: a complement, an adjective or adjectival phrase, that follows a linking verb and describes the subject: Ed is late.

predicate nominative: a complement, a noun, a pronoun, or a nominal phrase or clause, that follows a linking verb and describes the subject: Ed is the chairman

preposition: a word that typically precedes a noun phrase or pronoun (the object of the preposition) to create a prepositional phrase, used adjectivally or adverbially. One of the Eight Parts of Speech

present participle: the fourth principal part of any verb, marked by the -ing suffix and used to create progressive tenses: reading, listening, thinking

primary source: The *thing* being studied; for example, a lab report recording direct observations, a letter from a soldier to her father, or a poem

pronoun: a word that takes the place of a noun that appeared earlier in the context, as in Bob broke his arm. See antecedent. One of the Eight Parts of Speech

pronoun agreement: the condition of a personal pronoun when its number and gender is consistent with the number and gender of the antecedent: My daughters did their homework, and my son did his

proper noun: a noun that refers to a specific person, place, thing, or idea. In English proper nouns are typically capitalized: Lincoln, Illinois, Tuesday

quote: a passage from a source conveyed in its original wording

race: used as a distinguishing factor in humanity, a group of humankind who share distinctive physical features and belong to the same lineage

regular verbs: verbs whose principal parts follow a predictable pattern: The past and past participle forms are identical, and both end in -d (or, less often, -t). Talk, talked, talked are the parts of the regular verb to talk

relative clause: an adjectival dependent clause that is joined to another clause by a relative pronoun or relative adverb

reverse chronological order: arrangement of items in the reverse order in which they occurred in time; usually used in résumés (Also, see *chronological order*.)

rhetoric: the art of persuasion

scholarly source: see *peer-reviewed* source

secondary source: a source analyzing and interpreting a primary source; for example, a scholarly article about *The Sun Also Rises* or one synthesizing and interpreting primary studies of geriatric dog behavior

sentence: a unit of language that contains at least one independent clause

sentence fragment: a grammatically incomplete sentence. A fragment may lack a subject or a predicate, or it may be a dependent clause punctuated like a complete sentence: Because that's wrong

sequential order: arrangement of items in the order in which they occur or occurred (e.g., "First, sift the flour; next add two eggs and mix . . . ")

signal word or phrase: word or words attributing credit or ownership of language or an idea to its originator (e.g., "According to Smith," or "Jackson argues"); also called *tag word or phrase*

simple predicate: in any clause, the simple predicate consists only of the main verb and its auxiliary verbs, excluding any adverbials or verb complements. In the last sentence, the simple predicate is consists

simple progressive tense: the verb tense consisting of an auxiliary that is some form of be followed by a main verb that is a present participle: am explaining, are explaining, is explaining, will be explaining

simple sentence: a sentence consisting of only one independent clause and no dependent clauses

simple subject: the noun phrase or pronoun that is the subject of a clause, minus its modifiers

simple tenses: the past, present, and future tenses of a verb, in contrast to the perfect and progressive tenses

spatial order: arrangement of items in the order in which they are placed in a space (e.g., "At the bottom of the mountain, wildflowers grow in large patches, but as one makes his way up the path, the foliage begins to change.)

summary: a *condensed* reiteration in one's own words of a passage from another source

subject: the noun phrase or pronoun that indicates what (or whom) the clause is about. See Complete Subject and Predicate

subject complement: another term for the Predicate Adjective and Predicate Nominative

subjunctive mood: the mood of verbs in clauses about hypothetical situations (e.g., wishes, prayers, and speculations), often combined with conditional mood clauses: If I were you, I would learn about verb moods

subordinate clause: an adverbial dependent clause that begins with a subordinating conjunction

subordinating: joining items of unequal value

syllogism: A three part logical statement (equation) including

- A **warrant**, or major premise: All women are mortal.

- A **minor premise**: Cynthia is a woman.

- And a **claim** or conclusion: Cynthia is a mortal.

syntax: the order or arrangement of words or phrases

tag word or phrase: see signal word or phrase

tense: the quality of verbs, signaled by inflections and auxiliaries, that indicates the point in time when the action took place: e.g., past, present, or future

thesis: the central argument of a text which controls the text as a whole

three principal parts: a conventional way of summarizing the forms of a verb used to create tenses: the present, the past, and the past participle. A fourth, the present participle, is sometimes included

transitional adverb: an adverb that contributes to paragraph coherence. It indicates a relationship between the sentence in which the adverb appears and a previous or following sentence

transitive verb: a verb that is performing an action upon a direct object in an active-verb sentence, or performing an action upon the subject in a passive-verb sentence

transposed order: describes a declarative sentence in which the subject appears after the predicate: Gently fell the rain

two-word prepositions: also called Phrasal Prepositions. A single preposition consisting of two words: e.g., according to, because of.

verb: one of the eight parts of speech, verbs indicate actions (e.g., read, write, walk, drive, think, consider) or states of being (e.g., become, seem, and forms of be)

verbal: a verb form used for another function, as a noun, adjective, or adverb. See gerund, infinitive, and participle

warrant: the major premise or underlying assumption of a claim (or conclusion); for an example, see *syllogism*.

Endnotes

1. Thomas Paine. *The Crisis*. UShistory.org. http://www.ushistory.org/paine/crisis/c-01.htm. Accessed April 23, 2014.

2. John Mueller. "Changing Attitudes Towards War: The Impact of the First World War." *British Journal of Political Science* 21.1 (1991): 3.

3. Mueller, 3.

4. Bodil Stilling Blichfeldt and Malene Gram. "Lost in Transition? Student Food Consumption" *Higher Education* 65 (2013): 277-289.

5. Blichfeldt and Gram 277.

6. Blichfeldt and Gram 287.

7. Aristotle. Rhetoric. Trans. W. Rhys Roberts. 1954. Hypertext resource compiled by Lee Honeycutt. http://rhetoric.eserver.org/aristotle/. Accessed 21 July 2014.

8. Longinus. "On Sublimity." Classical Literary Criticism. Eds. D.A. Russell and Michael Winterbottom. New York, NY: Oxford UP, 144.

9. Aristotle. Book 1, Chapter 2, 1356a.

10. "Survey reveals half of autistic adults 'abused by someone they trusted'." theguardian.com. 16 June 2014.

11. Sir Arthur Conan Doyle. "A Scandal in Bohemia." The Adventures of Sherlock Holmes. Posted November 29, 2002. http://www.gutenberg.org/files/1661/1661-h/1661-h.htm Accessed July 7, 2014.

12. Ibid.

13. Park, Douglas B. "The Meanings of 'Audience'." College English. 44.3 (1982): 247-257. Print.

14. Ong, Walter J. "The Writer's Audience is Always a Fiction." PMLA. 90.1 (1975): 9-21. Print.

15. Elbow, Peter. "Closing My Eyes as I Speak: An Argument for Ignoring Audience." College English. 49.1 (1987): 50-69.

16. Ibid.

17. Aristotle. Rhetoric. Trans. W. Rhys Roberts. 1954. Hypertext resource complied by Lee Honeycutt. http://rhetoric.eserver.org/aristotle

18. Ong, Walter J. "The Writer's Audience is Always a Fiction." PMLA. 90.1 (1975): 9-21. Print.

19. United States Environmental Protection Agency. Waste—Non Hazardous Waste—Municipal Solid Waste. Environmental Protection Agency, 2014. Web. 14 June 2014.

20. "A Generative Rhetoric of the Paragraph." College Composition and Communication (1965). Rept. in The Norton Book of Composition Studies. Ed. Susan Miller. New York: W. W. Norton & Company, 2009. 285. Print.

21. This section relies on the work of Francis Christensen cited above and Erika Lindemann. A Rhetoric for Writing Teachers. 3rd ed. New York: Oxford University Press, 1995. Print. This method is also relevant to the parts of the sentence and emerges from that work, which is called the "generative rhetoric of the sentence." Christensen labeled paragraphs similarly calling it the "generative rhetoric of the paragraph."

22. McKoon, Katie. "A Day in the Life of a College Student." *CollegeXpress. com*. Carnegie Communication. 2014. Web. 21 May 2014.

23. Murray, Donald M. *A Writer Teaches Writing*. 2nd ed. Boston: Thomson Heinle, 2004.

24. Murray 26.

25. Murray 26; italics in original.

26. Murray 29-32.

27. Whelan, Lara. "The Topical Theme and the Analytical Composition: Paragraphing." Handout. (Dr. Whelan is still at Berry College, and if this is used, we can secure the proper citation information.)

28. Charlotte Perkins Gilman. "The Yellow Wallpaper." Posted 2008. Accessed 8 July 2014. http://www.gutenberg.org/files/1952/1952-h/1952-h.htm

29. Zora Neale Hurston. "How It Feels to be Colored Me." About Education. http://grammar.about.com/od/60essays/a/theireyesessay.htm Accessed 19 September 2014.

30. George Santayana. "Intellectual Ambition." About Education. http://grammar.about.com/od/classicessays/a/intellambition.htm Accessed 19 September 2014.

31. Harry Esty Dounce. "Some Nonsense About a Dog." *Modern Essays*. Ed. Christopher Morley. The Gutenberg Project. http://www.gutenberg.org/files/38280/38280-h/38280-h.htm#TRIVIA Accessed 19 September 2014.

32. In this section, I am using the term "Works Cited" because the style guide for English is MLA; however, other disciplines will have other names for this section of your document—References, Bibliography, etc. Always use the proper term for the discipline in which you are writing.

33. Steve Craig, "Men's Men and Women's Women." *Signs of Life in the U.S.A.* 7th ed. Eds. Sonia Maasik and Jack Solomon. Boston/New York: Bedford St. Martin's. 189. Print.

34. Shelley, Mary. *Frankenstein*. 1818. A Norton Critical Edition. 2nd ed. Ed. J. Paul Hunter. New York & London: W. W. Norton & Company, 2012. Print.

35. But what is "common" knowledge? Good point. Sometimes, it depends. Common knowledge for a specialist in any given field is not necessarily common knowledge for you, the student. If you didn't know the information already, you should just cite it.

36. There is one caveat here. You can't re-use essays or other material you already submitted for a grade for another class without permission. Even though this is your own work, you can't "double dip." Technically, this isn't plagiarism per se, but it is considered academic misconduct. There are cases when both instructors may give permission, but again, BOTH instructors must agree.

37. The Research Prospectus is a revised version of an assignment composed by Donna Gessell and Erin Wilensky Caldwell, influenced heavily by —— (textbook).

38. Gunther Kress. *Multimodality: A Social Semiotic Approach to Contemporary Communication*. New York, NY: Routledge, 2010. 79.

39. Jody Shipka. "*A Multimodal Task-Based Framework for Composing.*" *College Composition and Communication 57.2 (2005): 277-306.*

40. Emily Dickinson. "Wild Nights! Wild Nights!" Poetry Foundation. http://www.poetryfoundation.org/poem/173343 Accessed 25 September, 2014.

41. Hofmann, Angelika H. *Scientific Writing and Communication: Papers, Proposals, and Presentations.* 2nd ed. New York: Oxford UP, 2014.

42. Hofmann 2.

43. See Hofmann 228 for example.

44. See Hofmann 229 for a more comprehensive list.

45. Hofmann 262.

46. I am modifying Hofmann's explanation, 263.

47. See Hofmann 264-265.

48. See Hofmann 272 for a more complete list.

49. Hofmann 287.

50. See also Hofmann 298.

51. Hofmann 524.

52. Hofmann 526-527.

53. John Berger. *Ways of Seeing*. New York, NY: Penguin, 2009.

54. Omi, Michael. "In Living Color: Race and American Culture." 14 May 2014. Web. 12 August 2014. 628. http://writeverse.files.wordpress. com/2013/04/inlivingcolor.pdf

55. Image of More's map of *Utopia*. Library, St. John's College at Cambridge, England.

56. More, Thomas. *Utopia*. 3rd ed. Ed. George M. Logan. New York: W. W. Norton & Co., 2011. 36.

57. Nazaryan, Alexander. "Choose Your Dystopia." *Newsweek Global* 162.4 (2014): 154-160.

58. Charlotte Perkins Gilman. "The Yellow Wallpaper." Posted 2008. Accessed 8 July 2014. http://www.gutenberg.org/files/1952/1952-h/1952-h.htm

CPSIA information can be obtained
at www.ICGtesting.com
Printed in the USA
LVHW060047080119
603112LV00003B/20/P